Ellen Fader

THE
ANIMAL'S COMPANION

THE
ANIMAL'S COMPANION

❖

People & Their Pets,
a 26,000-Year Love Story

JACKY COLLISS HARVEY

BLACK DOG
& LEVENTHAL
PUBLISHERS
NEW YORK

Black Dog & Leventhal Publishers
Hachette Book Group
1290 Avenue of the Americas
New York, NY 10104

www.hachettebookgroup.com
www.blackdogandleventhal.com

First Edition: April 2019

Black Dog & Leventhal Publishers is an imprint of Running Press, a division of Hachette Book Group. The Black Dog & Leventhal Publishers name and logo are trademarks of Hachette Book Group, Inc.

The publisher is not responsible for websites (or their content) that are not owned by the publisher.

The Hachette Speakers Bureau provides a wide range of authors for speaking events. To find out more, go to www.HachetteSpeakersBureau.com or call (866) 376-6591.

Print book interior design by Katie Benezra

Cover Illustration "The Postman Only Rings," 2016 (oil on canvas), Watson, Gavin / Private Collection / Bridgeman Images

Library of Congress Cataloging-in-Publication Data

Names: Harvey, Jacky Colliss, author.
Title: The animal's companion : people and their pets, a 26,000-year love
     story / Jacky Colliss Harvey.
Description: First edition. | New York : Black Dog and Leventhal, 2019. |
     Includes bibliographical references.
Identifiers: LCCN 2018045116| ISBN 9780316466219 (hardcover) |
     ISBN 9781549168116 (audio download) | ISBN 9780316466189 (ebook)
Subjects: LCSH: Pets—History. | Human-animal relationships.
Classification: LCC SF411.35 .H37 2019 | DDC 636.088/7—dc23
LC record available at https://lccn.loc.gov/2018045116

Printed in the United States of America

LSC-C

10 9 8 7 6 5 4 3 2 1

This one is for my mum,
who first taught me how to play with cats.

CONTENTS

The animal looks at us and we are naked before it.
Thinking perhaps begins there.

—Jacques Derrida

My mother, me at age 3, and my cat Freddy, also age 3, in our garden in Suffolk.

REGARDING

In evolutionary terms, pet ownership poses a problem…

—John Archer, "Why Do People Love Their Pets," 1997

A few years ago I wrote a book on the history of the redhead, as part of which I found myself in the Dutch town of Breda, at the largest gathering of redheads on the planet. And there I met Daniel and Joe—redheads the pair of them, and not only that but dressed to match as well: identical yellow bandanas round their necks and matching sunglasses. And we got talking—or rather I, in that entitled way that writers have, began asking questions, and Daniel did his best to answer them. Were he and Joe always dressed alike? I asked. How long had they been in each other's lives? How did people react when they saw the two of them together? And given that what I saw was a settled adult pair, wholly at ease with each other and praiseworthily forbearing when it came to me, and that life for young redheads, especially young male redheads, can sometimes be a tad taxing, let us say, how had life been before they had each other, when they were younger and on their own? At which Daniel began describing the usual experiences of soft discrimination and of being marginalized at school, and Joe gave a wide, luxurious, and noisy yawn, settled his head on his paws, and went to sleep. Smiling, Daniel explained, "He's heard all this before," and reached out and patted Joe's head. And looking at the two of them, I found myself begin one of those idle inner ponders—in this case why, for millennia, as members of the dominant species on this planet, we have been so impelled to take members of other species into our homes and lives and (hopefully) cherish and indulge and care for them as if they are the exact thing they so unalterably are not—like us.

Beware those idle inner question marks. They start out as such unassuming little sprouts, and just what social media was made for. Why do we have the pets we have, I asked, and within hours my readers were sharing with me the pictures and the stories of every beloved pet you can imagine, from ginger cats and dogs to strawberry-roan horses and ponies, from auburn guinea pigs and hamsters to a tiny Rhode Island Red chick and even a henna-colored bearded lizard. And that momentary ponder with Daniel and Joe has become what this book is about. Or to be specific, Daniel, and all the other Daniels there have been down the ages, has become what this book is about. Because this book is an exploration of the history not of the pet (the handsome red setter) but of the pet owner.

I come from a family of animal lovers within a nation, so we are told, of animal lovers; much as that description would for centuries have amazed and baffled our neighbors on the Continent. My favorite TV program as a child featured a man called Johnny Morris, playing a pretend zookeeper in a permanent, *Columbo*-style state of dishevelment, voicing the thoughts and opinions of the animals he encountered. My favorite childhood reading included James Herriot, the Yorkshire veterinarian, and the naturalist Gerald Durrell—any story with an animal in it always interested me far more than one without, but they had to be the right sort of stories, those dealing equally with people and animals, about the interaction between the two, not simply an animal being made by the writer to behave in a human way (Babar the Elephant, for example, I always found creepy as heck). Some of those stories stuck, and some seemed to relate to each other in that curious way of two plus two equaling five. This is, I appreciate, no basis on which to begin the research for a book, yet looking back I can see that's what it came to be, and I was delighted to discover that when Katherine Grier began her research for *Pets in America*, it was by photocopying items of interest and stuffing the photocopies into a drawer.[1] In effect, this book is an unpacking of a similar drawer of my own. Perhaps, with a subject as diverse and wide-ranging as this one has proved to be, it was after all a valid way to set about it.

Most significantly, all the way through my childhood and my growing there were animals. The first that was truly mine was also ginger, a swaggering tomcat named Freddy, who had paws the size of my infant hands, a purr you could feel through the floor, and fur as perfectly marked as red onyx, and who is still, four decades after his death, there in the measure of all other cats for me. But there were also bantam chickens, deep-bosomed and high-sterned as tiny Tudor galleons, sallying forth across the lawn like a miniature feathered armada; guinea pigs with their squeaky Morse code of *wheek-wheek-wheeeek*; and two rabbits, one an albino and one as elegantly black-and-white as a two-tone brogue. There were temporary pets in the form of half-mangled fledglings and field mice still wet with cat drool; there were baffling pets in the form of silkworms, stick insects, and goldfish, and, at the other end of the scale entirely, an Irish wolfhound. My mother told me stories from her childhood of her animals, and on those joyfully grubby student train journeys across Europe, I in turn swapped tales with my girlfriends of the animals from their childhoods.

It was only as I began working on this book, and listening in that awakened, note-taking way, that I realized quite how frequently we animals' companions tell such tales. People would ask me what I was working on, and half an hour later the stories of them and their animals would still be flowing. Nor had I truly reflected on how profoundly such stories connect us, even between generations who never met. Both my grandfathers died long before I was born, but now I know that my mother's father, a sandy-haired man-mountain who went through the North Sea convoys of the First World War as a teenage sailor, and who was hard enough when fire-watching in the Second to pull out the severed tendons in his own forearm after he was hit by shrapnel, was also fond and daft enough where the household hens were concerned to walk around the garden summoning them by calling, "Come along, ladies!" Animals bond us—us to them and we to one another. If we are pet owners, that is true to the power of ten.

They also educate. The novelist Edith Wharton wrote of how ownership of Foxy, her first dog, made her a "conscious, sentient person," and so it was with me as well.[2] As I look back, all the most important lessons of my life were taught to me by animals: the realities of love and loss and the impenetrability of death, which could take a warm, breathing, living flank and overnight turn it into something lifeless, cold, and solid; the imperatives of sex; the largeness of care and of responsibility. The effortless teaching of these lessons was, I am sure, why my parents believed that to have pets was a good, indeed essential, part of any childhood, expanding the imagination and sharpening empathy, even if the precepts I drew from these experiences were not always those my parents had anticipated. Growing up with animals rounds out your understanding of the world. I had a glorious shimmering firebird of a cockerel who began building nests; while one of my rabbits, the black-and-white one, turned out to have a heart condition and every morning, after his daily digitalis tablet, which did indeed come in the form of a little blue pill and was served to him cunningly crushed up in warm milk, would leap aboard his guinea pig brother hutchmate. Animals are better educators, where sex is concerned, than any book. Growing up a redhead made me bold; but it was growing up with animals that made a liberal out of me.

They also made me a thinking, pondering, question-asking being. The animals I grew up with were like and unlike me at one and the same time. They didn't have to go to school, wear clothes, sit up at the table; but they also ate, slept, spent their days out in the garden, often in company with me, and were subject to human rule-making in their world just as I, a child, was subject to adult regulation in mine. They were not me, but they made me think about myself. They made me study me.

The strongest indicator for being a pet owner in adult life is to have had pets in childhood, but my adult life had also included an unplanned-for, peripatetic stage, of living emotionally as well as physically in rented space, where the less I was responsible for, I felt, the better. So while I was working on *Red: A History of the Redhead*, I was petless for the first time in my life, and writing that down, I share the astonishment of the writer Elizabeth von Arnim contemplating her own petless state at the beginning of her 1936 autobiography, *All the Dogs of My Life*. ("This, when I first began considering my dogs, astonished me; I mean that for years and years I had none."[3]) Now that period too was done with, and here I was with a permanent roof once more over my head, and under that roof there was a lack. Sitting on the sofa with my laptop on my knees, I wanted to be interrupted. I wanted to have an animal come in and make the sort of noise I could interpret as asking me what I was doing. I wanted a head to be pushed into my hand if I let it dangle to the floor. I wanted to have some other creature in my life to be concerned about. What I needed, I decided, as many writers had done before me, from the ninth-century scribe who immortalized his cat, Pangur Bán, all the way through Joachim du Bellay (sixteenth century), Christopher Smart (eighteenth century), Alexandre Dumas (nineteenth century), and Ernest Hemingway and Colette (twentieth century), to name but five off the top of my head, was a cat. A sensible middle-aged cat who would understand that her mummy, or parent, or owner, or guardian or caregiver or indeed companion, or whatever term is most acceptable to you, had to go out to work and who would be content to engage with the world through a window. What I came back with from the local animal rescue center were two half-starved, half-bald, tiny little scraps of cat, one of whom, the moment I opened the cat carrier, shot into the kitchen, ascended the kitchen cupboards like Spider-Man, and took refuge behind the microwave, and the other of whom, just as smartly, galloped into the bathroom and wedged herself under the loo.

What is a pet? The dictionary definition speaks of "any animal that is domesticated or tamed and kept as a favorite, or treated with indulgence and fondness." Samuel Johnson (noted cat lover) in his *Dictionary* defined "pet" in 1755 as "a lamb taken into the house and brought up by hand"; something orphaned or abandoned, and needing our human intervention if it is to survive at all. It's a dialect word, from the Scots and the north of England, where the long winters and unpredictable springs still engender such tender care—thinking of a childhood Easter holiday on a Yorkshire farm sets loose at once the memory of watching the farmer's wife striding down from the fell, wrapped up until she was as inflexible as a roll of carpet against the pelting sleety snow, and with her arms full of sooty-faced and sooty-footed lambs, still a little bloody from their birth cords. I remember how their black feet bobbed like musical notation against the whitening front of her khaki mackintosh and the whitening landscape. Following right on her heels (and right into the barn where a lamb nursery was speedily established), with their heads raised up and full of anxiety, came the lambs' two mothers. If you were to ask my own mother now about the same event, that is without a doubt the detail she would remember most vividly: the focus of that pair of ewes, their fleeces also bright with snow, on their offspring, and the inevitable parallel between their role and that of the woman carrying their lambs downhill toward shelter and warmth. The fact that animals reflect back at us so many aspects of ourselves, the universal and the individual, is yet another part of our conjoined history. We also have the words "petty" and "petit" or "petite," all three related one to another, and negotiating meaning between being little and being of little account. There is to pet, as a verb, meaning to pat or play with or fondle, and to be in a pet, or pettish, is to give way to the kind of behavior indulged in by the petted when that attention is taken away.

Our human activity around that word has expanded it enormously. Pets, after all, are made by us—they don't come into being on their own. That should make deciding what a pet is or isn't a simple matter, except that we not only define them, we define the definitions, too, which makes it anything but. This is rather fitting, in my view. Animal studies, which is where our activities as pet owners place us, is so new a field and is growing so rapidly that it can still almost get away with defining itself as it likes, so why should definitions of its subjects be fixed, either?

So: a pet is an animal we bring indoors—except when we don't. It is an animal we never eat—except when we do. It is an animal we name as an individual, but not quite with a human name, except when it is. Its relationship with us is individual and unique—just as are our relationships with each other. It is yours—your cat, your dog, your parrot, your pig. It can be a hedgehog or a horse. It is a creature to whom we present belongings that don't belong. It is animal-animal, distinct from us, who are human-animal, except that historically human beings have been kept as pets, too—the court dwarf in Europe, or in South America where the Aztecs kept human albinos in menageries, treating them as the kind of curiosities they would themselves come to be seen as by the Spanish conquistadores. It is a creature for whom the boundaries between human and animal have become blurred; and where it is we who do the blurring. We feed them in our kitchens, where we ourselves eat. They sleep with us on our beds, something that for most of us is a privilege granted to but one other member of our own species, but with our animals it is an intimacy granted without thinking (and certainly without being asked). Those, like me, who have a litter tray in the bathroom have created a variation on the animal latrine, or dedicated communal defecation site, behavior shared with horses, deer, raccoons, badgers, and dinosaurs. Our pet animals go with us from room to room, and when we go outside they frequently go with us there, too; we pick them up and carry them about with us; spontaneously caress them; and talk to them in what anthropologists term "motherese." We attempt to control and supervise their sex lives, much like the conscientious parent of a teenager and very likely with more success; and when they die, we mourn and memorialize them as if they were members of our family. Indeed for most of us owners, pets *are* members of the family and there is no question about it. And although you could describe them as artificial hybrids manufactured by us, the best, most fulfilling relationships with a pet involve engagement, cooperation, and understanding that is conscious and mutual, that happens on both sides.

It is a thing we know when we see it. Poor Baa-Baa-Black Sheep, obediently producing all those bags of wool, never attains the status of pet (any more than would my newborn Yorkshire lambs), but Mary's Little Lamb undoubtedly does, first because of the Möbius-strip equation of Lamb loves Mary *ergo* Mary loves Lamb; second, because he is allowed to follow her into human space—her school—from which Baa-Baa would have been shooed; and third, because in Kate Greenaway–esque illustrations in children's books without number, he has a bow of ribbon round his neck, like a collar, and the end of the ribbon is in Mary's hand, like a leash.

This business of connection, whether through a leash or no, is very significant, and is an excellent indicator that the creature attached to the other end is a pet, no matter how unlikely. Images of St. Margaret of Antioch (a sort of female Jonah, who probably never existed at all but who is nonetheless a favorite of mine) often show her with a fearsome dragon curled at her feet, from whose belly, according to her legend, she rose unharmed. In 1525, Girolamo Savoldo took this imagery the logical step further when he created a portrait of a matronly Italian noblewoman about to rise from her reading to take her eager greyhound for a walk. There he is, in the bottom left-hand corner of the painting—one of the traditional places for pets to find themselves—joined to his owner by a chain looped around her waist. Only when you register his strangely frilly ears do you realize who this "pet" and owner are meant to be.[4]

We have an almost constant experience of this type of physical connection with our pets, which of course means that they have an almost constant experience of contact with us. You might say the clue is in the name here, with "pet" being both noun and verb. This includes flourishing brush and comb to groom them, as if we were their animal, rather than human, parent; but then thousands upon thousands of us also brush our pets' teeth, as if it's they who were human instead. The fluidity of who is what in the relationship of pet and owner, the way in which each side contributes to it, the overlaps in behavior and the mirroring in our experience of each other recur over and over again, as true for an owner a thousand years ago as it is today. We choose them; but they seem to choose us, too. We make a noise to communicate with them; they make a noise to communicate right back, even if neither party, frankly, has a clue as to what has been said. We love them; they behave with trust and affection toward us in turn. And we lose them, but they lose us, too. And it is our pets, our companion animals, who in turn make that fascinating thing the animal's companion out of us.

To add even more variety to the mix, by no means all these definitions need be met all the time. As I researched this book I was often asked whether horses and ponies qualified as pets. They certainly don't share domestic space with us (something granted even to St. Margaret's dragon) but they are named, cared for, and communicated with, and anyone who has ever ridden a horse will know how profound the physical connection with them becomes. Moreover the outrage over the 2013 horsemeat scandal in the United Kingdom, where foodstuffs masquerading as beef were revealed to be anything but, left no doubt that in the public mind, horses, ponies, and donkeys too were covered by exactly the same taboo as cats and dogs, a taboo that had been quite horribly breached.[5]

Perhaps the only constantly reliable definition of a pet is that it is so to you, its owner. The 1854 letters home from the Crimean War of Lieutenant Temple Godman, one of the owners looked at in this book in detail, demonstrate how his three horses, to him, were not anonymous and replaceable beasts of burden but named and known and carefully tended individuals, which is how, in so brutal a conflict, all three survived.[6] (The letters also show how absolutely Godman's survival, in turn, depended upon them.) In the same way, the correspondence of historical owners often makes reference to indoor-living "house-dogs" and "parlour cats," within which groups the named and cherished pets were to be found.[7] These were exactly the same creatures as the anonymous mousers and moochers hanging around the stable or scullery door, except that to their owners, they were not. Some achieve pethood; some have it thrust upon them.

Historically, if you could move an animal into this category, you could also move it out. Neither of my grandfathers would have hesitated at any point in their lives to translate the rabbits and chickens and ducks with which they shared their back gardens from pet to pot, yet by the time of my childhood, seventy years after theirs, the idea of any of "my" bantams ending up on the dinner table was unthinkable. When my bantams died they were buried with honors. Go back to the time of my grandfathers' grandfathers, and the first animal welfare acts in the United Kingdom were being battled through Parliament, and both bull-baiting and cockfighting were still legal (just). The ways we think about pet owning are changing even as you read this; the casual understanding that these animals were for eating while those were not, that these mattered while those were expendable, which has carried the human race more or less comfortably through so many centuries, is today being closely and ever more anxiously examined, and the gap dividing us and our companion animals in terms of moral and even legal rights is in flux as never before.

Indeed, our relationship with the entire non-human world is being re-examined. Like many pet owners I find it absolutely abhorrent that dogs are farmed for meat in Korea (although Korea is not alone), primarily because the conditions in which the dogs are kept are so unnatural and so cruel but also because cultural taboos against eating dog go back centuries in Europe—it simply never happens, unless all social norms, as in time of warfare and starvation, have completely broken down. But here in the United Kingdom we farm pigs—animals that are also very smart and highly social—in conditions just as inhumane as those of a Korean dog farm; likewise chickens, ducks, rabbit, and calves for veal; and the United Kingdom is certainly not alone in doing so, either. There's a strange little moment in the movie *Moana* (2016) when the heroine, who has both a chicken and a pig as pets, praises the quality of the pork she is eating in her pig Pua's presence, and then apologizes to him. There you are, he has a name, he is a pet, and he is also food, and if the questions this raises about the categories we slot animals into can feature in a Disney cartoon, or in the universe of *Star Wars: The Last Jedi* (2017), where the puffin-like Porgs present Chewbacca with a similar dilemma, then they must have risen near the surface for us all. It is a challenging and fascinating time to be an animal's companion, and you're telling me that thinking begins here. My great-great-grandfathers, all farmers, would never have believed the natural world could fail; we know not only that it could but that if it does, it takes us with it, and one recent change in our awareness can be seen in the fact that sentimentality and its more scientifically minded cousin, anthropomorphism, both of which used to be thoroughly sneered at, are now being put forward as valid ways of entering and investigating that world.[8] I am unashamed in my use of both of them.

Inevitably, there is a Tweedledee, a contrarywise left hand to all this. Johnson's *Dictionary* also defines "tame": "not wild, domestick, subdued, depressed, dejected, spiritless, heartless," and the business of taming as "to make gentle, to subdue, to crush." There is an argument, passionately held, that to make any animal a domestic pet automatically means even the most loving owner is guilty of subtle cruelty. There are people to whom the term "owner" is offensive—to you I apologize, as after much head-scratching it is the term I find myself using most frequently here, and I ask your tolerance of it on the grounds that much of this book deals with periods when no concept other than "owner" existed. On the other hand, if you are dismissive of the idea of a sheep expressing anxiety, or of an animal coming to see what its owner is doing, I make no apology, and this book is not for you.

However, if you have ever heard yourself ask an animal where one of his or her possessions might be; if you have ever felt mysteriously flattered when an animal grooms *you* or reacted with delight when one appears to recognize you and to be happy to see you; if you carry a picture of your animal with you on your phone; if a line you have used on an animal has ever had you cackling at your own wit (and even more if you are in your most secret self somehow convinced that the animal got the joke); if you have ever insinuated yourself back into bed in the dark with the care with which a hot dog might squeeze itself into its bun and thought these contortions completely worthwhile if greeted by the thump of a tail or a purr, then this book is yours, and in it you will find yourself among very good company—adults and children, bohemians and bourgeoisie, artists and chroniclers, churchmen and aristocrats, naturalists and urban literati from one side of the planet to the other: all with this one thing in common—they were all pet owners, just as you are.

And owners, moreover, whose praise for and plaints concerning and lamentings of and celebrations honoring their animals have been constant from one age to the next to an extraordinary degree. That's the reason for this book being arranged not chronologically but by theme. If you look back at society through a telescope, then yes, there have been enormous changes, particularly in the last 250 years or so, in the way we behave toward and think about all animals, pet or no, but look through a magnifying glass at the individual owner, as this book sets itself to do, and our consistency is remarkable. Has the temporary disappearance of a pet ever thrown you into an undignified panic? Here is the diarist Samuel Pepys, writing on April 8, 1663:

> ...after dinner, by water towards Woolwich, and in our way I bethought myself that we had left our poor little dog that followed

us out of doors at the waterside, and God knows whether he be not lost, which did not only strike my wife into a great passion but I must confess myself also; more than was becoming me.[9]

Have you ever raised an animal's paw to another member of your own species, to pretend it was waving hello? Thomas Gainsborough painted the mild-looking 3rd Duke of Buccleuch doing exactly that in *c.*1770 waggling his dog's paw in greeting to the artist (one dog-man to another) as he encircles it in his arms and thereby created an image popular enough to be disseminated in a fittingly soft and furry mezzotint in 1770.[10]

Have you ever been placed in the dreadful situation of having to choose between pet and place to live? Here is Sir Walter Scott, author of *Ivanhoe*, contemplating the enforced sale of Abbotsford, his home, in 1825. Is it the loss of his house that troubles him the most? No, it is not:

...the thoughts of parting from these dumb creatures have moved me more than any of the painful reflections I have put down—poor things, I must get them kind masters...I must end this, or I shall lose the tone of mind with which men should meet distress.[11]

And if you have ever made the tearstained journey from vet's surgery back to your car, heart-, brain-, and soul-shocked at the profundity of what you have just done and carrying what will now never respond to being carried by you again, you will understand exactly the agonies recorded by this owner—

I am in tears carrying you to your last rest place as much as I rejoiced when bringing you home in my own hands fifteen years ago.[12]

—even if they were writing in Latin, and more than two thousand years ago.

A biologist would argue that the earlier a particular mechanical skill develops, the more fundamental its importance; perhaps we might also guess that the more unvarying a response, the further back its human history might reach. There were owners two, five, or ten thousand years ago whose relationships with their animals would be entirely recognizable as those we have today, and maybe further back even than that.

Most fundamentally of all, if you, as owner, have ever lain with your chin on your hands, nose to nose with your own possessor of muzzle, whiskers, or beak and wondered as you looked into its eyes what on earth it makes of you, then you are in company no doubt with them, and with philosophers from Michel de Montaigne in the sixteenth century ("When I play with my cat, who knows whether I do not make her more sport than she makes me?"[13]) to Jacques Derrida himself; and likely just as close as any of them have come to answering the question of why we, the human animal, persist in doing this. Never mind the cute ones, the ones with the big eyes and soft fur or crisp plumage; we have made pets of robots. We have made pets of Tamagotchi pixels. We have been invited to make a pet of the Qoobo wagging-tail headless pillow. We have made pets even of rocks.[14]

And therein lies the evolutionary puzzle. We are not, as a species, hard-wired for altruism. Like any other animal, we have learned a degree of tolerance and cooperation, which is perhaps our version of tameness and domestication, because it maximally benefits the greatest number of us and only minimally impacts the individual—anyone commuting into a major city and taking a moment to watch the flow dynamics of the herds passing through a tube or subway station in rush hour can grasp that. Like any other animal, and for the same obvious reasons, we nurture our own kith and kin, and our own offspring in particular. Where does the creation of the pet, this nurturing of other species, fit into the evolutionarily "worth it" box?

Animal studies may be a relatively new field, but it is vast—already reaching into psychology, biology, ethics, anthropology, philosophy, art, and film, to name but some, and this book examines only one tiny aspect of it—the owner, which is all I am. Even so, there have been times, in looking at our long, long history of doing this, when I have been driven to wonder whether one reason we do it is simply that we are still trying to understand it ourselves.

Just look, for instance, at all the complex nuances in our alternate terms for "pet"; all the knotty linguistic tangles these have brought into being. There is "companion animal," which is very pleasing but suggests an equality that, while it might be ideal, ignores the responsibilities in the relationship and whom they lie with and is a howling great contradiction in terms, too—what does it mean? Acceptance of the animal in all its animalness, or the very opposite? Elevation to status more human than pet? One unit, made of two? It's easy to mock—yet look how readily the term, once coined, was taken up.[15] We want a name for this, and we're still searching. "Fur baby" has its fans, although I can't say I am wholeheartedly among them—my cats are not infants, nor do I wish to think of them as being human in that way; the challenge and the fascination in my relationship with them is that they are not the same as me, by so many measures. The word most commonly used in ancient Greece to refer to a pet, from the period when in the West the written record of our activities as owners can be said to have begun, was *athurma*—a plaything, a toy, a producer of joy and delight, while for the Romans it was *deliciae*, something that brings happiness or pleasure, but which can mean "beloved," too. Isabella, Lady Wentworth, who was born in 1653, and who lived through the Protectorship and five subsequent monarchies, endured four decades of widowhood hugely enlivened by her dogs, her parrot, and her monkey, and in her engaging correspondence, deciphered from her family papers by Ingrid Tague, described these nonhuman members of her household as her "dumbs." An eighteenth-century dog groomer in Paris referred to his charges as *les cheris*, or "the darlings."[16] Edith Wharton called her dogs "the little four-foots," which is charming in its way but also to me takes something from their dignity. The term "emotional support animal" is in the news at present, mainly, sadly, because of its predictable abuse. In Japan, companion animals are *petto* or *aigando butsu*, animals to love, or play with, or take pleasure in, which just about covers it all.[17] The next time you greet your own possessor of muzzle, beak, or whiskers as "baby" or "sweetheart," give yourself a moment to marvel at what a deep current in human history you are part of and how much care and emotional importance is reflected in the terms we use to speak of our pets; the very same we use for those held within our innermost human circle. At the same time, let's not forget we have made other human beings our pets, too—those jesters and dwarves, the court "fool" (another term used by Lady Wentworth), and at our worst have chained and collared other human beings as well. Even at its most benign, ownership still makes one the master and one the underling. Alexandre Dumas, creator of *The Three Musketeers*, whose *Mes Bêtes* is as human and engaging an account of pet ownership as any, includes among his *bêtes*, or animals, a boy from Abyssinia, present-day Ethiopia, whom he had "collected" on his travels. Dumas writes of this boy with great affection, but then he does the same for his dogs and cats, his monkey and birds; and Dumas is a particularly perplexing case, as his own grandmother, Marie-Cessette, had been an African slave in what is now Haiti. There are fractal moral judgments in play here— simply consider the different meanings in putting a collar on an animal, in which case you are claiming and very often naming it and making explicit its value to you, and what you are doing if you place one on another human being, in which case you are annihilating all its human status at once and making of it a slave.[18]

Another Roman writer of an epitaph for a much-loved dog, this one inscribed on the animal's gravestone in *c.*150–200 AD, refers to the animal, Helena, as a "foster-child"—mine, but not; not by nature, but electively, by choice.[19] My two cats could in that case be defined as foundlings. Another borrowing from the dilemma-rich language of human ownership had an owner in 2000 speak of herself as being her dogs' "surrogate mother."[20] Each of us seems to find the term that fits our particular case, which again is saying something: that our relationships with the animals we share our lives with are as varied and as individual as the relationships we have with the humans with whom we do the same. I walk through the front door of an evening, and my first words to my cats are always "Hello, the little ladies," one of many bits of ritual language and behavior I (and they) employ, but why I call them that, other than that both are indeed female, and indeed smaller than I am, I would be hard put to explain. The puzzle of defining goes on and on and on. In truth, perhaps the experience of owning a pet is like nothing except the experience of owning a pet.

And any futzing of the difference between animal and child, and we are in the most perilous of minefields. One of the earliest recorded outright criticisms of the pet owner comes from Plutarch's "Life of Pericles" of the second century AD and has the Roman emperor Augustus taking aim at certain "wealthy foreigners" in Rome who supposedly lavished attention on their pets only because their women were barren. Clearly the emperor was happy to ignore all those imperial Roman pets that, judging by the archeological record, must have been frolicking just about everywhere he looked. But in acknowledging that we human animals have to have something to love, whatever it is and whatever we are, the emperor was speaking truer than he knew.

Criticisms of pet owners are always couched in these terms: as if we are born with a finite amount of love to dole out over our lives, and the giving of any of this to an animal means some more deserving human is left shortchanged. As an argument this is literally nonsensical, but it's astonishingly persistent—in 2017 it was even the plot of the cartoon *The Boss Baby*, with the villain's cunning plan to create the "Forever Puppy," which would never grow up and would monopolize all the love in the world. Yes, owners care passionately about their animals, but my picking up my cats as I would a child doesn't mean I think of them as being children, any more than their meowing at me means they think I'm another cat. We only have our human, two-upper-limbs way of doing this, and I pick them up in exactly the same way as I pick up groceries, bunches of flowers, and boxes of trash. They and I know we're different from each other; one of the most uplifting aspects of a relationship with an animal is that we take pleasure in each other nonetheless. (It would be wonderful to know somehow, someday, what a pet historian, as in a historian who was a pet, would make of this.)

And undeniably, the bond between animal and owner can be mighty; so strong that owners have died rather than break it. As a child I was deeply shaken by the story of Ann Isham, one of only four first-class women passengers on the *Titanic* to perish, who may have drowned because she refused to leave her Great Dane to its fate. (The story of Ann Isham resonates as no other with owners of canine companions— even today a colleague who regularly travels by sea from England to Ireland with her dogs tells me she always has a plan in mind for their survival should the ferry sink.) In the late 1970s in England, the great scandal was the Thorpe affair, when the nation was invited to consider whether the onetime leader of the Liberal party, Jeremy Thorpe, was, firstly, homosexual and, secondly, party to the attempted murder of his lover, Norman Scott. Scott too refused to leave the body of his dead or dying Great Dane, the only victim of the bungled shooting. My parents' outrage over the breakfast table at almost every detail of this story was as nothing to me compared to the misery of the image of the dead animal and the man cradling it in his arms. Had I, so I imagined, and my wolfhound Fergus been on the *Titanic*, I would have stayed with him as well. I wouldn't have known how to live with myself had I not. So many owners refused to leave their animals when Hurricane Katrina struck New Orleans in 2005, and lost their own lives as a result, and so great was the outrage at the number of rescued animals later killed by the authorities (an expedient solution, but an utterly wrongheaded one) that the event brought into being the Pets Evacuation and Transportation Standards (PETS) Act, as a result of which household animals had to be included in any future evacuation plan.[21] It's astonishing that after so many centuries of ownership, legislation was needed to recognize something so blindingly obvious. Animals do indeed matter that much—in fact in many a physical disaster, where human lives are lost and human livelihoods upended, the welfare of animals seems to gain almost a compensatory emotional focus and importance, which in itself has things to offer in answering that question of why we do this in the first place.

Whoever you may be, pet keeping is something you share with many cultures other than your own. It's far from unique to the West, nor as a phenomenon is it a recent one. Pet owning existed in tribal societies from South America to New Guinea and, where the tribespeople have survived, does so still; animal graves that speak of an emotional relationship between us and their inhabitants have been found in the archeology of some of the earliest civilizations in the Middle East; while between 269 and 232 BCE the emperor Ashoka, in Iron Age India, laid down edicts concerning animal rights, including "all four-footed animals that are neither useful nor edible," which as a definition of "pet" works better than many. Cats were treasured in Japan from the tenth century; while Thailand's *Tamra Maew*, or Cat-Book Poems, describes the most auspicious breeds of cat in verse that certainly goes back to the nineteenth century but may originate centuries before. Nor are pet owners only to be found among the wealthy and the aristocratic, the same privileged social class as the foreigners who so exasperated Augustus. Certainly there is less evidence of pet keeping from lower down the social scale, and almost none in the form of the firsthand accounts that exist for the aristocratic European pet owner—but lack of evidence is not the same as evidence of lack. Throughout history, most of humanity has left absolutely no trace of its passage across this planet; and all that can really be said here is that more written evidence of our activities as pet owners survives from after 1700 than from before. Where there is documentary evidence, it supports the logic that historically, pet keeping was as widespread across social classes as it is now. A handy register of households in New Romney in Kent, from the time of Elizabeth I, suggests that every single one of them, from the highest to the low, included a dog, and there is no reason to think of New Romney as being exceptional. When a dog tax finally entered the English statute books in 1793, a human population of about 6.5 million was keeping company with a canine population estimated at 1 million—there was "scarce a villager who has not his dog"; while Daniel Defoe, in his *Journal of the*

Plague Year, speaks of there being as many as five or six cats per London hearth in 1665.[22]

And if you look at the artistic rather than the written record, the lack is more than made good. In art, what William Blake described as "the Beggar's Dog & Widow's Cat" can be found disporting themselves just about everywhere, providing their own quiet commentary on our human doings simply by their presence.[23] Dogs curl up in the warmth of a cradle or wait patiently under tables, guard peasants' discarded clothes in the fields at harvest time or pad uncomplainingly home through the mud of winter at their masters' heels. Cats monopolize the warmth of a fireside, stare into mouseholes, sleep on serving girls' laps, eye up songbirds in their cages on the windowsill. One of the most timeless and most charming is the mackerel tabby in the illustration for February in the Grimani Breviary of *c.*1510. There it sits, slit-eyed with contentment, on the doorstep of the peasant's cottage as the snow comes down outside. It's a pet, there to complete the image of warmth and safety and security represented by that inside space, the medieval version of the "two cats in the yard," in the song by Graham Nash—or in this case, the one cat on the doorstep and the one small, well-mannered peasant boy, peeing over the doorstep into the snow outside, as he had been taught to do.

So art has a role to play in this exploration of the history of the pet owner, together with the words of the owners themselves. Where these relate to what is now thought about the psychology of pet owning they are so related, whether they bear it out or no. There are also examples of fictional owners, illuminating some aspect of ownership in real life. And inevitably, any discussion of pet ownership by a pet owner becomes a partial exercise in biography. Menagerists are by and large excluded unless they had that genuine, one-on-one relationship with a pet, which is why you will find the Renaissance painter Giovanni Antonio Bazzi, better known as Il Sodoma, mentioned here, but not much on the Renaissance popes, emperors, and kings and their private zoos. Public pets do feature, however, from Hanno, the elephant presented to Pope Leo X in 1514, to Grumpy Cat. And film will certainly enter into it, from the earliest days of cinema to *Rear Window* and *Jurassic World*, where the raptor Blue fills just about every definition of a pet, wearing a collar (albeit a radio-controlled one) and having an owner (Owen Grady). At the end of the film it is her loyalty to her owner that wins her freedom. Film deals in cultural shorthand—if a piece of symbolism or bit of behavior can play a part in a movie, it's pretty much a guarantee that it has entered the collective consciousness for good.

This book begins with what we know of the earliest pets, taken from the wild, and looks at how our role as owner might have come into being. It examines the processes of choosing a pet (something that many an owner is convinced happens to them, rather than the other way around) and how we have fashioned our companion animals to our liking and what that says about their importance in our image making of ourselves. Naming comes next—an act of such central importance that it alters both namer and named; and once a creature has a name, we construct for it a voice and a narrative, so the next step after naming is the chapter on communicating; and then "Connecting" explores how we use those narratives to connect to our animals and to each other. "Caring" examines all the ways in which we look after them, but they benefit us as well; while "Losing" explores what in any relationship with an animal is almost inevitable and why it hurts so ridiculously much. And this book ends with "Imagining," which thinks about where we go from here. It can't look back quite as far as the age of the dinosaurs, but it is a great shame that it cannot. Had man and dinosaur coexisted, it seems perfectly likely that we would have ended up attempting to make pets of them, too.

A boy and his dog from 26,000 years ago. The foot- and paw prints (on the right) from the Chauvet Cave, discovered June 7, 1999.

CHAPTER ONE

FINDING

Nothing feels better than being singled out by something that at best should fear you, and at worst would like to eat you.

—David Sedaris, "Untamed: On Making Friends with Animals," *The New Yorker*, December 17, 2016

Twenty-six thousand years ago, a boy and a dog took a walk through a cave. The dog, at one point, as dogs will, jumped onto a rocky outcrop sticking up from the cave's muddy floor. Then he jumped down again and the two resumed their journey, paw and footprints side by side. A little farther on and the boy, who was carrying a flaming torch, paused in the darkness of the cave to wipe it against the cave wall, perhaps to keep it burning cleanly, perhaps to mark the way back out. Thus from actual carbon we get carbon dating for what, in that trail of now-petrified twin tracks, is so far the earliest-known evidence of our role as an animal's companion.

The cave in question (in fact some half dozen galleries, with more still to be explored) was rediscovered in 1994 in a limestone cliff above what was once the course of the Ardèche River in southern France and was given the name "Chauvet," after one of its discoverers. It is not an easy place to reach today, nor would it have been so then, a scramble on two legs or on four: there is the cliff; there was the river. There was also the chance (impossible, with human imagination, not to have this in mind) of encountering one of the cave's original inhabitants as well—cave bears, who wore bowl-like depressions into the cave's floor over generations of hibernations and whose fossilized skulls and bones are still scattered throughout the cave wherever you look. So the Chauvet cave was difficult to climb up to, it was dark, and it was potentially a very scary place to find yourself. It is nonetheless a palimpsest of human-animal interaction from the point where, some 30–35,000 years ago, it became the canvas for some of the most accomplished and beautiful cave art in existence.[1]

The cave paintings at Chauvet are among the oldest yet discovered. We have nothing before them to explain where the artists developed their skills or how their particular aesthetic was arrived at—the black chalk line that mists in and out, the blur of movement in multiply incised legs and shoulders, the tiny individualized details of whiskered muzzle, keenly focused eye. But it's not only that the paintings manage to be both so realistic and to show such artistry at one and the same time; not even the presence of those twinned foot- and paw prints that makes Chauvet so significant; it's what the paintings say about our perpetual fascination and engagement with the world of animal-animal as opposed to, or as a complement to, or as the sur-round to that of the human-animal—us.

The animals depicted in the Chauvet cave are the big beasts: lions, horses, rhinos, bears; all the most impressive trophies of the hunt. Not the easy pickings of rabbit or game bird, in what at this period was a land-scape of tundra and steppe, frequently dusted with snow—very different from that of the South of France today. These were the animals that stood out, admirable in their ability to withstand the cold and in their size and power. And the way they are depicted, live, and in movement, and with that soft black line and the use of the bulk of the cave wall to suggest the weight and muscle of the animal draws us into a dialogue with them even today: What has that lion scented? Why is the horse whinnying? Has that rhino lowered its horn to charge at us? Their slightly unfinished quality might hint that the intention was always to lure the onlooker into com-pleting the drawings in their mind and with their inner eye, and thus to set up that debate within—to complete, if you like, the story the paintings begin. Perhaps this is one of the ways in which they were used originally and one reason for their creation, as a hook for the telling of tales. Beauty has always been a splendid way to attract human attention, a most effec-tive hook for any narrative; and in this case part of the message of the Chauvet paintings could have been that any animal is an infinitely more skilled hunter than we, and if we were to survive alongside them, above all if we were to hunt and avoid being hunted by them, we needed all our skills in interpreting these other creatures with whom we shared the world. We needed to learn to "think" animal, to project ourselves into another creature's head in order to answer the question: what would we do if we were they? And it's thought that this skill, the ability to enter the consciousness of another creature and the high degree to which we have raised it, is there as one of the drivers in our relationships with the animals we now make our companions, too.[2]

As such theories go, this one is pretty compelling—we owners do project ourselves into the heads of our pets; we do give them thoughts and characters and voices that we manufacture for them. It's one of the ways in which owning a pet is so singularly satisfying. Being conscious of that difference, between us as human-animal, and them as something else, most definitely (in my view) plays a part in our role as animals' companions. But there is a but, and it's this: all animals have to learn the creatures they hunt. The fox has to anticipate which way the hare will jink, the cheetah to learn the signs that one antelope rather than another is weaker and easier prey. Even a shrew has to learn that somewhere dark and damp might equal the hiding place for a juicy beetle. But other animals do not create pets, not even the most socially complex and intelligent of them. Eleven million years' worth of orcas circling the seas of this planet, and not one of them has ever yet adopted a baby seal. There are other factors in play here; factors in addition and peculiar to us.

Thousands of years after the first of the painters began preparing his charcoal pigments and smoothing the walls of the Chauvet cave of the claw marks of cave bears came the boy and the dog: foot- and paw prints, side by side.

To be wholly and scientifically correct, the dog at this early date is more accurately referred to as a "canid"—something between dog and wolf, but far enough away from the latter for the impressions of its toes, preserved on that muddy floor, to suggest that the side and middle toes differ in size and shape. This says dog. The four toes of a wolf are all the same size. The feet of the child—solid, no-nonsense little trapezoids—have a length-to-width ratio that make it likely he was a boy, maybe four feet six inches in height, and maybe eight to ten years old. The two sets of tracks do not cross, at least not in the 230-foot length of their walk that has been examined so far, so we cannot be absolutely certain that the two made these tracks together, but their pacing strongly supports the idea it had to be so. So projected now into *your* mind, or the mind of any-one who has ever seen a child walking with a dog, there might well be an image of this small human, either intrepid or terrified, making his way through the cave (did he climb up into it to see the paintings?) with one hand holding the torch aloft and the other, naturally, in contact with his companion's shaggy shoulder. Because this is how, if you are small, you walk with a dog, a sort of canine alternative to holding an adult's hand. Sir Anthony van Dyck painted something similar when he depicted Charles II at the age of seven with four of his siblings, plus a sort of proto-spaniel, and with an enormous mastiff sitting stolidly beside the young prince, Charles's hand and forearm resting on its uncomplaining head as on a plinth.

So we may only have his footprints, and he may have lived and died thousands of years ago, but we can imagine quite a lot about this little boy. First, as he walked, he was in physical contact with the dog, and second and most important, that the dog was trusted and familiar to him, and we might perhaps say "his," and third, that he took on the darkness of the cave in its company. Because big dogs change the world for you. They make you fearless. If you're a child, a dog becomes your bodyguard.

Or if you are a woman. The psychological effect of walking with a big dog padding along obediently beside you is intoxicating. The world opens up, no matter how timid by nature you may be yourself. The poet Emily Dickinson spent most of her adult life a-tremble at the rest of creation, but with Carlo her Newfoundland, her "shaggy ally" for sixteen years, beside her, she braved the woods and fields of Amherst, and only when he died in 1866 did her reclusiveness become complete. Elizabeth von Arnim (best known perhaps as the writer of *The Enchanted April*) would write of her Great Dane, Ingraban, "Those fears which I suppose most women know in solitary places left me…with Ingraban magnificently slouching beside me, I could go anywhere." Me too. Fergus, my wolfhound, and I used to set off into the murk of winter fields and winter evenings without hesitation. And then on one particular evening, cutting across a stubbled field, he off his leash and me holding a flashlight rather than a burning brand, Fergus saw something at the side of the field that caused a growl to rise from within his chest that was both the deepest and the most horripilating sound I have ever heard an animal produce. It was like listening to the ominous drawing-back of the sea before the crash of some terrible wave. My own hackles were up instantly at the sound of it, never mind his; my nerve ends soaked with adrenaline in nanoseconds—the kind of atavistic response you forget the modern human body is still capable of producing.

Wolfhounds are about as big as a dog can get. The Tudor physician John Caius might have been describing Fergus when he wrote in his *De Canibus Britannicis* in 1570 of hounds that were "vast, huge and stubborn...terrible and frightful to behold...striking cold fear into the hearts of men, but standing in fear of no man," although Fergus's behavior on this particular walk was the one and only time this side of his character ever sprang forth from whatever ancient Celtic fastnesses it ranged over, undisturbed within his doggy skull. Otherwise it was simply his appearance that gave people pause: Fergus was brindled as a timber wolf and three feet high at the shoulder, the living embodiment of the ancient Irish "slaughter hound," and no one messed with us. Other walkers swung away from us and waited till we passed; dogs fled before him, ears laid flat, bellies low to the ground and legs a-blur.

But we all have imaginations, and Suffolk, like any other place, has its cave bears, its animals of the mind, most famously Black Shuck, a shape-shifting hellhound complete with flaming eyes, the sight of which is meant to foretell certain death for the beholder before the end of the year.[3] And Suffolk fields at night are dark, dark, dark—as I remember this we had no starlight and only a thumbnail sliver of moon, and the edges of the field and ground ahead, beyond the parabola of the flashlight, dropped into that intensity of super-black that makes a mockery of trying to guess distance or form. I have no idea what Fergus saw on our walk, or what, more likely, in that darkness, his nose and ears told him was keeping pace with us. Whatever it was remained invisible to me, no matter where I directed the flashlight beam. It might have been a fox, it could have been a deer, it could have been a nothing. But I remember that walk as the purest experience of terror I have ever been through; and flashlight or no, I would not have continued crossing that field without Fergus beside me, vibrating with menace and aggression in a manner totally unlike his usual placid, slightly goofy self; and the boy in the Chauvet cave (home to those cave bears too, remember—the males ten feet long and weighing in at half a ton apiece) set out into the darkness with the same survival kit as me: light and a big dog. Perhaps we shouldn't think of ourselves as genuinely owning any animal. Our relationship with them has always had too much of symbiosis in it for that.

The track of paw prints in the Chauvet cave pushes the date for domestication of the dog back to 26,000 years ago; many zooarcheologists would opt for an earlier date even than that, arguing that the process of changing from wolf to dog was already underway tens of thousands of years before, minus any association with or indeed assistance from our ancestors. For those with a liking for such things, you could make a creatively bad translation of *Canis lupus familiaris* as "that dog-wolf thing—*you* know." In other words, they were around. They were on the edges of our early human world, sniffing and snuffling at our peculiar trash, backing off to watch our peculiar human doings, and occasionally, so the thinking goes, giving warning of the approach of some other predator nasty enough to put dogs and early humans on the same side. For thousands of years for our ancestors, in their camps and settlements, the sound of approaching danger would have been what I heard on that walk with Fergus—a dog's deep, rippling, primal growl. Maybe, predator dispatched, we rewarded them with chunks of its flesh.

Or possibly our doings were not so peculiar to them. It's conceivable that the reason why dogs so boldly became the founder species of "pet" is that we and they are not so very different. They lived in packs; so did we. They hunted; so did we, and that would have been another opportunity for our two species to rub up against each other. They had a social order—dominants, subservients—and territories, a home range; so did we. They also had (and have) a crucial socialization period in puppyhood, in which to get used to having us in their lives, and an enormous range of expressive behavior, with which to "talk" to us. And dogs are smart—which more than anything else seems to be the quality an animal needs if it is to flourish in close association with us. Even in our earliest contacts with them, we must have understood what they were telling us (front paws extended, tail aloft—happy and welcoming; backing off, teeth bared, and growling—not), and they could have read us, too: the tone of voice, the stance, the raised hand holding stick or stone. We learned each other, and our early communities were literally surrounded by theirs.

Naturally this Arcadian explanation for how it all began is thoroughly disputed, *but* there's something to it, that juxtaposition of human settlement and wildish animals orbiting around it, worth keeping in mind. Twelve thousand years ago in the Upper Jordan Valley, there lived a people now called the Natufians, who might have been the first to make their movable settlements into permanent villages, circular clusters of huts (circular, like every nest ever made by any animal whatsoever). They still lived as hunter-gatherers, not as agriculturalists, but they all came back to the same place to sleep at night, and when, in one such village, one of the members of their community died, he or she was buried with their legs drawn up, lying on their right side, and with their left hand under their head, like a pillow. It's always struck me as very poignant, how our first ancestors buried their dead in the same position as sleep, curled up like a newborn to enter the next world rather than laid out like an effigy, as we do it now; and in this one particular burial, under that left hand was the skeleton of a puppy, maybe four or five months old. So what this says is that the Natufians had dogs in their lives, importantly and significantly in their lives; and in this case not disarticulated as food nor, given its age and size, as a guard or hunting dog for the life after this. Instead the puppy appears to have been there in a relationship of close affection, of emotional importance that was seen as desirable in that afterlife, too. What do we do, those of us so minded to do it, once we have put down roots? We acquire an animal to live with us. Even if we can only guess and argue how, here, perhaps, is one of those loci where we can see it all begin. Domestication needs a domus; you can't transport another creature over the threshold physically or in your thinking without that threshold existing first. We still speak of rescue *shelters* for animals, and the largest refuge for strays in the United Kingdom is still known as Battersea Dogs *Home*—a place where animals are brought *in* from the outside world to an environment created by us.

And where there were permanent homes there were permanent food stores, and where there were food stores, there were mice and rats. Cats—*Felis silvestris*, cat of the woods—came into our lives chasing mice in the granaries of the Fertile Crescent around 10,000 BC. The first physical evidence of cat and human coexistence comes from a grave in Cyprus dated to just five hundred years later.[4] Again the grave contained the skeleton of a human of unknowable gender and, just sixteen inches (forty centimeters) away, that of a cat, about eight months old. The two were oriented to face each other, as if to watch and wait together for an afterlife, and both were buried as individuals—not disarticulated, not where they happened to drop, not tipped into the ground willy-nilly, but laid to rest with care. It's extremely useful that the dog in the Natufian grave was a puppy; it's just as useful that Cyprus is an island. Cats were not part of its native fauna and would not have reached it other than by human agency—more of our "carrying" them with us—and it's been suggested that such a carrying must be evidence of domestication and of tameness by this date, as no one would undertake a journey with a cat as an unwilling fellow traveler. That's not entirely convincing to any cat owner with a recent visit to the vet in mind, but no doubt those early Cypriots were as capable of manufacturing a cat carrier as we are, and the point survives: cats arrived when we did, so they had to be with us in some manner for that to happen at all.[5] In other parts of the world, no doubt monkeys were being tempted down from trees, parrots introduced to perches, and anything small, furry, and pick-up-able picked up by human hands. Or as William Service describes it in his memoir, *Owl*, "our retriever puppy discovered the fuzzball, beaky and glare-eyed, in woods behind the house, and bellowed at it until children came." There is a pyramid of sensory contact that we still have in common with our ancestors in our experience of other species. It begins with sight; at its apex is the moment of true meeting: of touch.

In the city of Harar, in Ethiopia, there are men who feed hyenas. Not merely feed them, either, but hold meat in their mouths and wait for the hyena to approach and swipe it from them. Hyenas have been a part of Harar-by-night for perhaps half a millennium, entering the city through holes in its walls and aided by jaws more powerful than those of a brown bear, feeding off its garbage.[6] Human feeding of them began only in the nineteenth century, in an attempt, it is said, by one farmer to stop them preying on his livestock. Let's put some scale to this: these are spotted hyenas, as intimidating as a canid can get, as tall as Fergus at the shoulder and, at 140 pounds, as heavy. Yet in Harar they are fed in this extraordinary manner, spoken with, and even named. Folklore has grown up around them. They have not crossed the absolute threshold into petdom—yet—but in 2010, one of the hyena men, Youseff Mume Saleh, was already describing them to a journalist as "family." In another part of Africa the photographer Pieter Hugo has recorded hyenas chained and muzzled yet still bristling with machismo and walking beside their muscular human owners. You can see what is happening here, and you can reconstruct the first action with which such an encounter thousands of years ago might have begun because we still perform it today. Walk around any pet show and you see it happening over and over again—to meet an animal we first crouch down, negating our strange bipedal height. Then we purse our lips and make what might just be one of the first call-names (so-called) in history, the sound of one of the oldest words in the world, a vocalized kiss—the squeaky plosive p, a softer ending. From which, just possibly, in Old English and German and Dutch, and Lithuanian, and Old Norse and Irish, we get eventually to our word "puss."[7] And then we hold out a hand. And the hand is not snapped at; it is sniffed. Hand to nostrils: it's the interspecies handshake.

Touch is the first of our senses to become functional, which it does even in the womb.[8] It does look to be worth noting, therefore, that we only feel we have "met" an animal if there has been this moment's physical contact between us. It's even more significant that such contact feels so good, and not only through the pleasing sensation of soft fur or plumage but emotionally as well. And this, if you unpack it, might start to explain something of the "why," the human factor in our taking companion animals into our lives.

Animals are like but not like us at one and the same time—a philosopher such as Jacques Derrida would call this their "alterity"—and part of the fascination we feel for them is this fact of their difference. So their reactions are not predictable or guaranteed—the dog that sniffs, then wags its tail at you; the cat that lifts its head and closes its eyes; the bird that rotates its pupils to watch as your finger strokes the back of its head may growl or hiss or peck at someone else. And when an animal approaches or accepts us, it makes us feel singled out, special in some way. Not for nothing have we made the ability to communicate or otherwise interact with animals so frequently an attribute of holiness or sainthood, and in some religions, we made animals our gods or our means of sacrificing to and accessing those gods. We read the future from their flight or sacrificed them, cut them up, and peered into their entrails. We esteemed them; and still today, to be the one whose finger the bird returns to, to be the one whose lap the cat adopts, to have the dog sit beside you and not someone else, makes us feel elevated among our peers. The animal enlarges and enhances us. It's not simply that we intertwined ourselves with them mentally in order to hunt them; there's this important emotional response as well. Why do we have pets? One reason is because we have egos. Paradoxically it bolsters our human status, our sense of ourselves, to have an animal interact with us.[9] Nothing feels better, as David Sedaris says.

Why it feels this way is part of the complexity of our relationship with the natural world "out there," as opposed to the human world that we, with our arrangements of huts and granaries and cities, have created. First of all, much that came from the world out there could kill us, so whatever emerged from it, it was wise to treat with caution or respect; second, as a result of this, whatever came from it we prized and privileged, as with our early decorating of ourselves with furs or feathers, teeth or claws, and as with our animal gods. As with our animals, too. If one selects our company, we react by seeing it as implying powerfully good things about us. It's very deep-rooted, this belief in animal intuition. It's part of the appeal of books such as Stéphane Garnier's *How to Live Like Your Cat* (2017). The animal knows something we don't, we say. And it knows who is a good person to be around, and who is not.

The experience of meeting an animal is also very one-on-one, a moment in the moment in itself, another rarity for most of us in the world as we have shaped it today, where nature may seem very far away and perhaps another reason why we so value this contact still. The animal watches you for exactly the reason you watch it, because you too are an unpredictable non-member of its species (it is perhaps the closest either of us will ever get to encountering an alien). It concentrates upon you as if it wants to learn you, as well as to ensure its own safety, and we meet, the first time that we meet, with twin impulses of investigation on either side. This is another example of the doubleness, the mirroring, found in so many aspects of our relationships with animals, and it's the one they all start with. It shouldn't be forgotten either that finding yourself the focus of such attention provokes it back—many of our human relationships come into being in exactly this way: intense regard, and its return.

And then they feel so good as well. Contact with fur or feather is a sensual pleasure; even the brush of a scaled belly has the attraction of novelty to it, let alone the sense of connection to the creature within. Rubbing, nuzzling, and above all the rhythm of stroking an animal bring specific physiological incentives into play, measurable benefits in terms of slower heart rate and lowered stress levels, for them and for us, something we seem to have known or to have intuited for a very long time indeed. "I have sent unto you...a beast, the creature of God, sometime wild, but now tame," writes Dan Nicholas Clement, a monk from Canterbury, to Lady Honor Lisle in April 1536, "to comfort your heart at such time as you be weary of praying." Lady Lisle was in Calais, England's last outpost on the Continent, at the time, where her husband, Lord Lisle, was Henry VIII's deputy and governor, and it would be very satisfying to know what kind of "beast" this was, but, sadly, we have no idea. We do know, however, that the Lisles shared their quarters with songbirds and falcons, with dogs, and with highly fashionable marmosets and monkeys. This is not the last we will hear of Lady Lisle in connection with her pets.[10]

Even the presence of an animal to watch helps calm us, whether we are in physical contact with it or not—hence the presence of tanks of tropical fish in dentists' waiting rooms. The well-being of patients with tuberculosis is supposed to have improved simply with the introduction of a pet turtle (hardly the most pet-able of creatures) to their hospital ward.[11] It's magical stuff, this alterity, and there must be something in it for them, too, to make tolerable the sheer weirdness of being a pet—the asking for food, the endless being picked up, the living and sleeping with these unpredictable creatures so unlike themselves. It took a year before Bird, the bigger, cannier, and the much more damaged of my two cats, came to sit on my lap—one tentative front paw, then the other, a pause to test that this new surface took her weight, then the slow, circular settling—but when she did, that was the point at which as her human, I could begin to feel confident there was a relationship of whatever sort coming into existence here that was being made by two. And that, really, for an animal's companion, is what it's all about.

Reading within the field of animal studies you often come across the assumption that the proliferation of pet owning at least in the West in the last three hundred years or so is because it rebonds us in some way with the natural world, that it maintains a contact that, living in cities as so many of us now do, we would otherwise lose. To have an animal in our homes, so this theory says, restores a kind of eco-mental balance, necessary to us as creatures who also once lived "out there." This is an assertion that has perhaps more of an emotional than a strictly historical truth to it, although it's one that we'll come back to (in Chapter 7). Thousands of animals followed us from the wild into these new habitats: the squirrels or raccoons in every roof space, the wild birds in the gardens, the mice and rats always and everywhere. As I look from the kitchen window of my partner's apartment, along with the cats dividing up the monorails of walls and fences, there are brown and black squirrels, once a mother raccoon and her three kits; there are blue jays, red cardinals, sparrows aplenty (far more than in London these days, sadly); there are pigeons and, unsurprisingly, given this furred and feathered bounty, there was once a red-tailed hawk. This is in Brooklyn. Peregrine falcons hunt from the top of the skyscrapers opposite my front windows in London; and in the waters of the dock outside, taunting me with its uncanny knowledge of when I'm there *not* with my camera, there is a seal. These wild creatures are more common in our cities than we think. Growing up in Suffolk, in all my childhood I saw one fox, one time only: just the brush of its tail disappearing into the exuberant verdant edge of an unharvested field. Living in West London, as I walked one evening to the pub, a magnificent dog-fox, booted and suited, sauntered nonchalantly past me down the pavement. And yes, I did feel singled out and touched by the experience, and my friends in the pub marveled at it, too.

For various hunter-gatherer communities around the world, the same small mammals provide both pets and prey. A hunter killing a nursing mother will take her infant back to the village, where it may be raised and cared for with great tenderness by the hunter's wife, even to the extent of nursing it at the breast as she would her own children. In this way, supposedly, the hunter propitiates any offense given to the true masters of the forest, the spirits who live there; balance is maintained, and the hunter "keeps right" with the powers that determine whether he lives and his own family eats.[12] Sinning against a taboo in the natural world has been with us ever since Eve ate the apple and is by no means limited to the West: in Buddhist Japan, the release of animals back into the wild was historically seen as so meritorious an act, so creditworthy in terms of individual karma, that their supply became a business, with birds, fish, and tortoises bred and sold specifically for the purpose. You may well feel this rather removes the point, but the gods were less judgmental.[13] Leonardo da Vinci, who according to his biographer Giorgio Vasari "delighted much in horses and also in all other animals," performed the same act for real, buying wild birds from their captors and releasing them there and then.[14] So here is another possible subconscious reason why we do this: that our own pets in the here and now, far from forests and their spirits, still serve some purpose in keeping us "right" with a natural world that yet exists in our heads.

So they may—but equally, for the animal's companion, our animals may also balance, if not offset, a world where others are mistreated, abused, and injured by us, all the time and everywhere. If our exploiting of animals somehow poisons the relationship between us and the natural world, is the keeping of and caring for pets an antidote? If we are at the top of the evolutionary tree, the responsibility of being there is something we still seem unable to support consistently, and depressing as this is to contemplate, perhaps the importance of pets in the lives of so many of us is also partly to compensate for all those animals we can't look after and fail to protect. It's part of that business of division into categories again. We can't take care of *those* animals—but these, we can.

Although there is another possibility. It may be doing no more than reinforcing our sense of having mastered nature, that we can take some animals from it and into our lives by choice. We seem equally able to support the two opposite beliefs—simultaneously, if need be.

Ultimately, of course, the wild is where all our pets came from, gathered up for centuries, willy-nilly. In ancient Rome, as well as the infamous lapdogs, they are supposed to have made pets out of crickets, locusts, hares, dolphins, cheetahs, and snakes, as well as turbot, lamprey, and moray eels.[15] The eighth-century Irish *Bretha Comaithchesa*, or Laws of the Neighbourhood, yields a list of pets taken from the wild that includes stoats, otters, cranes, ravens, rooks and jackdaws, red squirrels and badgers, all of them with owners responsible for fines for their animals' misbehavior. Medb (or Maeve), the warrior-queen of Irish mythology, is supposed to have had a pet pine marten that twined seductively around her throat and shoulders, a form of carrying that marks a truly exceptional degree of trust between owner and pet. Rather smaller, but historically rather more recent and reliable, Alfonso X, King of Castile from 1252 to 1284, kept a weasel for a pet, an animal that delighted him with its "scampering and jumping," enclosing it in "a pretty little wooden cage...for he was very afraid of the cat." Very wise, you may think, but in this case near-death came from Alfonso's own affection for the creature. Oh, the heartaches of being a pet owner:

He was riding down a road when he took the weasel from its cage, and being a very quick creature, it fell under the horse's feet…the King cried out in alarm "Holy Mary, save my little weasel and do not let death take it from me!" All those there were very distressed because the King's horse had stepped down on it very hard. The King cried "Oh, men, can you see it?"…

Holy Mary intervened as requested, and when the horse finally lifted its hoof the weasel came out from under it unharmed, and the episode became one of 420 songs of thanks to the Virgin composed or commissioned by Alfonso over the course of his reign.[16]

Weasels are tiny, but no one's told them. Lithe as a snake and hyperactive as a silicone-rubber ball, they seem to exist in a state of overpowering fury with most of the rest of creation. Over the course of my childhood interactions with critters in the wild, among the most non-cute memories are those of having an abandoned nestful of sulfurous bantam eggs explode in my face like a bomb, being bitten by a centipede, setting my four-year-old foot down on an adder, being pursued along the banks of the River Deben in Suffolk by wasps as by a lynch mob, and having my finger punctured down to the bone by a shrew, but the only one that bit and then hung on, swinging from my hand as I tried to rescue it from my cat Freddy, was a weasel. I don't think Alfonso need have been concerned. Yet where once we had *cantigas* to the Virgin, now we have Ozzy the Adorable Desk Weasel, YouTube star. It may be a cigarillo-size killing-and-eating machine, but someone will still make of it a pet.

But then badgers are formidable carnivores as well, and the artist

Giovanni Bazzi, aka Il Sodoma, depicted himself with two of them walking at his heels, obedient as dogs. The same 1502 fresco in which we find the badgers also contains the faint and faded ghost, as you might describe it, of his pet raven, a bird that had been tamed, according to Vasari again—

> to speak so well that in some things it imitated exactly the voice of Giovanni Antonio himself, and particularly in answering to anyone who knocked on the door, doing this so excellently that it seemed like Giovanni Antonio himself, as all the people of Siena knew very well

—which must have endeared him to them greatly, when they came knocking on the door to ask him to keep down the noise from his "badgers, squirrels, apes, marmosets, dwarf asses…little horses from Elba, jays, dwarf fowls, Indian turtle doves and other suchlike animals, as many as he could lay his hands on."

Birds were among the easiest of pets to abstract from the wild, and just about every owner whose experiences are examined in this book, certainly up to the turn of the twentieth century, seems to have helped themselves to one—as the historian Ingrid Tague puts it, "to respond to nature's beauty by trying to turn it into property." You get some idea of the almost limitless range of birds so adopted from Giovanni Pietro Olina's *Uccelliera* of 1622, which includes every tweeting, chirping thing from quails to nightingales. Olina was one of Europe's first ornithologists, gathering together much invaluable information on bird habits and bird lore, but he was also completely unself-conscious in presenting this information alongside an account of any bird's utility to us, whether as singer or indeed as foodstuff. "The bird is more esteemed for its loveliness than anything," Olina declares lyrically of the lapwing, then adds "they are also suitable for eating, being of quite good flavour and nourishment."

Birds may have been the commonest pets to be so obtained, but they were certainly not the only creatures we helped ourselves to. Gilbert White (1720–93), one of those leisured English parson-naturalists to whom the science of natural history owes so much, and inheritor, via his aunt, of perhaps the most famous pet tortoise in history, also kept at his rectory at Selborne in Hampshire a tame robin redbreast, tame brown owl, and another tame raven, as well as a tame snake and a tame bat "which pleased me much." White was of the opinion that "every kind of beasts, and of birds, and of serpents and things in the sea is tamed, and hath been tamed, of mankind," and who is to argue with him?[17] The poet William Cowper, White's contemporary and another country parson, kept three wild hares as treasured pets. He named them Tiney [*sic*], Puss, and Bess, and fed them on bread and milk and apple rind. A century later, the American poet and abolitionist Sara Jane Lippincott, who under the pseudonym Grace Greenwood penned *The History of My Pets* (1853; Nathaniel Hawthorne described it as "one of the best children's books he had ever seen"), kept a tame robin; a hawk, which she named Toby; and a raccoon.

Sara Jane's contemporary in England was Emma Davenport, a prolific children's writer and author of the rather alarmingly entitled *Live Toys* of 1862. Her pets included Puffer the pigeon, Pricker the hedgehog, a jackdaw, a sparrow hawk, and Dr. Battius, another bat. But both women are completely eclipsed by the Reverend John George Wood, a tireless advocate for the natural world and the closest thing Victorian England had to a figure such as Sir David Attenborough today. Wood wrote and lectured in both England and America and became so well known that he was referenced by Mark Twain on one side of the Atlantic and by Arthur Conan Doyle on the other.[18] His son, Theodore, described him as "never more happy than when surrounded by animals with which he was intimate, and which, to him, were not only companions but true and actual friends." And judging by everything he wrote, this was indeed true. Yet even Wood, although he could be passionate and even maudlin on the wickedness of depriving songbirds of their freedom, speaking of a lark in a cage as "a prisoner in solitary confinement...no more will it seek its mate and know all the joys of nest and children," could speak with a chuckle of how "to possess a tame squirrel is often a legitimate object of a boy's ambition," and inform his readers that the jay was "a rare bird, and seems yearly to be diminishing in numbers" without apparently for one instant connecting this with the very nest-robbing, trapping, and caging he was instructing them how to do.

As onetime editor of the *Boy's Own* magazine, Wood had clear ideas on how an English boyhood should be spent: abstracting animals from the wild ("every boy should be ashamed if he cannot catch a young jackdaw for himself") and constructing cages in which to keep them. His own pets from the wild in youth, again according to Theodore, included "bats, toads, lizards, snakes, blindworms, hedgehogs, newts and dormice." Reading Wood, who is in every other way something of an animal hero, you truly are brought face-to-face with one of those areas where attitudes toward the natural world and toward pet ownership have been totally transformed. Owls, Wood felt, also made pleasing pets, once the "chief drawback" of their "nocturnal habits" had been corrected.[19] One dreads to imagine how.

Ravens, such as Il Sodoma's, and other corvids (crows and jackdaws) are intelligent and adaptable, which would give them at least a chance of thriving in our ownership. They became particular favorites in the nineteenth century—Charles Dickens owned three, all named Grip, the first of which was both the inspiration for the raven in *Barnaby Rudge* (1841) and via *Barnaby Rudge*, the bird in Edgar Allan Poe's "The Raven" of 1845, which is a literary pedigree to be proud of. An unexpectedly harsh yet familiar-sounding squawk from the gardens behind me has just taken me to the kitchen window of the apartment in Brooklyn, and there on the electricity and telephone wires, along with the squirrels and the pigeons, were two parakeets, the first I have seen here. Parakeets in the wild are found almost anywhere with warmth and trees, across Africa, Asia, and Central America. They were popular as pets with the ancient Greeks and Romans, supposedly having been brought from India via the armies of Alexander the Great, and ever since have continued merrily hopscotching their way around the planet from one green space to the next.[20] Since the 1990s they have been found in flocks in West London, where their lime-colored presence and tropical squawk, so unexpected among the London pigeons, have given rise to urban myths to account for them.

Here is another of our human characteristics—that we seek to account for things. Supposedly the first London parakeets, having been taken from the wild, escaped from the set of *The African Queen* when it was being filmed at Isleworth Studios in West London in 1951. Alternatively, Jimi Hendrix is supposed to have released his pair of pet birds in Carnaby Street in the 1960s—a connecting of two new exotic species perhaps: the fashionable male of the 1960s and the psychedelic bird. (Something similar happened in the London of the 1760s, when the new exotic species of monkey arriving in the city as fashionable pets were linked in popular imagination with the dandies, or macaronis, arriving in the city fresh from the Grand Tour.) There are established flocks of feral parakeets in Brussels, Cologne, and Rome, in Chicago, and apparently most recently in Tokyo. They came from the wild and insofar as our cities provide "wild," the parakeets have returned there. They are an urban feral success story. Like the corvids, they are smart, and like the corvids, they find our human world accommodating; and you can see perfectly well what will happen next—chicks hatched in the wild will be adopted, fed from the nest, and raised as pets, and so the cycle will begin again. Like the old lady said, it's turtles all the way down.[21]

Raccoons, for example, were commonplace as pets in sixteenth-century Mexico and are still hopping merrily if unwisely back and forth across thresholds in the United States today.[22] I've walked within a couple of yards of a raccoon in New York's Central Park at dusk, and it appeared as unperturbed by my proximity as it was by the rest of Manhattan going about its nightly business around it. Judging by its girth, its choice of territory was serving it well (it was Halloween, and this particular raccoon was as round as if it had swallowed a pumpkin whole). In Australia it is dingoes that drift in and out of human lives and spaces. Aboriginal communities in Australia take in orphaned dingo pups—which, yes, they have often themselves orphaned by killing the mother—sleep with them for warmth, and use them as sentinels and as companions; once the pups reach sexual maturity, they are allowed to wander off—a sort of dingo walkabout—to go make more puppies and so repeat the cycle.[23] The suitability, or lack thereof, of a dingo (or, come to that, a raccoon) as a pet and the desirability or not of creating "tame" dingoes is an area of much scientific conversation and dispute, with some states in Australia still outlawing their ownership (but when did that ever stop anyone?) even as the Australian National Kennel Council published a breed standard for them. Are these the next two to cross the species line? Will there in future, along with wild and pet parakeets, be both wild and pet raccoons, and wild and pet dingoes? Just as there are wild (green and yellow) and pet (green, yellow, turquoise, blue, gray, violet, white, and even crested) budgerigars, and wild (round face, round eyes, small ears) and pet (triangular face, almond-shaped eyes, and ears the size of bird wings) Siamese cats? And how different might we make one type of raccoon, say, look to the other? Coloring, like the budgerigar? Or, like Siamese cats, their entire morphology?

It's the timing of the taking from the wild that is the crucial factor. If the animal is young enough—as happened with Ozzy the Desk Weasel, found half dead and almost newborn—you can make of it a pet, and for millennia, so we have. In the 2016 documentary *The Eagle Huntress*, the prerequisite for thirteen-year-old Aisholpan to acquire her eagle from the Altai Mountains in Mongolia is to find an eaglet sturdy enough to survive being taken captive but still young enough to accept captivity. But if the creature taken from the wild has progeny, the process of accustoming them to domestication will have to be gone through all over again. Being tamed is not the same as being tame; wild stays wild. My mother treasures a photograph of my brother, on a trip to London in the early 1970s when he was about six years old, holding a lion cub in his arms. They had gone into Harrods, which for two East Anglian children was the equivalent of landing on a different planet, one composed of escalators as tall as our house and so much gilt and marble that even Kubla Khan could not have asked for more, and with a pet department, the Pet Kingdom, that, before the Endangered Species Act of 1976, would sell you lions and tigers as happily as designer dogs and cats. Noël Coward bought a baby alligator there in 1951 and Ronald Reagan a baby elephant in 1967. This is the very small part the Harvey family played in the game of How Times Change: my mother took my brother up to the top floor to see the animals, and there was a man with a lion cub and a photographer, and she handed over five shillings, perhaps, or its new decimal equivalent, and in return got a photograph of her son hugging a real live lion cub as if it were a favorite teddy bear.

Come to think of it, the 1970s were a different planet. Pet Kingdom has closed (albeit only in 2014), and nothing in that encounter could be repeated today, from the presence of a wild animal of a vulnerable and decreasing species in a department store to its being handled by a child; and you have to say, good thing, too. Yet you should see the delight in my brother's grin. And looking at the photo recently, looking at the cub and then looking at my brother, what I was seeing was the same—the same high, rounded forehead, the same oversize eyes, the same big head on small body. And when we started to pick and choose among those adoptees from the wild, when we made the passage over our threshold permanent, that look, that baby face, was part of what we made permanent, too.

JACK BLACK, HER MAJESTY'S RATCATCHER.

"Jack Black, Her Majesty's ratcatcher," from Henry Mayhew's *London Labour and the London Poor* (1851). Note the "VR" on Jack Black's baldric, together with the silhouettes of two rats, and his indispensible companion, his terrier.

CHAPTER TWO

CHOOSING

Almost any animal can be tamed with enough human contact, but only a domesticated one remains tame generation after generation.

—David Grimm, *Citizen Canine,* 2014

One of the first books I put together as an editor was a celebration of surviving breeds of traditional farmyard animals. Not black-and-white Holsteins but cherry-red Lincoln cattle and mighty Long-horn bulls. Not pork as in run-of-the-mill pork chops in the supermarket fridge but pork as in piebald Gloucester Old Spots, the pig that spends its life rootling around for wind-fallen apples in cider orchards, and whose meat is every bit as delicious as that description would suggest (and which, at this event at least, had been obtained as it always should be: from mature animals, slaughtered on their home turf, instantly and painlessly and out of sight of their fellows). The photographer for the book, his two assistants, and I spent a weekend at the Rare Breeds

Survival Trust annual fair, up in the English Midlands, where my job was to race around the pens minutes behind the judges, convincing owners of the prize-winning animals that what they really wanted to do now was not celebrate with a pint but bring their prizewinners to be immortalized in our makeshift traveling studio: a canvas draped over a wall where to left and right the photographer had set up two immense, fizzing spotlights.

It was like being a model's booker for Noah's Ark. By eleven a.m. we had a line of rare breeds and their owners, all queuing like starlets waiting for their close-ups. There was a Clydesdale horse (the Russian weight lifter of the equine world) waiting patiently behind a Tamworth pig (streamlined as a ginger seal, but with a snout), waiting behind a Scots Dumpy cockerel (exactly as its name sounds), waiting behind a Leicester Longwool sheep. Leicester Longwools have fleece that spirals down in dreadlocks to their ankles—Rasta sheep, complete with a suitably mellow outlook on life (or on what one assumes they can see of it, through their jaw-length fringe of ringlets)—and rapidly became my favorites. My other favorites were the Middle White pigs, who sport the sort of chinless faces and turned-up snouts only achieved by generations of careful breeding within the human race, too. The Rare Breeds fair was also where I discovered that if you find the sweet spot to scratch on a pig's back, they uncoil their tails and stand there wagging them in ecstasy, like dogs. And they had plenty of time to do so, too, all because one little Soay sheep, after its fifteen seconds in front of the camera, was refusing to find first gear.

Soay sheep are not among my favorites. Munchkin size but vastly overendowed with 'tude, they are rumored to be the descendants of animals that swam ashore from wrecked vessels of the Spanish Armada, so to call them "tough" barely begins to do them justice. Genetically they are linked to the ancient Mediterranean mouflon but have been living semi-wild on the St. Kilda Archipelago, beyond the Western Isles of Scotland, for so long they have turned into something else altogether. That something has a remarkably solid skull and satanic yellow eyes with pupils like the machine-gun slits in a pillbox. There are species where those horizontal pupils seem to speak of ancient wisdom, but with the Soay they speak of knee-high malevolence and the trigonometry of the head butt, for which they also come equipped with a pair of sharp little horns. I tried to encourage this particular Soay out of the spotlight; it butted. I clucked my tongue, crouched down, held out my hand; it butted. I turned my back on it; it butted—and then at once returned to the prime spot in front of the camera. We had a dozen animal portraits we were hoping to knock off the list in that one morning, and the photographer was getting restive. The photographer's assistants were getting restive. The Clydesdale was getting restive. Even the Leicester Longwool looked as if it might ask, if it could, who was harshing the vibe. And under those fizzing spotlights it was much more than comfortably warm. In desperation I turned to the Soay's owner, a young woman with the kind of complexion only possible if you have forty miles of running sea between you and all sources of urban pollution. "Does it have a name?" I asked, thinking that calling it might do the trick of getting it to move.

"Nooo, it does nae," came the reply, in tones of withering contempt. "They're nae *pets*."

No indeed. The value—and genetically, it's immense—of these rare breeds is their ability to withstand disease, do well on scrappy pasture, not succumb to foot rot, recycle wind-fallen apples, calve or foal without supervision, and preserve a chromosomal treasure chest of riches; but to be petted, named, and tamed is not a part of the plan. If you want to make a pet, you start by looking for something else altogether.

Writing a book makes you a hermit, a troglodyte, a recluse—no wonder St. Jerome (also an animal's companion) kept his lion in his study. It might have been the only creature he spoke with all day. To remind myself that the outside world still exists, I go running. On such a run I found myself approaching one of the many lengths of railing near my flat in London that separate quayside path from water, one that in this case had been adopted by a mix of seagulls who had arranged themselves along the rails both high and low. Naturally as I drew nearer they took off with the usual squawks and squabbling, but not all of them did. Those that stayed in place were of all types and shapes, but the one thing they obviously had in common was the ability to tolerate my proximity without feeling threatened by it. When they saw me, their flight-or-fight reflex was not immediately drenched in cortisone, and their wings did not at once lift them up into the air.

Cortisone is the battery acid of hormones. It's released by the adrenal gland in response to stress—a deadline, say; a growling dog; pursuit by a hungry lioness or by your Stone Age neighbor armed with a flint axe. It makes your heart thud and your blood pressure soar. Its opposite is oxytocin, which is the hormonal equivalent of mother's milk—literally so, in that it's produced in response to breast-feeding. It helps us bond, it helps us trust each other, and it's one of the feel-good endorphins released for both of you when you pet your dog or cat. And just as with those seagulls on the railing, there are those individuals in any species who produce it more readily, who are simply a little more chill than the rest. Puss, one of the poet William Cowper's three pet hares, took happily to life indoors—"gentler Puss," the poet calls him, while "Old Tiney" remained "a wild jack-hare":

Though duly from my hand he took
His pittance every night,
He did it with a jealous look,
And, when he could, would bite.[1]

During the 1950s a Russian scientist called Dmitry Belyaev played a hunch along this line of thinking and began an experiment with a population of silver foxes to test it out. Belyaev's work is much better known now than it was, but a quick recap, just in case. Belyaev suspected that the progression from wild wolf to tame dog could have come about simply and logically by breeding for tameness—the quality that means an animal will neither attack nor run from you, but will at worst tolerate your nearness and at best might even be actively welcoming of you.[2] Obviously, the animals that displayed this characteristic most strongly would also be the ones early humans would have encountered most frequently around their dwellings and with whom they would have had the most contact—interesting, in this context, to discover from Marion Schwartz, in her *A History of Dogs in the Early Americas,* that the word the Amazonian Achuar people used for "tameness," *tanku,* means exactly that, having the capacity to live with people. So Belyaev began selectively breeding from among his silver foxes, choosing those animals that seemed least ill at ease around him and his workers.

Tameness, it turns out, is one of those elegant states of being that reinforces itself. Before Belyaev's experiment, it was assumed that the process of moving from merely tolerant to wholly tame would have taken thousands of years of accident and happenstance. But Belyaev and his right-hand woman, Lyudmila Trut, who supervised the breeding of the foxes, saw a difference in behavior within just four generations, which is less than the blink of an eye in evolutionary terms, and within forty fox generations, or about twenty-five years, they found they had a population who displayed all the behavioral changes seen in domesticated dogs—wagging tails, seeking physical contact with humans (all that lovely doggy business of leaping into arms and licking faces), yipping and whimpering to attract attention, responding to the sound of a name, and coming when called. And what would have been the expected cortisone levels in these foxes had halved.

All that is groundbreaking, but it didn't stop there. As the foxes grew tamer and their cortisone levels dropped, there were changes in their appearance as well. Their ears began to flop and those wagging tails to curl. Some were born with parti-colored coats, with splotches of white or light brown among the dark gray. Their skulls changed shape—shorter snouts, higher foreheads. They even lost that rank, wild-garlic fox smell, which is the closest many of us come without even knowing it to an encounter with a fox in the wild: just its scent on the air.

These changes in appearance and behavior—the higher foreheads, the yipping and whimpering—are characteristics of infancy in the wild, but in these foxes, and in our other companion domestic species, they become fixed. They persist into adulthood and are passed on to the animals' offspring. And because they go along with docility and tameness and cooperation, and because we find their effect on an animal's appearance pleasing, we breed for them still. We like animals with short snouts and high foreheads, because we associate these characteristics with all infants, our own included, and they set off that good-feeling, oxytocin-producing response in us. We even select for them in the toys we buy our children—Mickey Mouse has grown progressively cuter over the years, from the rat-tailed, small-eyed, dunce cap–nosed original; while the first toy teddy bears did indeed look like bears, some of the earliest coming with Hannibal Lecter–type muzzles, just to prove these were wild and unpredictable animals for real—very different from the short-nosed, squishy creatures of today.[3] We also like smallness in our pets—we find this cute and a catalyst to our nurturing side, as well as smaller animals being so much more tractable (unless they happen to be Soay sheep). There is evidence that even as early as the Natufians, we were breeding dogs for smaller size.[4]

And we like light, pale colors, which we associate with domesticity and tameness, in an animal's coat as opposed to dark. Pangur Bán, the cat immortalized in the ninth century by his Irish scholar-owner in the poem beginning

I and Pangur Bán my cat,
'Tis a like task we are at:
Hunting mice is his delight,
Hunting words I sit all night... [5]

was in all likelihood named for his desirable white fur, as the "pangur" part of his name refers to the word for a fuller, or one who bleached wool using Fuller's earth, a natural clay that has some of the cleansing properties of soap. The fullers using it became covered in its white dust. (Pleasingly, one of the uses for Fuller's earth today is in cat litter.) Pangur sits close to the beginning of a long tradition of monks and cats—with monastery scriptoria full of expensive vellum and edible animal glue, hungry mice were a constant hazard.[6] Not that choosing to keep cats in the scriptorium was without its dangers, either—a fifteenth-century manuscript from Dubrovnik still bears the inky paw prints of the cat who walked across it all those centuries ago, thus proving that cats have been walking across our keyboards since before there were keyboards for them to walk across.[7] There is another white cat in the illustration for the month of February in the *Très Riches Heures du Duc de Berry* of *c.*1410. This work inspired the later Grimani Breviary, and both include the charming incidental detail of wild birds, pecking in the snow for the grain scattered there—in the *Très Riches*

Heures by a peasant who has left only his footprints behind, creating a small historic testament to our care for the animal world from six hundred years ago.

White as the color of tameness, as an outward sign of an inner evolution, changed our attitudes toward even those creatures that in their natural form were loathed and feared, such as the urban brown rat. Jack Black, who in mid-nineteenth-century London styled himself as Rat-Catcher to the Queen, bred from any variegated rats he caught and would sell them as pets "to well-bred young ladies to keep in squirrel cages." Black was one of the celebrities in Henry Mayhew's *London Labour and the London Poor* of 1851 and could in fact have preempted Belyaev by a century: interviewed by Mayhew in his Battersea sitting room, complete with pet gray parrot, pet white ferret, pet linnets, and a cage of captured sparrows, Black missed by only a whisker the connection between his specially bred rats with their coats of "fawn and white, black and white, brown and white, red and white, blue-black and white, black-white and red," and the fact that "they got very tame, and you could do anythink with them."[8] It's as if tameness and everything it has come to mean to us—in behavior, in coat color, in the lineaments of the baby face—was all there behind the one single door. And then you begin to look at the effect opening that door had on us, and it all becomes rather more complicated.

So long as both we and the animals we lived among were equally likely to be hunter and hunted; so long as either dog or boy might provide supper for a cave bear (the thinking goes), there was a sort of equality between us. If we tried to work out what went on in animals' heads, it was as our peers—different, but not inferior. Domestication changed all that.[9] On the one hand it introduced "social" relationships and made possible what has been described as the "durable bond of domestic partnership" between us and those animals we took into our lives.[10] On the other, it set up a hierarchy. It separated the human from the animal, and it put the human in charge. Those dogs who hunted the same prey animals as we did, and who supposedly became our tools in the chase, would have been of very little use to us if they had simply piled in and started pulling the prey to pieces themselves, as foxhounds do unless prevented with riding crop or whip. For this reason the theory that wild dogs at first simply hunted alongside us, and thus our deep association began, has never struck me as convincing—you had to train the dogs to wait to be fed, and they had to trust that they would be. In other words, you had to have tamed before you could have trained. And at that point there is a dependency and authority in the relationship that was not part of it before. J. G. Wood used the metaphor of guardianship, one that we still resort to:

> Let us enjoin on every intending rearer of a pet to consider well before he takes on the sole guardianship of any creature... [it] ought to incite in every right-feeling heart a strong compassion for the helpless state in which the creature is placed, and an unshakeable resolution to make it as happy as it can be...[11]

And there is responsibility as well. In Antoine de Saint-Exupéry's *The Little Prince*, a fable whose continuing fame strongly suggests we

are all just as sentimental as one another, the strange little Fox encountered in the desert by the strange little Prince explains to the Prince
that "you are responsible for ever for that which you tame."[12] As a child
Antoine de Saint-Exupéry supposedly stepped off the path in his grandmother's garden to avoid treading on caterpillars, which is charming;
but as an adult he would also plaintively ask his soon-to-be wife, "Don't
you want to tame me?," which is rather less so. It does at least make no
bones about who gets to abnegate responsibility for being in charge in
the relationship and who is meant to assume it.[13]

The philosopher Yi-Fu Tuan, in his essay *Dominance and Affection* (a
work you will find quoted in every history of the pet there ever was), is
blunter, arguing that it is dominance plus affection that makes the pet.
Dominance without affection, on the other hand, without that sense of
responsibility to the other, creates a slave. There is a sad and subtle
portrait by Velázquez, from about 1645, of a dwarf from the court of
Philip IV of Spain, standing beside one of King Philip's hunting hounds,
which leaves you to decide for yourself on the similarities between the
two, and which has a greater degree of autonomy over his own life. Isn't
it extraordinary down what deep and overgrown paths being an owner
can take you; and how indicative they are of the profound significance of
animals in our lives.

There is a logical connection between understanding an animal in order
to be able to hunt it and entering its mind in order to create with it what
Jessica Pierce, author of *Run, Spot, Run*, calls "a meaningful friendship."
That's the ideal, but if an animal becomes one of an owner's significant

others, you have to ask who that otherness is most significant to. On one side of the relationship there is control and selectivity and choice; and on the other, there is not. Instead, there is a tamed creature and with all it has come to symbolize, there is the baby face.

We like animals with faces we can read, that strike us as expressive in the same way as ours. The particular proportions of the baby face are our own. We like dolphins not simply because they are warm-blooded mammals like us but because they have high-domed foreheads bespeaking large brains and they seem to be smiling. The larger the brain, the higher we believe an animal's intelligence to be, and thus the more "like us," which as soon as you think about it, is the oddest possible yardstick by which to measure an animal's smarts, but still, we do. And we like best those animals, in fact we like them very much indeed, that have what appear to be engagement with us, some mutual understanding, some human aspect to their face or behavior. One of the things we all do as owners is read into our pets, endlessly, emotions that we suppose they share.[14] It's been described as one of the characteristics that marks us as human, this assigning of human values to non-human entities. After all, anyone can approach an animal—you don't even have to like them to do that. What registers and matters to us is their engagement in response to ours. We want them to reciprocate, which is exactly what we look for in our human relationships, too. It's telling in this context that the one indigenous animal not represented in the Chauvet cave is the human one. We know all about us; it's they, the animals, who fascinate, and whom we try so hard to understand, and who so delight us if we feel we can read into their physiognomies (or thoughts, or actions) something in common with our own.

One such being Purkoy, a small fluffy white dog (note the size, note the coat color) originally belonging to Lady Honor Lisle but made over as a gift to Anne Boleyn. Purkoy earned his name from what, to his human owners, was his inquisitive expression and habit of tilting his head, "Purkoy" being a kind of balky Tudor French for *pourquoi*, or "why?" and it does sound as if he was very cute indeed. I feel there should be a round of applause here for all such little fluffy white dogs, in recognition of the enormous role they have played in our history as our companions. They could form a line that would extend from Issa, the little white dog owned by Publius, governor of Malta in the first century AD, and praised by the poet Martial—"When she whines, you would think she was speaking!"—right up to Nero, the boon companion of Jane Carlyle, wife to the historian Thomas Carlyle, in London in the 1850s. Indeed Jane and Nero formed a unity as tightly bound to each other as the better-known pairing of the poet Elizabeth Barrett and her spaniel, Flush.

Both Issa and Purkoy may have been early forms of the Maltese; but it's been suggested that Purkoy's famous inquisitive expression implies that he could have been a proto-Havanese, from the newly discovered island of Cuba, or Isla Juana, as it was then.[15] The Lisles had marmosets from the New World, so it's conceivable they might have had a dog as well. Owners in the nineteenth century had Maida, Sir Walter Scott's "Scotch greyhound," who was also celebrated for his "human" expression, in this case a dog grin so famous it got an honorable mention in Charles Darwin's *The Expression of the Emotions in Man and Animals* (1872).[16] We in the twenty-first century have Grumpy Cat (more than

8 million followers on Facebook, 21 million views on YouTube, 1.54 million followers on Twitter). One of the bantam hens I grew up with, Cookie, is there in my head infinitely more vividly than all her brood of sisters or chicks, but not for the gorgeous golden lacework of her feathers, nor for her comely feathered feet, but for the aggrieved old-lady manner in which she would tap on the kitchen window when she wanted feeding. If that didn't work, she would walk into the kitchen, into human space itself.

You do have to ask yourself, looking at some animals and their owners, if choice of the uniquely privileged animal in the uniquely close relationship is not predicated in some way around shared characteristics—in which case you could argue that we are again choosing our animal companions in the same way we choose our human ones, and place right there the beginning of the idea that people grow to be like their pets—or that, rather, they choose pets that are like them in the first place. We all have our personal aesthetic for what is attractive and what is not, and we can all think of a case similar to the novelist Barbara Cartland, with her dandelion-fluff hair and her kohl-rimmed eyes, and a Pekingese with dandelion-fluff fur and black-button eyes perched on her lap. Like choosing like has certainly been true of some of the owners in this book. Horace Walpole, for example, was eighteenth-century London's most irresistibly bitchy chronicler, and in his own infirm old age notably favored "small, tetchy dogs with chronic illnesses."[17] Walpole's near contemporary, the painter William Hogarth, bore more than a passing resemblance in both character and features to his pet pug. The artist Dante Gabriel Rossetti, who was plumply built, had a particular affection for the rotund little wombat, of all unlikely creatures, declaring them "a Joy, a Triumph, a Delight, a Madness," and owned two as short-lived pets, celebrating them in pen-and-ink sketches and mourning them in verse. Elizabeth Barrett's likeness to her spaniel, Flush, is unmistakable, with her hair falling around her face in those annoying nineteenth-century ringlets just as Flush's silky ears fell about his, and further would write to her lover, Robert Browning, "He is my Flush, and I am yours." The Royal Photograph Collection includes a snapshot of George V holding a pug in his arms, over whose head he has carefully draped his handkerchief. I defy anyone looking at the dog, with its dew-laps and protuberant eyes, not to be put in mind of the famous portrait of George V's grandmother Queen Victoria, in old age and wearing her white lace widow's cap, which is no doubt why this supposedly irascible monarch is smiling quite so broadly. (It's startling how subversive you can get away with being if the vehicle for that subversion is an animal. It's how *Ratatouille* gets away with asking questions in a children's cartoon about the mentality that allowed the Holocaust to happen and how *War for the Planet of the Apes* can reference the murder of Eric Garner.)

Which all raises a rather interesting possibility. Maybe there is more at work here than simply our choosing the pets who look like us. We select for the characteristics of the baby face in our own mates, too, passing over those with low foreheads and unbalanced proportions to their faces as unattractive in the extreme, and opting for those with big eyes, big foreheads, small noses, and regular features instead. So maybe this "reading into" has become reciprocal as well, although we know it not. Dogs in particular, our first and oldest animal companions, are exquisitely, almost painfully good at reading human faces, picking up tiny clues to our mood and intentions from changes in expression or body language of which we may be completely unaware.[18] If we are breeding not only them but ourselves to have this irresistible baby face, this particular neotenized cast of features, is it possible that our dogs are now reading us, with our uneven gait, our high, smooth foreheads, our short snouts, and our big eyes, as great ungainly infants of some sort?

The less readable, hence less reachable, animal has nearly always had bad press. Now that, in Bird, I own a black cat myself, I wonder if one of the reasons why they are so often the first to be abandoned, the last to be adopted, isn't solely to do with the fact that along with all the associations around their color (witchcraft, bad luck, death, and mourning; the opposite to the hearth-and-home of white), their faces with dark mouth and nose are just that bit more difficult to read. I wonder too if Bird's impressive vocabulary of squeaks and creaks and chirrups, along with the regulation meows, isn't the result of my being otherwise too dense to work out what it is she's after.

But then there are animals that we all, for the most part, seem instinctively to react against. Contrast our affection for dolphins with our loathing for sharks; our bafflement at so many cold-blooded creatures in general. At one pet show in 2017, I watched as a tiny baby, who couldn't have been more than a few months old, encountered what must have been its first snake—a ten-foot albino Burmese python, a vast curved mound of white-and-yellow marble as sculpted by Gaudí, a creature of such grandeur it would have excited the natural admiration, you'd think, of anyone. As the baby's father held it up to the side of the snake's vivarium, where the python dozed under a bank of lights, the baby put its hand against the glass. One Burmese ruby-red python eye opened in its mighty skull at once, it minutely adjusted the weight of its coils—and that was all it took. The baby instantly produced a clinically perfect shudder response and began to wail.

Those animals we have tamed are in fact by far the minority. There are five species of wildcat: we have succeeded in taming just one, *Felis silvestris lybica*. We have tamed horses, ponies, and wild asses, but no one has ever been successful in reliably taming a zebra. Queen Charlotte was presented with a zebra, which lived in an enclosure outside the then Buckingham House, in 1762. It was the first ever seen in London and became one of eighteenth-century England's favorite public pets—due no doubt to the number of opportunities it gave ribald Londoners to joke about seeing "the Queen's ass"—but the only other thing the unfortunate beast is remembered for today is the unalterable vileness of its temper. The Asian water buffalo has been domesticated for about five thousand years, but the African buffalo remains not only wild as the wind but one of the most dangerous animals, by repute, in the whole of Africa. Possibly almost any animal can't, in fact, be tamed; perhaps the essential predisposition to lower levels of cortisone and to all the changes that come in its wake are rarer than we think.

As for Soay sheep ("*Semi*-wild," I kept telling myself, "only *semi*"), it transpires that the way to get them moving is to grasp their horns with one hand, and with the other give them a wallop on the rump. Our pushy little star allowed itself to be led away by the girl with the wonderful skin as obediently as if it were a dog.

Of course it is not simply a question of us choosing them. In the aptly named *If You Tame Me,* Leslie Irvine quotes a study from 2003 in which "the most common reason people adopted a particular cat was the belief that the cat had chosen them." Culturally we put great value on this notion of spontaneous attachment, of "love at first sight."[19] As I write, in the United Kingdom there is an entire TV advertising campaign for the Dogs Trust animal adoption agency, geared around the idea of dogs looking for their #specialsomeone, but it's an idea with a long history. Pepys was less than enthused when his wife's little black dog, Fancy, first joined them in their London home as a gift from his brother-in-law (whom Pepys didn't entirely approve of, either), but even he is tempted in August 1661, while visiting Hatfield in North London, to make off with "a pretty dog that followed me." John Hogg, creator of *The Parlour Menagerie,* a best-seller of the 1880s, walks into a dealer in birds and spots a ragged-looking nightingale, and is captured instantly. "There was something about this bird's eye—something in his bearing," he writes, "that won my heart over at once." Elizabeth von Arnim, encountering Cordelia the dachshund for the first time in her new marital home in Germany, writes of how "we immediately loved. At first sight we loved." J. R. Ackerley, a man of letters in the England of the 1950s who created not so much an Arnim-style biography by dog but a co-biography *with* dog in his account of his relationship with his German shepherd, Queenie, wrote:

> I came late in life into the domestic pet world, and I had no intention of entering it at all...but I chanced to do some kindness to Queenie when she was very young and in need of help and from that moment she marked me as her own.

In fact, enchanted by her beauty, he relieved the parents of one of his gay pickups ("some working class people") of her, while Freddie Doyle, the young man to whom she originally belonged, was serving a prison sentence.

Even the scientists among us are not immune to this idea of being chosen. Alexandra Horowitz, author of *Inside of a Dog*, found the successor to her beloved Pump when an anonymous puppy leaned against her in the noisy chaos of the animal shelter. Irene Pepperberg, who conducted one of the most important experiments in animal-human communication and whom you would anticipate having as rigorously objective a stance in such matters as could be asked for, meets a baby parrot who waddles up to her foot, and all scientific detachment falls away: "The little seven-and-a-half-week-old had chosen me. I simply could not resist."[20]

If such judgments are indeed being made on the animal's part, then they are not always in our favor. There is something particularly demor-alizing in being rejected as an owner, again, I think, because of the weight we put on an animal's judgment. We've been found wanting in ways we can't even recognize. John Caius can therefore use the tale of a greyhound belonging to Richard II that, even before Richard was deposed in 1399, "utterly left the king," and swapped its allegiance to Richard's usurper, Henry Bolingbroke, to make a political point about Richard's inadequacy as monarch; Charles Dickens uses the same trope in *Oliver Twist* (1839) to signify Bill Sikes's final desertion of and by all that's decent by having even his dog, Bulls-eye, turn its back on him. Emma Davenport, along with Pricker the hedgehog, Puffer the pigeon, and Dr. Battius the bat, lists among her *Live Toys* two kittens, although Blacky, to her distress, made a selection of his own and "was pleased to be much fonder of my sister than of me," while Dash, the beloved pet of the young Queen Victoria, was originally her mother's dog and not Vic-toria's at all. In 1835, Victoria notes in her journal that her mother, the Duchess of Kent, had a new pet parrot "of which Dash is very jealous," and by the end of the same year, Dash had bonded with Victoria while she was recovering from illness at Ramsgate. Dash, Victoria wrote during her convalescence, in a perfect example of pet/owner identifica-tion, "passes his little life with me upstairs."[21] No wonder she was so attached to him. You may spoil and indulge them all you like, but our pets can be so fickle.

Sometimes the animal seems to come looking for us. Alexandre Dumas acquired a favorite black-and-white cat, Mysouff, when it simply wandered in one day; the same happened to the curator and broadcaster Sir Roy Strong. "A new black cat has adopted us," records the entry in his *Diaries*. "Large and furry and affectionate...We call him Muff."[22] The artist Louis Wain owned a black-and-white kitten, Peter, "a series of irregular circles, such as a geometrician might have made in an absent moment: two round eyes, one round head and one round body," who was either a wedding present or was discovered mewing in the Wains' garden during a rainstorm. In either case, Peter became the solace for Wain's mortally ill wife, Emily, and a vital element in the artistic inspiration of Wain himself, and for a now undeservedly forgotten memoir *Peter: A Cat o' One Tail*, which Wain wrote with the journalist Charles Morley in 1892.

Cats seem to have a particular propensity for wandering into our lives, no doubt linked to their original solitary character. There can hardly have been a month in my mother's life when she hasn't been feeding a stray from somewhere, or someone else's less than happy former pet, sharing her seventeenth-century cottage with them in a manner that, when her cottage was newly built, would very likely have brought the Witchfinder-General to her door. I joked with her that she must have the cat equivalent of the tramp's mark on her fence—whatever arcane symbol serves to pick her out as the one whose kitchen floor will always sport a saucer of cat food—then discovered that the real hobo sign for "kind lady lives here" is, you guessed it, a drawing of a stick cat. Bob the Street Cat chose James Bowen, rather than have James choose him, but then Bob is plainly one of those very chill cats with an extraordinarily positive attitude toward people and toward his person in particular, with his trick of traveling happily (and calmly) on James's shoulders. According to J. G. Wood's son, Wood's cat spent mealtimes on his owner's shoulders, too; while in 1939 the novelist Elinor Glyn caused a sensation at the Savoy Hotel in London when she attended a literary luncheon wearing her Persian cat, Candide, around her shoulders like a stole. I have tried this with both of mine, and they were having none of it.

And as before, it is so often touch that seals the deal. Dumas came away from a trip to Le Havre with a new pet monkey and macaw, convinced it was they who had chosen him, the macaw simply by a look, the monkey by reaching out a hand through the bars of its cage. As he put it:

> I am very amenable to demonstrations of the kind, and those of my friends who know me best declare that for my own good name and my family's, it is a very lucky thing I was not born a woman.[23]

We might say today that Dumas, whose vast, good-humored sonic boom of a personality comes across unhindered by the filters of time or of translation, supports the suggestion put forward in 2000 by James Serpell that "studies [of pet owners] may in fact be registering some genetic predisposition to be more emotionally responsive to the apparent emotion of another," and by Margo DeMello in 2012 that "some very preliminary studies are showing that there is a link between positive attitudes toward animals and a more compassionate attitude toward people."[24] Unfortunately, no matter what the hoboes hoped, these studies are very preliminary indeed, with no proof one way or the other that the animal's companion is different from other members of their species in any specific way—other than that we all go on believing that we are.

It is a different thing if the relationship with an animal is chosen for you. Fancy joined the Pepys household in early 1660 and first makes an appearance in Samuel's diary as the cause of "high words" between man and wife, "upon my telling her that I would fling the dog her brother gave her out of the window if he dirtied the house any more."[25] Predictably, his attitude was to change. Horace Walpole, who really must have had "dog man" written all over him, received two of his favorites as bequests. The first, Patapan, another little white dog like Purkoy, was a gift from a friend in Florence, Elisabetta Grifoni, while his final favorite, Tonton, was bequeathed to him by another female friend, Madame du Deffand, in October 1780. Walpole was sixty-three at this point, and Tonton was spoiled, bad-tempered, and boisterous; nonetheless it is not inaccurate to describe the dog as being the central, stable relationship of the next nine years of Walpole's life.

The most famous tortoise in all tortoise history was also a bequest, this time to Gilbert White from his aunt Rebecca Snooke. Timothy, who was in fact female, was already some thirty years old when White took charge of her, she having been purchased by his uncle in 1740 from a sailor in Chichester on the South Coast for two shillings and sixpence. In White's famous *Natural History of Selborne*, she is referred to resolutely as "it" throughout and seems to have lived the whole of her life outside, yet was the object of the most attentive observation by White, who knew her favorite foods ("milky plants, such as lettuces and dandelions"), remarked how she recognized his aunt ("as soon as the good old lady comes in sight who has waited on it for more than thirty years, it hobbles towards its benefactress with awkward alacrity"), and was highly amused by the tortoise's dislike of rain:

> No part of its behaviour ever struck me more than the extreme timidity it always expresses with regard to rain; for though it has a shell that would secure it against the wheel of a loaded cart, yet does it discover as much solicitude about rain as a lady dressed in all her best attire, shuffling away on the first sprinklings, and running its head up in a corner.[26]

Hard not to see this as typical of the attention and "reading into" of the indulgent owner, no matter how man and tortoise had been put together. One of the dearest and most entertaining cats I have ever been privileged to care for, Miss Puss, was chosen from a pet shop but not by me, and initially our relationship needed the kind of active work on my part that I hadn't experienced before with an animal, and still didn't truly settle. Then I came down with atrocious and maddeningly persistent eczema, and she did the same, and we bonded, as partners in adversity. Whatever gets you there.

The pet shop, which is now such a ubiquitous element in the bringing together of pet and owner, is in fact a fairly recent development. If the surrounding fields, woods, barns, or neighbors couldn't provide you with what your heart yearned for as a pet, there was always the peddler, selling them door-to-door. George Morland's 1789 oil painting *Selling*

Guinea Pigs shows such a transaction in progress and incidentally demonstrates that the pester-power of a child for the small, furry, and pick-up-able was as much a feature of acquiring a pet two hundred years ago as it has always been. I looked for something on the selection and care of the non-human members of the well-run household in the writings of Mrs. Beeton, whose *Book of Household Management* of 1861 made her the Martha Stewart of her day, but there is disappointingly little, and guinea pigs Mrs. Beeton anathematizes as "rats without a tail." Morland, however, seems to have rather liked them, painting them at least twice.

Not until the nineteenth century did the practice of going to a pet shop become one of the means of acquisition, and even then it was uncommon. In 1877, Sarah Tytler (in fact the Scottish writer Henrietta Keddie) could still write that in the whole of her own connection with dogs, only one, Rona, "became ours by purchase."[27] Even as late as the 1950s, buying a pet was unusual. Shirley Jackson, author of "The Lottery" and *The Haunting of Hill House*, also wrote two extremely funny memoirs of family life in which her cats figure largely. Jackson was the creator of some of the scariest prose in American literature and had a lively personal interest in witchcraft, so with one exception the cats were always black, and either given to her by friends or found as strays. In *Raising Demons* (1957) she recounts her one and only experience of purchasing a cat, a supposed expert mouser, Ninki, an "elegant gray golden-eyed cat," who declares war on all the other household animals but catches not a single rodent.[28] Of course not. After Ninki has created chaos throughout the household, her daughter suggests it might be simpler just to adopt the mice as pets instead.

Acquiring a rescue animal, which is where many (but still nothing like enough) of our pets come from today, is a very different matter. Acquiring a rescue animal is, in the long, long history of the pet owner, a relatively new phenomenon. Princess Alice of Albany, whose Jack Russell terrier, Skippy, was adopted from Battersea Dogs Home in the 1880s, was a trailblazer. Today, at least in my experience, choosing a rescue animal is so regulated, so carefully sequenced, that it sits somewhere between going to a matchmaker, going on a blind date, and being checked out by an adoption agency. "We have to vet *you*," as the administrator explained to me, straight-faced. It was by no means either a short or simple process; and it was one that involved my being in orbit around my local rescue center for weeks. When would the right cat for me be there? (Matchmaker, Matchmaker, make me a match!) And what would they be like?

For Bird and her sister Daisy, their trajectory into my life was much more straightforward—after they were rescued from the cupboard in which they were locked whenever their owner wasn't around, a volunteer at the center attached my name to theirs as soon as they entered its care. But *I* was the one who had to pass muster for suitability; I was the one chosen for them. Which you can only say is how it should be. And yes, the matchmaker made a great match. And yes, I do feel that they chose me, and yes, again, it was touch that sealed the deal, in that I knew the mangy, pissed-off-looking little tabby and her skinny black spider of a sister would be coming home with me, despite the fact that they were everything I was *not* looking for, when the tabby let the weight of her exhausted head rest on the finger I had placed beneath her chin and simply closed her eyes.

It was no surprise after that to learn that along with online sites that will "match" you with your ideal pet, there are pet-dating sites for the single pet as well as people-with-pet dating sites for the single owner. At the time of writing, Date My Pet, PetPeopleMeet, Doggone Singles, and Leashes and Lovers are thriving. Twindog ("It's Tinder—but for dogs and their people") takes it further and will set up a date for you *or* your canine companion.[29] Because we want to get that match right. The pets we choose say important things about us to others of our own species, too.

Two young men, possibly brothers, with that shared dimple in the chin, who chose to be photographed in 1910 with their baby raccoon. And very appealing they look, too, as a result.

CHAPTER THREE

FASHIONING

Ye tasteless sons of men, is nature such a bungling performer, that her works must submit to your improvements in almost every instance?

—*Memoirs of Dick the Little Poney*, supposedly written by himself, 1799

In 1529 Federico Gonzaga, 1st Duke of Mantua, was busy wooing Margherita, heiress to the Marquis of Monferrato, and as one of the chess moves in his campaign to make Margherita his wife, he had his portrait painted by Titian, no less. The Gonzagas were both dynastically and territorially one of the great families of Renaissance Italy, yet when Federico came to have his portrait painted, it was not in some grand interior, with his lands visible through a window and a mighty hunting hound of some sort leaning against his legs. It was against a plain, dark wall, with a table beside him and, lifted up onto that table, a fluffy little lapdog.

Federico was the son of Isabella d'Este, and Isabella was passionately fond of pets, which she collected as she seems to have collected just about anything. Guests were warned of her imminent arrival among them by the yapping of the many lapdogs who ran along at the hem of her skirts. So Federico would have been brought up with animals, and as we know, being brought up with them is more or less a guarantee that you will have pets yourself. But the fluffy little dog in this painting is not there as a companion—it's there as an ad. Margherita was hesitating; the Gonzagas were notoriously bad husband material; and the little dog is there to say that she has nothing to worry about, that as a husband Federico will be both faithful and protective. It's there, in other words, to help Federico fashion the image he wanted her to have of him.

Whether we intend it or not, those animals we take into our lives say things about us in the same way as the places we choose to live and the clothes we choose to wear. The qualities we attribute to the animal reflect on us, just as they did when our clothes were their skins or they were painted on our shields. At one end of the scale are those muscular young men photographed by Pieter Hugo, using their pet hyenas to declare that they are themselves just as powerful, macho, and not to be messed with. Or Herbert Gustave Schmalz, a raffishly handsome Pre-Raphaelite painter, who was extraordinarily successful in his day but is practically unknown today, was in the habit of leaving his enormous mastiff, Sultan, on the pavement outside the Grosvenor Gallery in London's West End, to advertise the presence of the virile owner within. At the other, there is Federico Gonzaga, using that fluffy little dog with its supplicating paw to reinforce the message that he was benevolent and trustworthy, neither of which in fact was true.[1] The mechanism of image making, even if we are unaware of it, is going on just the same.

As you might expect, the individual owner has been the subject of much research by the pet food industry, in particular what the pets we have say about us as people, so here is an overview. In brief: women who own cats are seen as submissive and gentle (I'm not *entirely* sure this is so); whereas people who own pet birds are seen as unpretentious and sociable. Men who own horses are seen as dominant and aggressive, and men with large, ferocious dogs are said to be compensating for something very intimate and very small. The list goes on: owners of snakes, such as my awe-inspiring Burmese python, are seen as unconventional, which seems fair; indeed so-called pariah pets of all types (cockroaches, tarantulas) have become the living heraldry of the unorthodox, the free spirit, the punk and the Goth, whereas rats and even hermit crabs, which used to be unusual, are now almost commonplace.

Those who share their lives with turtles are seen as hardworking and reliable, which is nice, since as we know there are a lot of them—all the way down.[2] Amusing to speculate how appalled the flaneurs of nineteenth-century Paris, those idle young men who walked turtles up and down the Parisian shopping arcades at the reptiles' own pace as a symbol of their detachment from all around them, would be by this assessment. Moving on: owners of ferrets are seen as careless; of rabbits as complex, yet relaxed; and of hedgehogs (it really is extraordinary how specific some of these surveys have been) as unsympathetic and sloppy.[3] So much for Beatrix Potter's Mrs. Tiggy-Winkle.

In every case the animal is seen as defining the human owner. In this way our relationship with our pets, which seems so much something that happens on our side of the front door, is in fact public and communal, and society as a whole claims a role as stakeholder and the right to give its opinion of you in response to whichever of the above you snuggle up with on your sofa. As James Serpell puts it, "In our relationships with animals…emotional and materialistic considerations are both important and, at the same time, frequently in conflict."[4] All this is doubly true if the animal is rare or unusual in some way.

John Caius, the dog man of Elizabethan England, typified the English in 1570 as being "marvelous greedy gaping gluttons after novelties, and covetous cormorants of things that be seldom, rare, strange and hard to get," but our appetite for the seldom, the rare, and the strange is far older than that. Archeologists have unearthed the bones of a Barbary ape from Navan Fort in Northern Ireland, a hill fort in use from the Bronze Age to the first century AD, where it must have been some high-ranking owner's pride and joy, although as Barbary apes are native to the high, dry regions of Morocco and the Atlas Mountains, you do worry a little how this one adapted to the gentle wet of Ireland. But you can only conclude that for as long as there have been people to marvel at them, exotic pets from far away have been desired and sought for and marveled at. Which brings us to Isabella d'Este, Federico's mother, and her hunt for a "Syrian kitten."

Isabella was one of the most determined collectors Europe has ever seen, and as a state of mind, obsessive collecting is its own feedback mechanism—each acquisition proves you deserve it but, to preserve that sense of self-worth, must be joined by others. The more, in other words, the more.[5] This is the spiral that, much lower down the economic order, ends in those sad souls who harbor animals in the dozens in conditions of revolting squalor; but in Isabella's case was joined to a hefty disposable income and a European-wide network of agents ready to do her bidding. So when in 1496 Isabella decided that what she wanted was this alluring-sounding cat, the hunt was on. But what is a "Syrian kitten," and what made it so exotic and desirable?

It takes a little detective work. We have a description of the "common English catt" as being "white with some blewish piednesse…a gallipot blew," and there is an example of this kind of cat in a painting by Gillis d'Hondecoeter (*c.*1575–1638) of *Orpheus Enchanting the Animals*.[6] The cat, splotched with a bluish-gray on its otherwise white coat, crouches just to the left of Orpheus and looks none too impressed with his musicianship. These exotic and unusual Syrian kittens, as advertising for Isabella's own status and resources, must have looked very different from d'Hondecoeter's, therefore. They were valued completely differently as well—the chronicler John Aubrey, to whom we owe the description above, records William Laud, Archbishop of Canterbury, as paying five pounds for one. It's a challenge to relate purchasing power from one era to another, but that might equate to as much as £8,800 or more than $11,000 today. Their cost, and the mention of the Near East, makes one think these cats might have been Persians, as being one of our own most expensive and exotic contemporary breeds, but no. Persians were unknown in Europe until the 1630s, so Isabella would have needed to be supernaturally well informed to be aware of them. Syria, however, was known as an exporter of watered silk, the type that reveals its patterns of dark and light as the material moves; "tabby" silk, as it was known, named for the Attabiya district of Baghdad, where it was perhaps first made. And genetic research on feline DNA has revealed that sometime in the Middle Ages, somewhere in the Middle East, we began breeding, or you might say, "fashioning," cats with fur patterned in stripes and spots.[7] In other words when we look at the cat in the Grimani Breviary, we are looking at exactly what Isabella's agents were looking *for*, and Isabella's exotic Syrian kitten is today's garden-variety tabby. You hear that, Daisy?

Much of the activity of Isabella's agents in tracking down her Syrian kitten was focused around Venice, the great entrepôt for all things luxurious and Oriental. If you were looking for the highly fashionable, the rare and exotic, then a seaport such as Venice would be a very good place to start. The speed at which demand drove supply was extraordinary: a mere two years after Columbus landed in the West Indies, parrots from the New World were being traded on the other side of the Atlantic in the port of Cadiz.[8] In the years before you could Google a likely list of breeders, or simply walk into a pet shop, almost any harbor would have a local dealer in foreign exotica. In her memoir of her childhood pets, Emma Davenport writes of walking along a quayside where "many vessels used to come in from different parts of the world, and I suppose the sailors brought with them all sorts of animals and birds, for the houses looking on the quay…were almost entirely shops of birds and monkeys."[9] Dumas's monkey, Mademoiselle Desgarcins, who so captivated the writer when she reached out her hand to him, together with her friend the parrot, was acquired in this way, in the port of Le Havre, from a "dealer in animals." (The real Mademoiselle Desgarcins graced the Paris stage for a scant decade as one of its greatest tragediennes and died insane in 1797. It's tempting to imagine that the monkey's pathetic situation, when Dumas found her, suggested the name to him.)

Or one might entrust a naval friend with a specific commission. J. G. Wood would write of the African Grey parrot that there were "several modes of obtaining this bird, such as requesting a naval friend to bring one home on his return."[10] An African Grey, with its white clown face, steely black beak, and shocking pink tail, could be worth as much as six months' wages to a common seaman, well worth the trouble of acting as courier.[11] Frances Stewart, Duchess of Richmond (1647–1702), renowned for her beauty, famous as the model for Britannia on British coinage, and reputedly one of the very few women to turn down Charles II, owned what must have been one of the first African Greys in England. The bird died shortly after its mistress and was stuffed and displayed besides Frances's own wax effigy in Westminster Abbey, which Frances had dressed in her coronation robes and set up as her memorial, and which suggests just how much the presence of the bird had become a part of the public image of its owner.[12]

A few decades later, and you need go no further to view such exotica than your favorite London coffeehouse. Here, as you blitzed your brains on caffeine (the designer stimulant of the day) and caught up on all the latest gossip, you might be further entertained by the antics of the creatures kept in the coffeehouses themselves. Birds of every description, a live crocodile, monkeys galore, opossums, and rattlesnakes were all being exhibited in London coffeehouses in the 1730s and 1740s.[13] Is this the precursor to the cat café of today? You could even buy one of the animals watching you take your coffee, if you wished, and take it home. Many of these creatures would have arrived in the London Basin on slavers making the return Atlantic leg of their journey, some of them mooring in the dock now overlooked by the front windows of my flat, where I stand on many a morning, holding my once so fashionable, then discarded, then recycled-as-a-rescue little tabby cat in my arms, the two of us part of one of those overlapping Venn diagrams in human history that leaves you marveling quite how much of it can map onto the same few hundred yards. And how narrow the line between status as living creature and disposable piece of property can become, too.

We refashion them through breeding, fashion ourselves with them as exotic possessions, and then set about styling them with the latest uber-chic accessories, too. Patrons of those eighteenth-century coffeehouses, perusing the newspapers also on offer, would have found in them advertisements not only for ever more exotic animals but for all the extras to go with them: a monkey offered for sale with a suit of clothes "and a neat house," for example.[14] Indoor-dwelling lapdogs also had their own exquisite little houses. Marie-Antoinette's gilt and pale blue velvet doghouse, or *niche de chien*, is of such artistry that it is today preserved in the Metropolitan Museum of Art. In 1768 Jean-Jacques Bachelier painted what may well be another Havanese like Purkoy with such a *niche de chien* behind it, plus what looks suspiciously like its owner's well-chewed slippers, thus suggesting that no matter how long we have been presenting them with possessions of their own, the belongings our animals have always preferred have been those that used to be ours.

The Havanese in this painting has also been "clipt," in fact it has virtually been topiarized. Clipping and grooming is another means of styling a pet, and again of elevating the public image of the owner. The first dog "barbers" appeared in Paris in the eighteenth century. Being French, they were roundly satirized by the British, notwithstanding the theory that the fashion originated when poodles were hunting dogs for waterfowl, and their heavy coats were clipped to stop them becoming waterlogged as they forced their way through marsh and reed bed.[15] J. G. Wood positively splutters with outrage at the notion of barbering your dog—"Do not on any account clip his hair in the stupid and ugly fashion that is so often adopted and which was first imported from France," he thunders, but he was fighting a losing battle. Browns of Regent Street was already offering the same service in London.[16] There were summer and winter cuts for fashionable dogs in Paris (one was the "lion cut," now seen on both cats and dogs), and with an eye, no doubt, to the difficulties of bathing your dog in a small Parisian apartment, dog bathing was also offered along the banks of the Seine to rid the animals of fleas and odor.[17] A tiny and no doubt sweet-smelling little black dog sits beside two women, one older and one younger, in the foreground of Édouard Manet's *Music in the Tuileries* of 1862. It has its own chair, and despite the fact that it looks as if it would be hard put to force a path across anything more resistant than a deep-pile rug, it, like they, is accessorized with blue silk ribbon, holding back the hair over its face as if it were growing out a fringe. Does this mean the animal was seen by its owner, one of those two women, as no more than a fashionable accessory itself, as consumer goods? Or does it mean that it was seen, and benevolently, as a small human? Bachelier's Havanese also sports a bow—pink, in that case. Supposedly again the fashion had a hunting origin, to make dogs easier to spot. That sounds suspiciously like special pleading to me.

A hair bow is one thing, but what on earth would the Reverend Wood have made of the fashion of dyeing a dog's coat to match your own? What are any of us to make of it? Cora Pearl, a notorious Parisian courtesan, was at the height of her fame in the 1860s when Manet was painting in the Tuileries, and was notorious for having dyed her dog blue to match her gown. The dye was toxic, and the dog succumbed. In the 1920s, the Marchesa Luisa Casati, a professional exotic herself, prowled the streets of Venice with her cheetahs and blue-dyed greyhounds. We have, thank God, moved on from this, at least by a little. When Parisian model Lia Catreux appeared on Instagram in 2015 with her Pomeranian dyed fuchsia pink, the response was anything but impressed. "Our pets are living creatures," said a statement from the Royal Society for the Prevention of Cruelty to Animals (RSPCA), "and dyeing them in this way sends out an extremely worrying message that they could be viewed as novelty accessories rather than intelligent, sentient animals." PETA also had a view: "PETA would urge people to let dogs be dogs:

Love and appreciate them for their natural beauty and leave them out of our confusing human shenanigans."[18] Quite.

Writers train themselves to live pretty frugally, for the most part. We have a quietly paranoid relationship with our incomes—no monthly topping-up, just a steady whittling down, one fat year followed by seven lean ones. But where I hesitate on purchases for me, I readily buy toys and treats for my cats, partly because it's an expression of the affection I feel for them but also because watching them play is a source of huge amusement to me. It surprises me how infrequently you find this given its proper weight in studies on the nature of our relationship with our companion animals, as a reason for us having them about us in the first place—simply, that they make us laugh. Watching Bird and Daisy rolling around as they press catnip mice to their muzzles like Victorian ether addicts, or pursuing a Ping-Pong ball madly up and down the hall, tails a-fuzz with high spirits and feline electricity, has me in tucks of laughter every time and costs me almost nothing, nickels and dimes. This market in "extras" gives the pet trade a second engine, if you like, and reaches from one end of the economic scale to the other, from Marie-Antoinette's *niche de chien* right down to the street described by Louis Wain in 1892. No Swarovski-studded cat flaps ($1,644/£1,250) or dog tiaras ($4.2 million/£3.1 million—seriously) here.[19] Instead, somewhere in London's East End, there was this, a narrow thoroughfare:

> occupied by shops where birds, dogs, cats, pigeons, fowls, guinea-pigs, mice, rats, goats, rabbits, and fish, were on sale at the lowest market rates. If the quantity and quality of the livestock was

remarkable, the number of articles which was necessary for the comfort of their daily life was nothing short of staggering, especially in the bird line. Cages for birds, fountains for birds, nests for birds, seeds for birds, baths for birds, musical instruments for birds, paste for birds, nets for birds, traps for birds—the catalogue is endless...[20]

Many of the birds for sale down such a street in 1892 would have been canaries. You may think there is little to say about canaries as an example of the fashionable pet, but you would be wrong. The pet canary is a perfect example of manufactured exotica. The canary was once a small greenish bird, about the size of a sparrow and almost as nondescript, whose only noteworthy characteristic was the volume of its song. Louis XI of France bought canaries as songbirds in 1478, and there is nothing like a royal owner to raise an animal's prestige. Canaries also have a natural color variation in their plumage, which we were quick to exploit. By 1657 all-yellow canaries were in existence and as rarities much in demand; that man of fashion Samuel Pepys received two from a naval friend, Captain Rooth, in January 1661. Only a couple of decades later, however, yellow canaries need no longer come via an obliging sea captain. By the 1680s they were being bred in England and were available widely and cheaply enough to be sold like Morland's guinea pigs by street vendors door-to-door.

For centuries the canary breeders par excellence were the miners of the Harz Mountains in Germany. For them canaries were sentinel birds—canaries are extremely susceptible to toxic gases and would self-lessly keel over at the least trace of methane or firedamp in the air of a coal tunnel, thus giving the less susceptible human miners a chance to make their escape and creating the folk belief that these delicate little birds could be used to absorb human ailments like so much feathered blotting paper.[21] But the miners also bred and trained the birds as singers, as did the exiled French Huguenot weavers of the English city of Norwich.[22] Tim Birkhead, in his *The Red Canary*, makes the wholly believable suggestion that for homeworkers such as the weavers, the canary's song provided the kind of company now to be found by having a radio burbling away in the background.[23] And what songs: a top Harz Roller can trill its way through an entire tropical forest of notes and calls, plus a sort of falsetto imitation of a tommy gun and one that sounds to me exactly like a squeaky toy being trodden on. Malinois canaries produce "Klokkende," which sounds like water drops, and "Flu-itenrolle," like a long breath on a flute, and all, coming from such tiny birds, are mesmerizing. In the eighteenth and nineteenth centuries, a good living could be made by professional trainers of canaries, or *sif-fleurs*, who were employed by the most fashionable owners to expand their bird's repertoires with flutes and water-whistles. So by this point we had not only changed the bird's color, we had changed its voice as well, and somehow, in the cultural subconscious of the day, separated it entirely from its natural origins. So ubiquitous was the canary's caged presence in drawing rooms across Europe and America that bird and cage came to be seen as one.[24] "The cage is its native element," writes J. G. Wood:

Even the genuine British soldier can hardly be more helpless when deprived of ordinary military routine than is a canary-bird when set free and forced to fly alone in the world.[25]

The precursor to the pet shop of today was perhaps to be found in Paris in the twelfth century, with the bird sellers who plied their trade around the door of the church of St. Geneviève la Petite or on the Pont au Change.[26] The precursors to the PetSmart or Petco of today were the brothers Charles and Henry Reiche, who founded a commercial empire on the import of canaries from Germany and then their export right across the United States on the new transcontinental railroad.[27] Ten million canaries were imported into the United States in the first four decades of the twentieth century alone. This was perhaps the high-water mark in the pet canary's fortunes—Robert Stroud, the "Birdman of Alcatraz," who was possibly the most untypical owner a little canary bird has ever had, published his best-selling *Diseases of Canaries* in 1933 with as many as three hundred of them sharing his cell. (But then Stroud, a two-time murderer who spent fifty-four of his seventy-three years incarcerated and forty-two of those in solitary confinement, is possibly the most untypical best-selling author who has ever lived, to match.) And then, still not satisfied, we changed the canary's color once again. You can turn canaries orange, as the breeders in Norwich discovered, by feeding them red peppers; and if you interbreed with red siskins, after decades of experimentation that has left the siskin itself as an endangered species with maybe no more than six hundred pairs left in the wild, you can produce the red-factor canary, which looks like a grenadine cocktail balanced on a pair of hat pins. What Nature gives with one hand, however, she takes with the other. For all its beguiling-sounding chirps and trills, compared to a Harz Roller, the red canary can't sing worth a damn.

It is all so much easier for us now. Today, if you wish to discover what is new, what is exotic, and what is newly fashionable, you simply go to a pet show.

The first official dog show was held in Newcastle in the north of England in 1859, the first cat show in London in 1871. Here is a little historical connective tissue: the man who organized the 1871 show was Harrison William Weir, who would have been well known to his contemporaries as an engraver and illustrator of, among other works, the highly popular *Illustrated Natural History* of the Reverend J. G. Wood. Such shows were small and regional, but they were an instant hit, and they grew to be very large and international; and among other breeds introduced the general public to Chihuahuas, Pekingese, and the Persian cats that were first exhibited at that London show in 1871. I went to farming shows that were small and regional as a child and spent hours in the tents devoted to rabbits and guinea pigs, or in fascinated terror, nose pressed to the pane of glass that was all that separated me from the interior of a real live beehive, trying to spot the queen. Such shows had a breezily amateurish quality to them; they were punctuated by deafening announcements for lost children, and many of those showing their prize sheep or pigs or bulls or pots of lemon cheese, or the prowess of their offspring on a Thelwell-shaped pony, wore exactly the same suits to do so, if they were men, that they had worn to their own weddings, or if they were women, their one and only hat. I miss them. When I found myself at the Rare Breeds fair up in the Midlands, I felt at home at once.

The pet show today is a different thing altogether. It is as sophisticated an experience of commerce and marketing as is walking into a major department store. It is so stage-managed that you come out of it with head awhirl and feeling like you, the consumer, have somehow become a product yourself.

Just as in a department store, the first stands you are likely to encounter are selling the small stuff, the impulse-buy belongings, the toys and beds and feeders; fencing to keep your indoor cat indoors; litter for anything that poops; "eggloos" that enable you to turn the balcony of your flat into a hen run for bantams. As a necessity in the well-regulated household, even Mrs. Beeton had time for bantams, no doubt because of the glorious golden color imparted to anything made with their eggs.

The first living creatures you are likely to encounter are fish, which could be something of a disappointment, except that I think they are there to keep the unwilling male, trailing behind his cat- or dog- or rabbit-obsessed female partner, happy. Fish don't need cute little coats; they need manly stuff like pumps and filters and LED lighting. They need the kinds of things you can putter about with in sheds and improve at your workbench. They need (apparently) miniature landscapes to swim over of the sort you might create as background for a model railway. According to my friend Eve, fish are décor, but if that's so, they are very beautiful décor, and the kit for them is praiseworthily imaginative. At one show I was very taken by a tank that could liven up your tropical fish's day by simulating a tropical storm. Would the fish—tiny, darting little gummy bears, zipping about in their tank in strict formation—ever have experienced a real tropical storm? "Not in the wild, no," said their breeder. So we would be creating an artificial version for them of a natural phenomenon that they had never, naturally, experienced? "That's about it."

Next stop on from the fish are usually the birds. If my observations hold true for all pet shows, you will know when you have reached the bird section because these brilliant, squawking, sulking, teeter-totter, paint-box-colored creatures inspire a livery among their owners, too. Thus my notebook for one such show reads "lots of funky hair colors on the parrot people." Well, fine—if anything is to have dyes of one sort or another applied to it, to declare its solidarity with the animal that shares its life, then far better us than the pet. One aisle on from the parrots at this same show and I found myself deep in the territory of the background artistes from *Indiana Jones and the Temple of Doom*—the Death's Head cockroaches and Curly-Hair tarantulas; a giant African millipede named Mollie (which to my thinking is simply perverse); a Rose tarantula, which looked just like a little curled-up pink sea anemone; Cuban tree frogs; and a Red Tegu (for the unfamiliar, a breed of lizard that grows to the size of a large dog or small child, brick-red, and with jowls like a Victorian alderman). It was being admired by an outsize fan, glinting with studs and chains himself and wearing a lumberjack shirt the breadth, across his back, of a picnic blanket. "What a beauty," he was saying, as I passed by, "I need one," thus encapsulating the entire arc of why we do this in two sentences. And yes, there were plenty of Goths and punks among the crowd of onlookers, too, eyes a-shine with desire for a cockroach or tarantula of their own.

You have to persist, guided by those unmistakable Oriental meows, or the odd deep woof, to reach the sections of such shows devoted to what most of us would think as being our animal companions. I may be imagining it, I may have been biased, but it did seem to me that everyone in the crowd in the "World of Cats" at my first such show had a broad grin on their face—everyone, that is, except for the male half of the couple walking ahead of me. "Anna," he announced as he peeled away, "I'll be in the fish." The other thing that always strikes me, compared to the size (now) of my two, is how *tiny* the pedigreed cats are. I have a quick sketch I did of a Cornish Rex, half of whose head was ears, which were far and away the biggest thing about him. It always makes me wonder, must pedigreed cats be like supermodels and stick to a diet all the time?

The other thing you notice at once is how everyone crouches down to get on eye level with the animals at such shows. Katherine Grier makes the point in *Pets in America* that a portrait of an owner with pet on lap is saying something very different about that relationship than one where the heads of pet and owner are level with each other.[28] We don't want to look down on the animals at these shows as specimens in cages; we want connection with them as individuals. It was also notable how children were at once admitted to the front of the crowd. In 1763, in his *Jubilate Agno*, the poet Christopher Smart, owner of Jeoffrey, defined his cat as "an instrument for the children to learn benevolence upon," and it seems it's a lesson we still value. At this particular show I saw one small girl in the crowd, face-to-face with a Somali, quite clearly falling in love: her eyes wide, her expression smoothed of everything but joy. There were Somalis, there were Siamese, there were Thai cats, Ragdolls, Maine coons, and Burmese. Seated in a baby buggy, sleeping peacefully away, was a Sphynx. "She's a rescue," said her owner. How on earth does a completely hairless cat become a rescue? It's not as if this was an animal you would bring into your home without realizing what you were getting into.

From treasured exotic to rescue cat—where had I come across that before? I reached down and touched the Sphynx's pink flank and have to report that it was as soft and as dry and as pleasing to the touch as a rose petal. The little girl nose-to-nose with the Somali was still there, enraptured, when I moved on, her parents standing behind her, the father with a look of comedic resignation on his face, and his wife's hand upon his arm. She was *stroking* it.

Time, as they say, to go to the dogs.

Everything we have done to the canary has been doubly endured by the dog. We have bred them this way and that, up or down, out and in; changed their coats, changed their color; and then intervened mechanically if that was the only way to get the animal we wanted. We have clipped their ears into more pleasing shapes (more pleasing to us) and docked their tails. We have inserted "neuticles" into empty scrotums so that a castrated dog might still look as if it has its bollocks, even if only, one assumes, to any of us sniffing its butt—talk about confusing human shenanigans!—and we have removed their troublesome claws.[29] I chewed my fingernails as a child, and declawing is the equivalent of solving this problem in your offspring by amputating the top joint of their fingers. Seriously, if the state of their furnishings means more to an owner than their animal's paws, they should stick to soft toys. If they need a pet, go get a Furby.

There were just fifteen or so distinct breeds of dogs at the beginning of the nineteenth century; there are some 340 as I write. Breeds fashionable in Darwin's day, such as the Dandie Dinmont, popularized by Sir Walter Scott in his novel *Guy Mannering* of 1815 (an early example of later crazes for Dalmatians following Disney's *101 Dalmatians*, perhaps, or of clownfish after the release of *Finding Nemo*), are now worryingly rare; while new breeds are being created at a rate that is equally troubling. There are now even "wolfdogs," an attempt to turn the wheel of evolution full circle, which has produced a rangy, gray-and-yellow German shepherd–type dog that does, yes, remind one instinctively and immediately of a wolf. I've seen a pair of Czech wolfdogs being positively mobbed by admirers at a dog show. Just the name was enough to draw a crowd. Meanwhile the Pomeranian, like Lia Catreux's, which was once a sizable dog itself, had its size decreased by half and more than half during the nineteenth century and became the toy breed familiar today. Queen Victoria was a great fan of Pomeranians and had much to do with popularizing the smallest versions of the breed; she and her German consort, Prince Albert, also introduced the dachshund to the fashionable fireside, and again, favored smaller and smaller variations. Nothing, as we know, like the royal seal of approval; then along came World War I, and any "German" breed fell completely out of favor. Poor dogs; we have even made them subject to our human politics. How insane is that?

You can argue, obviously, that owners have always bred from favored animals, else where does the whole notion of pedigree come from? Pepys, once he had settled down into the role of owner, soon came to pride himself on his eye as a dog breeder, too, organizing an assignation in his closet between Fancy and a dog belonging to "Mrs. Buggins": "by holding down the bitch helped him to line her, which he did very stoutly, so I hope it will take, for it is the prettiest dog that ever I saw."[30] There is always someone who will be left unhappy: breeding, according to Yi-Fu Tuan in his famous essay, has made of the Chow "a stodgy teddy bear," but I would not expect any owner of any Chow to agree.[31]

You could also take the view that this is no more than dogs doing what dogs have always done. J. R. Ackerley was fascinated by Queenie's coming in and going out of season and determined that she should experience motherhood—just as soon as he had managed to locate a suitor. His telling of the hunt for the perfect mate for her reads almost as a knightly quest. (In the end, Queenie took matters into her own hands with a mongrel from next door.) I used to know a very elderly and dignified Pekingese named Wilfred who, years before and on the day his people moved to the other end of the country, managed to impregnate a neighbor's standard poodle by making use, so the story went, of a convenient field stile.

The difference is that then, this would have got you crossed off the Christmas card list, whereas today, it creates a designer puppy with a premium price tag attached. Money is involved. The changing whims of fashion are involved. The dog's agency in the matter is minimal; ethical issues of respect and dominion and control are involved. I hope no one is genuinely breeding a Brat (American rat terrier × Boston terrier), a Shocker (cocker spaniel × Shiba Inu), or a Poxer (you can, I am sure, work that one out yourself), simply because you can give such a cross-breed an amusing name, but I am far from confident they're not. I found one website with seventy-six such hybrids listed under the letter A, and 169 under the letter B, and there were twenty-four more letters of the alphabet to go. The vast majority come with photographs, to prove someone's really gone and done it.

It must be acknowledged that some of the dogs produced by these crosses are cute (or *kawaii*, as the Japanese, the nation that pretty much invented postmodern cute, would describe them) to the nth degree. Others do not shed or provoke allergies, thus making pet owning possible where it would not have been before. And it is reassuring that every owner who posted a photograph of their crossbreed described their animal with great affection and with the conviction that no dog could be better, and the website has its own warning that "choosing a dog simply for its looks is a foolish way to choose a dog." But equally, so is breeding for them. Wally Conron, the Australian who bred the first Labradoodle in 1988, has spoken of his regret, now, at doing so, at the tsunami of homemade hybrids his act unleashed, and the fact that, as he has put it, conditions such as hip dysplasia or breathing difficulties or eye problems might unknowingly be bred *into* dogs, as opposed to being bred *away from*. This is a serious concern, and I'm sure I'm not alone in being left uneasy at the idea of dog DNA being mixed as if by some crazed bartender let loose on the cocktail cabinet. How far are we from the dystopia of Margaret Atwood's rakunks and pigoons—or how near? And this is even before we get into the true Victor Frankenstein–type activities of those who deliberately breed for deformity because it has income-generating qualities of rarity or cuteness, and create dwarf cats with shortened limbs and kangaroo cats or squittens with forelegs they cannot use at all—or, indeed, El Rey Magnum, the Arab foal who looks (to me) like the result of some dreadful collision in the gene splicer between a horse and a Barbie doll.[32] Whether his extraordinarily distorted profile compromises his ability to breathe or not, it certainly compromises his ability to look like a horse. It won't make him gallop faster (it may indeed have exactly the opposite effect), it won't make him stronger; it has nothing whatsoever to do with augmenting his primary abilities as a horse and everything to do with making him correspond to a human aesthetic. His breeder has described him as a step toward perfection.

Not that any of this is new. In Japan in the eighteenth century a favorite pet was the "waltzing mouse"—mice with a neurological disorder that caused them to bob and tilt their heads and to run in circles. Waltzing mice were bred to be better and better waltzers, never mind the distress in which the mouse itself lived out its days. One of my girlfriends lives as the willing slave to an elegant black cloud of a Persian cat, Mrs. Peel, who was bred with a nose of such exquisite minuteness that every so often Mrs. Peel has to stop whatever bit of devilry she is about and clear her airways with a tiny sneeze. There are teacup Chihuahuas—minuscule, hand-size creatures that do indeed seem to spend their lives like the beasts listed in Jorge Luis Borges's *Celestial Emporium of Benevolent Knowledge*, trembling as if they were mad, but even in 1875 a French journalist was writing in alarm at the *"terrier microscopique"* to be met with on the streets of Paris.[33] We want *kawaii* and we will have it (just ask El Rey Magnum), with nothing but the ever profounder concerns of animal welfare and our own ever deepening insecurities as checks on our pursuit. It's comforting, in a way, to find that back in 1792, Carl Linnaeus, the father of modern scientific taxonomy of animals, was already complaining that the "dog of Malta," the literally archetypal lapdog from Roman times to the present day, had been bred down to the size of a squirrel. Yet the Maltese is with us still. Hooray for the human race that our level of acceptance is so much higher than it was, that Grumpy Cat, who was born, *not* bred, with feline dwarfism, wasn't immediately drowned in a bucket and instead became so well loved a public pet and such an Internet star. God help us that somewhere out there you can be sure there will be someone deliberately trying to create her successor.

And yet, and yet—devoted breeders have also preserved animals that would otherwise have vanished and been lost. Wolfhounds were saved by Captain George Augustus Graham in the 1880s when, there being no more wolves in Ireland, these huge dogs were rapidly following them into extinction. Wolfhounds now have the blood of the Borzoi, the Great Dane, the Scottish deerhound, and the mastiff in their veins, along of course with that of the original wolf. Here we are again with the difference between the generality "out there" and the specific animal one knows personally: the only Labradoodle I have known was a gorgeous dog—loyal, companionable, smiley-faced, and with a lion's mane of wayward curls around his shoulders, who took on the empty role of alpha male within his family without hesitation.

The question remains, however, why? Why turn a greenish bird yellow, and then a little yellow bird red? Why breed the African Grey to be shocking pink all over? A perfect Red Factor African Grey today can be worth as much as $150,000.[34] Is it simply because we know we can? Are we all obsessives, like Isabella—the more, the more? Why pursue the fashionable and exotic at all?

Because the irony here is that if we want the best life with and *for* our companion animals, the way they look is very low down the list of component factors. If we want that one special animal, the difference is made by the quality of our relationship with them, the depth of our comprehension of them, and the strength of our connection to them. Fashion has absolutely nothing to do with that.

Back in the late seventeenth century, many of the first London coffeehouses were businesses with Dutch connections, and it was the Dutch king of England, William III, and his English spouse, Mary, who began one of the early documented crazes for a fashionable pet when they brought their pugs into England with them in 1689. How very different these dogs looked to the pop-eyed, flat-faced little snorters of today: those first trotting around Hampton Court Palace had protuberant snouts, bigger, terrier-like bodies, and longer legs, too. Times changed and the craze for them ran its course, and Dutch pugs fell out of vogue, such that Dr. Johnson's friend Hester Lynch Piozzi, traveling in Italy with her second husband in 1785, would single out for special note the fact that pugs were still popular in Padua:

> the little pug dog or Dutch mastiff [of] which our English ladies were once so fond…has quitted London for Padua, I perceive; where he is restored happily to his former honours, and every carriage I meet here has a pug in it. That breed of dogs is now so near extirpated among us that I recollect only Lord Penryn who possesses such an animal.[35]

Fashionability mattered not a jot to William Hogarth, however. The English painter left us not only a perfect record of the pug's appearance in the mid eighteenth century but also one of the finest "animal's companion" portraits you could ask for, with the animal very much center stage and the companion minding his place in the background. There is Hogarth, in cap and wrap and with a noticeable dint in his forehead, gazing out at us with challenging mien from a fictive self-portrait, and there, seated before it in all his four-legged and three-dimensional reality, is his pug. The owner here is reduced to the piece of property, available to buy or sell; the dog is the active, living creature.

Hogarth's liking for pugs was attributed by the man himself to his own pugnaciousness and the tenacity with which he held to his own beliefs. (In one work, his pug became his actual proxy, and was shown peeing on the words of one of Hogarth's critics.) Hogarth was also one of the first, in his etchings *The Four Stages of Cruelty*, to put forward a link between cruelty to animals and cruelty to your fellow man, a connection still being debated by psychologists today. "I am a professional enemy," Hogarth declared, "to persecution of all kinds, whether against man or beast." But London in the eighteenth century was what it was, with its *Carry On* humor and all those jokes about the Queen's ass, and Hogarth's sense of irreverence was as broad as that of any man of his times. When it came to naming his unfashionable little pug, etiquette be damned. His dog, so beautifully and honorably elevated in their double portrait, apparently had a specific habit for which Hogarth wanted it to be remembered, and he named his dog Trump.

"Trump" had various meanings in the eighteenth century. According to the *Oxford English Dictionary*, one well-known definition was to cheat or deceive; and another, to sing one's own praises. But another of the word's most common uses was as jocular slang for a fart.

And so we come to naming.

Lieutenant Temple Godman of the 5th Light Dragoon Guards, his servant
Kilburn, and "The Earl," photographed by Roger Fenton in 1855.

CHAPTER FOUR

NAMING

Sulley, you're not supposed to name it! Once you name it, you start getting attached to it!

—Mike Wazowski, *Monsters, Inc.*, 2001

A ccording to the first chapter of the Book of Genesis, having created heaven and earth, the stars, the sun, and the moon, and greened the earth with vegetation, God filled the sea with fish and the sky with birds, and then the land with "living creatures according to their kinds."[1] When man and woman came along, as the final act in creation, it was specifically so that they might rule over this thus far nameless cornucopia. The four rivers of Eden all had names, but not until halfway through chapter 2 of Genesis does God bring "all the wild animals and all the birds in the sky" to Man, who is still unnamed himself, and watch as "whatever the man called each living creature, that was its name." Adam acquires a name immediately thereafter; Eve, despite the importance of her role in the event, remains merely "the woman" until after the Fall, when Adam names her himself. So according to the categories identified in this book, Adam becomes the first animal's companion in history—one, he lives with the animals; two, he names the animals; and three, he doesn't eat them. This, so far, was a vegetarian or maybe even a vegan Eden, where man might eat of any tree in the garden bar one. The birds of the air, the fish of the seas, the living creatures of the land, were off the menu; man was there to work the ground, and that was all.

Robinson Crusoe finds himself cast ashore on another, later Eden. Rather than giving it a name, he shoots the first bird that comes close enough to him, an act that seems absolutely typical of our relationship with the natural world since the Fall. "I believe it was the first gun that had ever been fired there since the creation of the world," Crusoe, or rather his creator, Daniel Defoe, writes in 1719. Defoe equips Crusoe with a dog and two cats from his shipwreck. The dog becomes "a trusty servant to me for many years...I only wanted to have him talk to me," says Crusoe, "but that he could not do." He also acquires a parrot and gives it a name—the rather uninspired Poll—teaching it to sit upon his finger and say his name in turn. Meanwhile, the two ship's cats simply go about filling the island with kittens, as cats have always done. Crusoe's real pet on the island is, without doubt, Man Friday, or "my man Friday" as Crusoe describes him, "a servant and perhaps a companion."

From Adam onward, to name something has been to make explicit your dominion over it. If you are the namer, the one who assigns something an identity, you establish a primary relationship with it, too. Any number of canny owners have solved the issue of a partner or child unhappy at the presence of a new cat or dog by giving them the privilege of naming. Naming is claiming—*my* man Friday. It's something else we understand so well that it can be used as movie shorthand—in the 2014 thriller *The Drop*, it's clear that the disconnected, enigmatic Bob Saginowski will assume responsibility for the injured pit bull puppy he found the moment he comes up with a name for it: Rocco. And in the act of naming, he has to relinquish some of his disconnectedness, and thus the rest of the movie unfolds from that point onward.

So in answer to the question "What's in a name?," where the animal's companion is concerned: a lot. First, there is that question of ownership and thus of responsibility. Second, there is the type of name—generic, such as Poll, or specific and individual; and what that implies about the relationship with the creature named. And then there is the whole business of naming in the first place. Why do we do it? Why is a name so significant a thing?

One way of approaching this is to look at animals who are within human space but whom we intentionally *don't* name. The scholar and feminist Donna Haraway calls this "the extreme showing the underside of the normal," and she's right.[2] Lab animals remain rigorously unnamed. In part, this is explained by the fact that one lab animal is meant to be as undifferentiated from the next lab animal as possible; that's rather their point. But the lie is given to this by the fact that when sociologist Mary T. Phillips began investigating this phenomenon of un-naming, she found that any rat taken home by a researcher, thus crossing the border into pethood, would be named and that researchers in the lab were keen to show they cared about the welfare of the animals in there with them even if they didn't name them. "There is a direct connection," Phillips writes, "between naming animals and developing emotional ties to them." Of course there is, as Mike Wazowski could confirm. "This," Phillips continues, "is a consequence of... the social construction of the individual, and it is a consequence researchers consciously wish to avoid."[3]

Equally, so do whale conservationists. While I was with a whale-watching group off Cape Cod one summer, the fact of our being interlopers within the whale's space was unmistakable. Carl Linnaeus described our entire human existence as taking place within a fragile bubble; drifting off the Cape, surrounded by fog and riding over a sea whose inky darkness told you how deep it was, I felt not only an interloper but an alien: vulnerable and very far from all that was familiar. Up the whales came, white flippers visible long before the enormous dark bulk of the creature itself was comprehensible. There is an etiquette to the naming of whales: the names are meant to function as pure identifiers, labels, created solely for the watchers' benefit. So they're almost always genderless, to begin with—"There's Tear!" our guide called out over the sound system. "There's our friend Salt! That one's Tornado!" And as labels they are as devoid of human association as human language permits, because whales are wild creatures and should stay that way.

With what looks to be the same kind of reasoning, Aisholpan, the Kazakh girl at the center of the documentary *The Eagle Huntress,* never once names her eagle. Although she is heard declaring, "I already love this eagle," within what appears to be a day of its capture, although she feeds it and talks to it with great tenderness, although the eagle lives inside with Aisholpan and her family, neither she nor they ever give it a name, even with the necessity of having to utter urgent commands in its training and have them understood. "Secure your eagle!" Aisholpan's father warns her when they go hunting, as the novice and panicked eagle flaps about upside-down from Aisholpan's hand, like a broken umbrella. There's no name for the eagle because after seven years the tradition is that it will be returned to the wild. It is only a long-term loan within our human space. It remains a wild creature; the whales of Cape Cod are the same—even as those creating the names rely on them to make the whales matter that little bit more to us, enough for us to donate that little bit more to their conservation, at any rate. Because that's another of the drivers for us, where names are concerned—this business of mattering.

We humans are inveterate namers. We give names to our cars, which are hardly likely to answer to them; we give names to our houses, despite the fact that all one needs to identify a house is its numerical address; some of us even give names to our private parts. Horticulturalists name and rename and rename again the plants in our gardens (something that not even Genesis attempted—all that naming going on, and not a single plant in the garden of Eden gets one, other than the Tree of Knowledge). As I was working on this book, Storm Doris was putting whitecaps on the waters of the dock outside—this naming of storms is new to those of us on Greenwich Mean Time, but the explanation from the Meteorological Office, when they were taken to task for this seemingly needless bit of anthropomorphism, was that if a storm is given a name, there is more engagement with it and hence more preparation. People take its likely threat to life and limb more seriously. It has more being-ness; it matters more; it is more real.

The underside again: when Ham the chimpanzee was sent into space by NASA in 1961, the first hominid ever to leave this planet, he went up known only as "Number 65." Those in charge of public relations for the program rightly foresaw the far greater problems they would face if a named animal, with all the attributes that creates of character and biography, not to mention human responsibility for him as an individual, failed to make it back to earth alive. Number 65 was only named Ham on his successful return. (His handlers, however, to whom he evidently had all those attributes already, always had a name for him. They called him Chop Chop Chang.)⁴ Four years later, London Zoo had its own lesson in names mattering when one of their eagles escaped—an event of importance to them alone, so the staff at the zoo initially thought, but public interest in the bird's exploits as an escapee in Regent's Park reached such a fever pitch that a name for him became a necessity, and thus Goldie the Eagle was created.⁵

Goldie the Eagle, Guy the Gorilla, Clara the Rhinoceros, who toured Europe from 1741 to 1758...Naming public animals is particularly important, because the name is how we take them figuratively and symbolically into our homes and make them ours and why their fates become something in which we share. It's why football teams name their mascots and how it is possible that for so many of its visitors, the emblem of the mighty Metropolitan Museum of Art in New York, completely unofficial as he may be, is a blue faience model of a hippopotamus, some four thousand years old, just eight inches (twenty centimeters) long and known universally as William.⁶ And to bring in a single, tragically notorious contemporary example: Cecil the Lion, shot in a pantomime of masculin-

Giovanni Savoldo, *Portrait of a Woman as Saint Margaret of Antioch, c.*1525.
Musei Capitolini, Rome.

One dog-man to another. Henry Scott, 3rd Duke of Buccleuch with a favorite dog, painted by Thomas Gainsborough *c.*1770, and as engraved in mezzotint by John Dixon before 1771.

A peasant family in relation to the natural world from 500 years ago, as depicted by a Flemish artist for "February," from *Grimani Breviary*, *c*.1515.

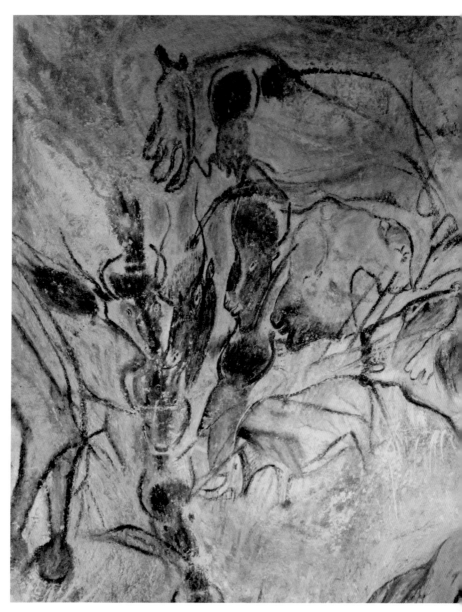

The Panel of Lions from the Chauvet Cave, created 35,000–30,000 BC.

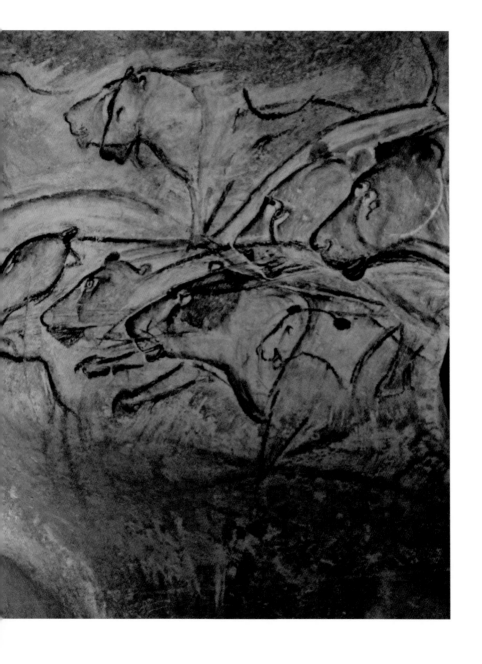

Sir Anthony van Dyck, *The Five Eldest Children of Charles I*, 1637.

Pieter Hugo, *Abdullahi Mohammed with Mainasara, Ogere-Remo, Nigeria*, 2007.

Il Sodoma (Giovanni Antonio Bazzi), self-portrait with badgers and raven in the Life of St. Benedict frescoes, Monte Oliveto, 1502.

My brother cuddling a real-live lion cub in Harrods's Pet Kingdom in the
early 1970s.

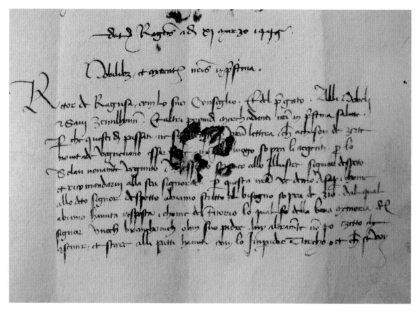

More paw prints, from 500 years ago, photographed by Emir O. Filipović
in 2011.

Diego Velázquez's *Dwarf with a Dog, c.*1645. Less than a decade separates this from Van Dyck's *Five Eldest Children of Charles I*; in essence, the elements of the paintings duplicate each other, yet their messages and implications could not be more different.

George V when Duke of York, caught by an unknown photographer in *c*.1895 being extremely irreverent with a pet pug.

Alexander Bassano, *Queen Victoria*, c.1890.

George Morland, *Selling Guinea Pigs*, c.1789.

George Piner Cartland, *Princess Alice of Albany with Skippy the fox terrier*, photographed in April 1886.

Titian, *Federigo Gonzaga, Duke of Mantua*, c.1525–30.

ity by the American dentist Walter Palmer in Zimbabwe in July 2015. Without a name, Cecil would have been merely another casualty of the recreational trophy hunter; with a name, assigned to him as part of a study being conducted by Oxford University, he was an individual in his own right, a symbol of wildlife conservation, the father figure of his pride, and the cause of an extraordinary moment of international outrage that encapsulates both the multilayered challenges of our relationship with the natural world in the twenty-first century and the instinctiveness of our response to its being traduced. What's in a name? As much, when we name an animal, as when we name ourselves.

So if you name your Alexandrine parakeet Kevin, as had the owner I met at the National Pet Show in London, or Echo, as friends of mine in California named their Jardine's parrot, it is saying something different about your relationship than if you had named it simply Poll. As a child I was the owner of two rabbits—one, a Dwarf Netherlandish, he of the daily little blue pill, I named Van Dyke, and I adored him. I loved the human way he splashed his warm milk about, and I was fascinated by the little pink beansprout that grew out of the fluff on his tummy after he'd dosed himself up. But the other rabbit I never bonded with at all— the poor unfortunate was an albino with, to my childhood sensibilities, alarming pink eyes, and all he ever got as a name was Bun.

What they lack in originality, however, these generic names make up for in staying power. Here's a quick trot through the most common: Bunny, which has been around at least since the seventeenth century; Jenny Wren, Robin Redbreast, Jack Daw, and Mag Pie, which have been with us much longer. Since they so often feature in nursery rhymes, they are often the first animal names in the West any of us learn.[7] For centuries the generic name for a sparrow was Philip, as in the early-sixteenth-century poem (by Henry VIII's poet laureate, John Skelton, no less), in which a schoolgirl bewails the death of her pet. Three centuries later, Beth March's canary in *Little Women* is still named Pip. There's Polly for a parrot, and in medieval England any random moggy (a term still widely in use in the United Kingdom for a non-pedigreed cat) might be referred to as Gib, a short form of Gilbert. It was a "Gyb our cat" who did for Philip Sparrow, and in his *Diary* entry for November 29, 1667, Samuel Pepys records how the night before "our young gibb-cat" leaped down the stairs "from top to bottom, in two leaps, and frighted us, that we could not tell well whether it was the cat or a spirit, and do sometimes think this morning that the house might be haunted." Any cat owner startled from their slumbers to find themselves part of a feline assault course will sympathize. Among the cartoon moggies, Felix and Sylvester both derive from the Latin genus for the domestic cat, but Tom Cat seems to have been coined only in 1760, in *The Life and Adventures of a Cat*, which may or may not have been written by Henry Fielding. Kitty came along a little earlier in the eighteenth century. The gloriously named Pussy Meow in *The Autobiography of a Cat* (1901) would not have been impressed:

> And right here let me tell you, a cat with a respectable name feels a sense of dignity and self-respect that is impossible to one only known by the general name of "kitty."

No, because while a generic name will do as a label, for the one-on-one relationship between specific owner and specific animal, a unique, "proper" name is essential.

One of the earliest such names to have come down to us is that of Abuwtiyuw, a Tesem hound who died before 2280 BC, so was around a couple of centuries before William the Hippo, and whose name was preserved on his gravestone, found in what might have been the tomb of his owner. We can be confident Abuwtiyuw was important to his owner in a way we would recognize today not simply because they seem to have been buried together but because the gravestone describes how his owner had him laid in a coffin and wrapped in fine linen perfumed with incense. It's been suggested that the *bu* of his name is onomatopoeic and may suggest a sharp, ferocious bark.[8] Or, it might refer to what would have been his pointed ears, a feature of the Tesem, which were greyhound-like hounds, prick-eared and with splendidly curly tails. This naming from a physical characteristic is an obvious and time-honored way of going about it, and many of our own last names came about by exactly this route. There is Klein ("little") in Germany; Kozlov in Russia ("bearded," or literally "he-goat," and another example of our thinking animal in order to think ourselves); Takenaka in Japan, "one who dwells among bamboo"; worldwide any number of Browns, Longs, and Shorts.

It would be pleasing to be able to track a progression in names for our animals from those inspired by a simple characteristic—Anne Boleyn's Purkoy, with his inquisitive expression, Queen Victoria's Dash, for his dashing about, perhaps—to more elaborate forms and then perhaps even to something closer to the names we give ourselves. This would parallel very neatly the supposedly increasing emotional importance of our animals in our lives and homes, coming up to the present day, which has sometimes been put forward. Only I just can't find that such a pattern exists. In fact the only thing consistently true about the process of how we name our animals is that as soon as you think you have found a rule, you find an exception to it. There are names a bit like ours (Gib), names that are identical to ours (Philip), and names that are nothing like any of ours at all—Cruibne, or "Little Paws," who is recorded in the early medieval *Corpus iuris hibernici* as a cat of the barn, and her friend Meone or "Little Meow," a kitchen-cat.[9] *The Master of Game*, written between 1406 and 1413, suggests for hunting dogs the wonderfully Gormenghastian "Nosewise," plus "Smylefeste," "Clench," "Holdfast," and finally "Nameless."[10] It would seem that the dog with no name preceded the horse with none by five centuries. Isabella d'Este's best-beloved of all her little dogs was named Aura by her mistress and was perhaps either as precious to her owner as gold, or yellow-coated, or both. Shakespeare, in *The Two Gentlemen of Verona*, gives us a dog named Crab, for his crabby nature; his owner, Lance, declares:

> I think Crab, my dog, be the sourest-natured dog that lives: my mother weeping, my father wailing, my sister crying, our maid howling, our cat wringing her hands, and all our house in a great perplexity, yet did not this cruel-hearted cur shed one tear.[11]

Very roughly, very tentatively, you might suggest that we are more likely to use names for animals that we would not use for each other—

and then along comes Christopher Smart and his cat Jeoffrey, just to show you how wrong you can be. Or Krook, the appalling villain of Dickens's *Bleak House,* who has a vicious gray alley cat he has ennobled as Lady Jane, which makes him perhaps the original evil mastermind with cat on lap, from James Bond's Blofeld to Austin Powers's Dr. Evil. The only conclusion I feel safe in drawing from all this is that the range of names we used historically is so close to the range of names we use today that as evidence, if they support any aspect of our dealings with our companion animals, it's that the way we regarded our animals in the past is very similar to the way we regard them now.

"If you do not know the names of things," said Carl Linnaeus in his *Philosophia Botanica* of 1751, "the knowledge of them is lost, too," which is true enough, but for us a name is not merely a handy scientific tag. As with Crab, it confers personality as well as identity. When Emma Davenport gets to the description of her Shetland pony in *Live Toys,* the pony in question is referred to as "it" until "it" is named. Thereafter in her narrative, Bluebeard is always referred to as "he," thus making it far easier to recount his biography, too.

The act of naming is as significant as the name itself. Naming creates a relationship, and it makes that relationship visible to others. As anthrozoologist Margo DeMello puts it, in *Animals and Society,* "naming an animal incorporates that creature into our social world."[12] The giving of a name to a pet marks a rite of passage, of entrance from the outside world into our own specific domestic realm. It brings an animal into our human space and our human way of doing things. In fact, without a name, such incorporation is virtually impossible. That's why in the movie *Breakfast at Tiffany's*, Holly Golightly's reuniting with Cat and her promise to give him a name marks her renunciation of her own rootless status and why in the original book, when Holly runs off to some unknown future, Cat remains unnamed and has to be abandoned, too. Again at the National Pet Show one of the stallholders explained to me that all his "small furries" had names riffing on the idea of "chew." Chew Guevara, Chew En Lai...Why did he think naming an animal was important? "Because it persony-fies them." So it does. So paramount is the persony-fying, personality-giving aspect of naming that to some tribes in the native people of northern Alaska, the giving of a name to a dog is what allows its soul to enter it for the first time; while for some Amazonian people, an animal killed as prey is called one thing, whereas the same animal taken from the wild to be kept as a pet is also given a different species name, as if it has become an altogether different creature.[13]

Something not so very different happened with my two cats. I have no idea what they were called by their original owner—like foundlings, their original names were discarded along with the owner's identity when they were taken into the rescue shelter. There, as with all the animals at the shelter, they were christened anew, as Georgie and Ginie, the new names being a reflection of their presence in this new place, this halfway house from which a safer and more healthful life might be found for them, and the discarding of the old, in which they had been malnourished to the point of losing their fur and terrified by every noise and everything that moved. Then I came along, bringing with me my own history of associations and preferences and a view that Georgie didn't suit the little black one at all and that Ginie for her even smaller, stripy sister had an uncertain pronunciation and unpleasing overtones of speculums and stirrups and being asked to shuffle down the examining table. And they were my cats now, which meant that the privilege of naming them was mine as well. As far as I can tell from the updates on the shelter's website, most owners do exactly the same—take their new pet home and rename it forthwith. The same thing happens to Tom Cat—halfway through his adventures, a besotted new owner names him Prince. It's a "material remaking," if you like, a sort of rebirth.[14] So Georgie and Ginie became Bird and Daisy, with Daisy being named by my mother, after my grandmother. It's a family name, if you like, short and small and simple, much like Daisy herself, and so it stuck. While Bird, who is quite the noisiest and most conversational cat I have ever come across, acquired her name from her polysyllabic chirping.[15] Friends in Brooklyn christened their rescue cat Mulligan, so he in your head, whether you have seen the musical *Hamilton* or no, is very likely both handsome and streetwise; and then there is the ineffably classy Mrs. Peel. We cannot, for ourselves, have a sense of self without a name; and because our companion animals are just as important to us, we have to give them names, too, to confirm and enrich our sense of *their* selves.[16]

And so we hit one of the two great conundrums, as owners, in our naming of our pets. The first is that it is *we* who are giving out the names—so we are making our dominion over them explicit even as we are conferring on them an independent identity; and as if that were not brain-tickler enough for you, the next time you sit there contemplating cat on lap or dog resting muzzle on knee, the second conundrum is this: these same names, which are so essential to us, could very well mean nothing to them whatsoever.

One could get very deep into the workings of language here. Names are so essential to us that we have sometimes struggled with the idea that, beyond being a familiar sound made by a familiar voice, it might mean nothing to the animal involved at all.[17] Jane Loudon, writing *Domestic Pets, Their Habits and Management* in 1851, is deeply critical of the intelligence of rabbits on the grounds that, as she writes without irony, they "do not appear even to know *their* names" (my italics). Yes, the names of our animals may be "their" names—but only so far as we are concerned. Byron named his Newfoundland Boatswain for the breed's connection to life at sea; Mr. Rochester's dog is Pilot, for the same reason, but neither dog would know or care what a boatswain or a pilot is or does. Sir Walter Scott's Maida was named after a battle in the Napoleonic Wars, which may seem a strange choice to us but would have troubled Maida not at all.[18] (Even more bizarrely, my father grew up with a farm dog named Bapaume, after a battle in the First World War that might just have been the one where his own father lost most of his right hand.) J. M. Barrie and his wife, Mary Ansell, owned a Newfoundland named Luath (the name appears to have been taken from the Irish for "early," or perhaps "in good time") who changed sex to become the inspiration for the dog Nana in Barrie's *Peter Pan*, but despite Luath patiently enduring close study by the actor who played Nana on stage, of all those people in the rehearsal room as the role took shape, the only creature without the idea of such a thing as a "nanny" in their head was the dog. And Queenie the German shepherd was not remotely bothered by any connotations her name might have had in the human world, but when Ackerley, who was gay, came to publish her biography, his—in my view—majorly oversensitive publishers made him call her Tulip instead. And of course naming is done in one direction only—our animals do not (so far as we know) name us back.

One advantage to the name meaning so little to the animal is that not only is changing it perfectly possible, so are multiple names. The philosopher Jeremy Bentham, who has been called the first patron saint of animal rights, owned a cat known successively as Sir John Langborn, the Reverend John Langborn, and then the Reverend Doctor John Langborn. Muff, the stray who adopted Sir Roy Strong, ended his days as the Reverend Wenceslas Muff, with a walk, Muff's Parade, named in his honor in his owner's garden. My partner's cat is Millie, Millie Malou, Mills! (when she's barfed on something), and Shoulder-Cat, for her favorite resting place, and then has her pick of nicknames, too, which include Baby Girl and Batface. Intriguing to put this habit of ours with our animals against our behavior with the humans who share our lives. Having another name imposed on you by a member of your own species is so odd and rare a piece of behavior that it would almost be an act of aggression, except if you are a parent, giving a nickname to a child, or (and these are the circumstances in which I think this happens most frequently) you are a lover, giving a new pet name to the one you love. Over the course of a relationship, we wear any number of variant names, each one marking some subtle shift of emphasis or shading in our relation to each other. As our relationships with our animals deepen and evolve, we do the same with them.

"It is my custom," declares Alexandre Dumas grandly, in *Mes Bêtes*, as if he were the only owner to have hit upon this idea since the world began, "to bestow surnames and nicknames on my protégées according to the merits or demerits, physical or moral, which I observe in them."[19] So let's look at some specific examples. Let's start with Rover.

Rover is one of the most familiar animal names and first appears in the eighteenth century. It's descriptive of a canine lifestyle—dogs rove about, having adventures. Rover must have caught on very speedily, because Jonathan Swift could use it satirically as the name for "A Lady's Spaniel" in 1725, so it must have been common enough by then for the satire to have its sting. By 1882, in her novel *Donovan*, the British writer Edna Lyall has a character, faced with the task of naming a dog, complain that "Rover would do, only it's so common." Then in 1905, early cinemagoers were entranced by *Rescued by Rover*, a short British film about a kidnapped baby, who is indeed rescued by Rover, the family dog. The film was produced by Cecil Hepworth, who also painted the scenery; starred his wife, who also wrote the screenplay, as the distraught mother; the baby was their baby; and their family dog, who was in real life named Blair, played the heroic canine. It was so successful that Hepworth had to shoot the entire thing twice as the prints wore out, and Rover became the name that is to dogs as Tom is to cats. (I can't honestly see this being the case with the name "Blair" for some time to come.)

The poet Alexander Pope (1688–1744) owned a Great Dane named Bounce.[20] Pope was crippled by Pott's disease, a form of tuberculosis, from the age of twelve; and as a viciously witty poet in a viciously witty age, he bore his share of outrage and insult, much of it in that unenlightened eighteenth-century way directed at his physical weakness (he never grew taller than four feet six inches). At one point Bounce, and a pair of pistols, one in each pocket, were felt necessary to preserve his safety if he left his house. You get a pleasing mental image of this fragile, child-size man (Pope presented himself in at least one of his poems as a "spider"), walking along the banks of the Thames at Twickenham in the company of a hound as irrepressible as A. A. Milne's Tigger, and relishing his dog's size and energy. And Pope must have liked the name, as he passed it on to at least three of the original Bounce's successors.

Dr. Johnson's most famous cat, who is commemorated by a statue outside the Dr. Johnson's House Museum in London, was named Hodge. In the famous *Dictionary*, "Godman [or 'good man'] Hodge" occurs as an example of "a rustick term of compliment," which might lead one to suppose that Hodge was originally a cat of the countryside and that his owner had his cat's virtues at the back of his mind when writing this particular definition. A "hodge-podge" is also there, defined as "a medley of ingredients, boiled together," so we might infer that Hodge himself had somewhat mixed ancestry and was maybe also a calico cat, with a coat of many colors. James Boswell, Dr. Johnson's biographer, might have settled the question for us, but Hodge's appearance was of no interest to him:

I am, unluckily, one of those who have an antipathy to a cat, so that I am uneasy when in the room with one; and I own, I frequently suffered a good deal from the presence of this same Hodge. I recollect him one day scrambling up Dr. Johnson's breast, apparently with much satisfaction, while my friend smiling and half-whistling, rubbed down his back, and pulled him by the tail; and when I observed he was a fine cat, saying, "Why yes, Sir, but I have had cats whom I liked better than this;" and then as if perceiving Hodge to be out of countenance, adding, "but he is a very fine cat, a very fine cat indeed."[21]

So we might be left none the wiser, were it not for the fact that after Hodge's death, Percival Stockdale (churchman and amateur poet and satellite to Johnson's inner circle) wrote an elegy in Hodge's honor, which contains the couplet

And never failed his thanks to purr
Whene'er he stroked his sable furr[22]

So there you have it. Hodge was a black cat, with "golden glare"— much like Bird, in fact.

There is also what one might call the rule of opposites in our naming of animals. Helen Macdonald explains in *H is for Hawk* how this works in falconry:

There's a superstition among falconers that a hawk's ability is inversely proportional to the ferocity of its name. Call a hawk Tiddles and it will be a formidable hunter; call it Spitfire or Slayer and it will probably refuse to fly at all.

She calls her hawk, who is by her own account an indefatigable huntress, Mabel, and as soon as she has named the bird, introduces herself to it: Helen.[23] That is the equality of companionship in one, and it brings us neatly to the story of "The Earl."

In 1853, Britain, France, Russia, and Turkey went to war over the territory of the Crimea, now part of the Ukraine. Among the troops sent out to fight was a young man named Richard Temple Godman, a lieutenant in the Fifth Light Dragoon Guards. Lieutenant Godman had been born into a wealthy family and grew up in a house known as Park Hatch, in Surrey. He arrived at Varna in the Crimea in June 1854, when he was twenty-two years old, and immediately started writing home.[24]

From the start, Godman's letters display an interest in the natural world and its inhabitants in short order—during his time in the Crimea his attention is caught by frogs, lizards, insects, orioles, hoopoes, eagles, storks, and hawks (his younger brother, Frederick, would become a noted ornithologist), wild dogs, deer, and boar, and what may have been marmots—"small animals between a rat and a stoat." Above all he talks about horses, including his own, who land in the Crimea distinguished only as "the Cob," "the chestnut," and "the brown one." In almost his first letter back to his family at Park Hatch, Godman describes "righting" horses all night long during a storm at sea; he also notes that the horses of Britain's allies, the French, show "no breeding or spirit," but then he also describes the French ships as being "such as an Englishman would only expect to see a fisherman in"—the Battle of Waterloo was well within living memory in 1854, and Godman shows all the xenophobia you might anticipate. Where he stands out is in the care and concern he displays for his mounts; equal to that he shows for his own human welfare. On June 18, 1854, he writes in the same sentence that he and his servant, Kilburn, breakfast on eggs, and his horses on "barley and chopped straw," and is already noting how they are "not so fat as when we left England."

There is a confidence throughout Godman's letters that his family back home (as with so many of the owners in this book) will share his interest and concern. By August he has tasked them with sending out a packsaddle for the Cob, who sounds to have been quite portly, at least upon arrival, as those available in the Crimea didn't fit. The gulf between Godman's attitude and the treatment otherwise meted out to horses in the Crimea is vast: within months, if not weeks, of the conflict starting, those sailing into the harbor at Balaclava knew they were getting close to it by the number of dead horses floating in the sea. So notorious was this conflict to become for the suffering endured by the horses in particular that thirty years later, in *Black Beauty*, Anna Sewell could still make reference to it. Godman, writing only in August 1854, describes how

The other evening on the march I had to forage for my horses, for they had not had a mouthful in 24 hours…after much trouble I found a stack of barley sheaves of which I bought as much as I could carry on horseback, and I am sure my horses would have thanked me if they could.[25]

In Godman's first seven months in the Crimea, the nineteen officers of the Fifth Light Dragoons were reduced to ten, and Godman himself suffers from chilblains, rheumatism, dysentery, and "brow ague." Then in October 1854, two of his horses suddenly acquire names: Chance, who seems to have been the chestnut, and "the brown one, now 'the Earl.'"

Chance does only second-hand duty such as when I take a ride...the Earl has all the honour in that I mount him whenever I expect any work to be done...

The "work," in this case, being a cavalry charge, such as that on October 25, 1854, after which, writing home to his family, Godman for the first time gives his horse a name:

I rode The Earl—an excellent mount for anything of the kind, he has such pluck he will go anywhere, while I can easily manage him with one hand. He is much faster than the Russian horses...

No doubt thanks to his better condition after Godman's care of him. The Russian horses Godman mentions here were those of Lieutenant General Ivan Ivanovich Rhyzov, and the charge was that of the Heavy Brigade—a rare episode of military success that has been completely overshadowed by the disastrous Charge of the Light Brigade on the same day. The Earl was only one among thousands of horses in the Crimea, most of whom saw much less tender care than he did; but at the point in their relationship where his and his owner's survival depended upon their mutually preserving each other, then he is given a name. And then just as suddenly, in the letters that come after, right up to the point when Godman and the three horses return to England in June 1856, the Earl is back to being "the brown one" again.

One postscript to this. The Crimean War was the first to be covered by the news media of the day, and at one point Temple Godman refers to a visit to his regiment from "the photographer man." This was Roger Fenton, one of the first war photographers, and Fenton's list of plates from the Crimea does indeed include one of "Temple Godman of the 5th Dragoons," standing next to his horse the Earl, with his servant Kilburn standing to the left. Kilburn's beard is as full as the bearskin hat hanging from the Earl's saddle; the Earl, tail neatly trimmed, has turned his head but looks sheeny and full of muscle. Temple Godman, in full uniform and slightly top-heavy out of the saddle, is looking back at the photographer. And there they are.

One thousand years ago, the Chinese scholar Chang Tuan owned five cats, among whom were White Phoenix and Drive Away Care. Both are truly splendid names for cats, but the reason the names are so inventive is that in China, giving an animal a human name is seen as mightily disrespectful. Not so in the West. Lying in bed one night— stapled in place, just about in a manner familiar to any pet owner, with sleeping cat whiffling peacefully to either side—I listened to the broadcaster Michael Rosen comparing eighteenth-century dog names to the names we give our pets today.[26] Rosen's list of the top ten dogs' names for 2016 ran, in ascending order, Jack, Daisy, Bob, Rex, Sam, Charlie, Alf, Poppy, Max, and Ben. The top ten cats' names were Thomas, Sam or Sammy, Felix, Smokey, Poppy, Jess or Jessie, Molly, Charlie, Bella, and—at the top—Bob. So out of twenty names, seventeen are those we might call ourselves or give our children. Meantime, according to the website Mumsnet in 2017, there is an ever-growing trend to call children by the kinds of names we might once have given to our pets: Trixi, Bambi, Peaches, Blue...we can all think of more. It is as if the animals and the children are swapping places. "C'mon Paul!" says the cat-loving Mayor West in *Family Guy*. And then, laughing, "What a ridiculous name for a cat!"

Giving an animal a human name could be seen as saying something very significant about the relationship between owner and pet. It may be more prevalent today, but it was by no means unknown before. The poet Joachim du Bellay, who died in 1560, gave his "little grey cat," to whom he was devoted, the name "Belaud"—a pun on the idea of "laud," or praising, perhaps, but also close to the name he had himself. On Belaud's death, du Bellay was heartbroken. Christopher Smart was just as devoted to Jeoffrey, who inspired him to pen one of the best verse portraits of a cat ever created, beginning:

For first he looks upon his forepaws to see if they are clean.

For secondly he kicks up behind to clear away there.

For thirdly he works it upon stretch with the forepaws extended.

Dumas gave his two favorites among his dogs human names as well: Flora and Pritchard. In the 2008 film *Wendy and Lucy*, the two named protagonists share the same food, the same car to sleep in, the same experiences, and have the same dependency upon each other, but one walks on two legs, one on four. (Don't, by the way, watch this film without a box of tissues.) If we want to elevate an animal, but in a mock-serious manner, we give it a mock-serious human name—Ralph Waldo Emerson once owned a kitten he named Johann Wolfgang von Goethe Hippens, and the joke hasn't worn out yet: a tiny ginger kitten, whose photograph was sent in response to my inquiry about ginger pets, was named Frederick Gaylord II. In 2014, the Wisconsin Humane Society, no doubt alert to the psychology of individualization at work here, was offering up for adoption Professor PuddinPop, Colonel Snazzypants, and the Good King Snugglewumps.[27] The US Veterinary Pet Insurance Company, in its annual competition to find the "Wackiest Pet Name," unearthed in 2016 such gems as McLoven the Stud Muffin and Scrappin Scruffy Macdoogles of the Highland Macdoogles. Names for cats included Princess Poopy Paws and Claws von Stauffenberg Sachs. All these are gleefully subverting the notion of the pedigreed, multibarreled aristocratic name or the professional human title (as indeed Sir Roy Strong's beloved "The Reverend Wenceslas Muff") yet at the same time, you might argue that all are also claiming a superlative level of social importance, at least in their owners' eyes, for the pet. So just how confused are we? Do we really see our pets as having the same importance to us as, or maybe even more importance than, our children?

Well, probably not. The thing about naming is that it says something about the namer, too, and if you give your child an outlandish and unorthodox name, yet your dog has the same name as your brother, maybe what you're really trying to get across is that you want to be seen as outlandish and unorthodox yourself. And choosing a daffy name for your child and a human name for your pet is one of the safest, most conservative ways of doing so. It's still the act of naming itself that matters most. Because if you were to try to define the human-animal, as opposed to the animal-animal, along the lines of a Jorge Luis Borges list, one way in which you could do so is by describing us as the animal who tells stories. We do so endlessly, relating one event to another, trying to make sense of the utterly random and bring it into some kind of pattern of which we are in charge. It's exactly what I have done at the beginning of this book, relating it to the one before. And in order to bring all these other creatures into the narrative of our lives, as we seek to impose order on what has been called the "multifarious and contradictory stuff of life,"[28] we must have something to call them. Which is why naming, communicating, and connecting are all so intimately linked.

Louis Wain photographed at his drawing board in the 1890s. The date makes it possible that the cat photographed with him is indeed Peter.

CHAPTER FIVE

COMMUNICATING

Between them lay the widest gulf that can separate one being from another. She spoke. He was dumb.

—Virginia Woolf, *Flush*, 1933

In 1736, Alexander Pope's dog Bounce gave birth to a litter of puppies, one of whom the poet then presented to Frederick, Prince of Wales. Supposedly the pup was sent complete with collar, on which was engraved the couplet

I am his Highness' Dog at Kew;
Pray tell me, Sir, whose Dog are you?

A collar means ownership. Dogs in the past seem to have spent much less time on leads and much more roving about the place than they do now, so placing a collar around the neck of your dog was particularly important if it might otherwise be rounded up and suffer the horrid fate of the urban stray—mass execution by whatever means was cheapest, and be damned to the cruelty involved. The Winterthur Collection in Delaware includes a brass dog collar inscribed "Pray kind people let me jog/For I am Josiah Smith's good dog." From rather lower down the social order, one would guess, and from the late eighteenth or early nineteenth century, comes this: "Jere Stebbins Esq Dog W. Springfield/Who Dog Be You."[1] Victor Hugo, author of *Les Misérables* (1862), used this around the collar of his greyhound: "Profession: Dog. Master: Hugo. Name: Sénat. I wish someone would take me home." The collar, not the dog, was regularly stolen by souvenir hunters.[2]

In every one of these examples, the collar reads as if it were the animal itself speaking, not the human owner. We just can't stop ourselves from putting words into their mouths. It's as if, as far as the owner is concerned, the very first recorded conversation of all between human and non-human, between Eve and the serpent, had simply never happened. Supposedly in Eden we all understood each other perfectly; it was the Fall of Man that deprived animals of human speech (which hardly seems fair), and it was the birth of Christ and every Nativity thereafter that, according to European legend, briefly restores it to them again.[3] There is a similar story in Chippewa mythology that recounts how in the beginning, when we were all animals together, we could all understand each other, and it was summer. When animals lost the power of speech, as the legend describes it, with sad dignity, then winter followed.[4] Maybe we owners, we animals' companions, see ourselves on some deep-buried level as trying to restore this long-lost equality. It's good to think so.

Humans acting like animals is a staple of the horror film, but an animal acting as if it were human makes us laugh—think Shakespeare's cat "wringing her hands." In particular, we like the notion of animal speech. There's something irresistibly subversive about the whole idea. Once one of those animal mouths has opened, anything is possible. In Tudor London, a printer named William Baldwin created an extraordinary piece of surreal Tudor comedy entitled *Beware the Cat* (its earliest surviving publication seems to have been in 1570), in which the unnamed narrator is first enraged and then intrigued by the noise of cats doing what cats do all night on the roof above his bedchamber. Deciding that "it doth appear there is in cats, as in all other beasts, a certain reason and language, whereby they understand one another," he concocts a magic potion so disgusting that it makes Shakespeare's eye of newt and toe of frog sound like a probiotic, but which does enable him to comprehend the speech of the "great cat" on the tiles above his bed "as well as if he had spoken English." Unfortunately so superhuman does the narrator's hearing become that he can also hear literally every noise in the city and is almost deafened by the wails of crying babies, the complaints of countless wives nagging their husbands, the scouring of pots and pans in innumerable kitchens, the crowing of cockerels, the songs of drunken revelers staggering home, and even the cheeping of mice in the walls of his room.[5] What was just about tolerated in Tudor England in low comedy was viewed rather differently in real life, however: when Elizabeth Francis, an Essex farmer's wife, claimed in 1566 to understand the "strange hollow voice" of her white spotted cat, the rather unwisely named Satan, she narrowly escaped becoming the first woman in England to be executed as a witch.[6]

This all seems very ridiculous to us today, blithely nattering away to our cats and dogs as we do, but the association between animal speech and unnatural magic cast a long shadow. When the first stories for children appeared in print in the eighteenth century, in the age-old format of the moral fable, the business of putting words into animals' mouths caused much heavy-footed moralizing and breaking of the fourth wall. Hence this piece of scintillating dialogue from the catchily titled *Fables in Monosyllables* of 1783:

Lady: Can ants speak?

Boy: No, Aunt.

Lady: Can flies talk?

Boy: No, Aunt.

Lady: Why then does this book talk of what they say?

Boy: I do not know, Aunt.[7]

And nor do I. What such killjoys would have made of *Antz*, or *A Bug's Life*, or *Madagascar*, or all their many successors, heaven only knows.

So was the historical pet owner suitably abashed and circumspect in putting words in their animals' mouths? Of course they weren't. Antoinette Deshoulières, noted beauty, variable poet, and crazy cat lady to the court of Louis XIV, penned a series of verse-letters between her cat, Grisette, and Grisette's friend Tata, who belonged to the Marquise de Montglas, in 1677. Tata, who in real life had apparently been neutered by the Marquise, bemoans the fact that (to put it delicately) he is now fit only to play Abelard to Grisette's Heloise, but Grisette assures him that she will

> *flee rooftop haunts, unfit…*
> *For proudly, I am one of these*
> *Lady-cats of most proper breeding*[8]

Unfortunately, Grisette was clearly a minx, and Tata was discarded. By 1688, the *Letters* had been followed up in epic fashion with "La Mort de Cochon," in which Grisette, throwing herself about the scenery, bewails the loss of her Cochon, the most recent love of her life: "No, it is not enough to weep for what I love, His death demands mine!" To the horror of the other cats gathered on the Paris rooftops to commiserate with her, Cochon is then revealed to have been *canine*.[9] Move forward to 1726 and Pope's friend and fellow writer Jonathan Swift is at it, too, this time on behalf of a male successor to the original Bounce, who we are to believe was busy penning his own "heroick epistle" to Fop, a spaniel at court.

> *To thee, sweet* Fop, *these Lines I send,*
> *Who, tho' no Spaniel, am a Friend.*

Tho, once my Tail in wanton play,
Now frisking this, and then that way,
Chanc'd, with a Touch of just the Tip,
To hurt your Lady-lap-dog-ship...

And so on. In 1784, it's the Reverend Gilbert White, composing a letter from Timothy the Tortoise to Miss Hecky Mulso, in which Timothy attempts to account (and apologize) for a weeklong disappearance:

It was in the month of May last that I resolved to elope from my place of confinement: for my fancy had represented to me that probably many agreeable tortoises of both sexes might inhabit the heights of Bakers' Hill or the extensive plains of the neighbouring meadow, both of which I could discern from the terrass. One sunny morning therefore I watched my opportunity...[10]

Hester Lynch Piozzi ends a letter to a friend in 1791 with the casual sign-off of her own best wishes and in the same breath the words "The indoor dogs send duty."[11] A century later, Emily Dickinson includes hopes for improved good health from her Newfoundland Carlo in a letter to an ailing friend.[12] My mother used to send me letters at university from my cat, commenting on the idiocies of the other cats (and dog), and very funny, read aloud, and much enjoyed they were, too. When Dr. Dolittle, in the person of Rex Harrison in the 1967 musical, sighs, "If I could talk to the animals..." pet owners across the planet answer, "But you can! And we do!"

In fact, 79 percent of us, according to one survey, talk to our animals on an almost continual basis, no matter how puzzling or even pointless an activity this may at first appear to be.[13] Even the scientists and anthropologists among us do it. "I talk to my cats a great deal," says Professor Kay Milton, then adds the properly distancing scientific rider, "but it would never occur to me that they understand my words; I take whatever powers of understanding they display to be feline in character."[14] Few owners, I suspect, could boast of such objectivity: 80 percent of us (again, is it really only 80 percent? Not 99 percent?) believe our animals respond to such communication, despite this being expressed in what one might suppose to the animal to be mere random noise.[15]

We talk because we walk, or so one theory goes. Standing upright allowed the tongue and jaw and organs of the human throat to develop in ways that not only made speech possible but positively boosted its development.[16] Thus the two factors that for so much of history have been cited as making us superior to every other species arrived hand in hand: first our upright stance, the noble locomotion of gods and angels (from Anubis to Ganesha to Pan, even when we have worshipped animals as deities, we have always stood them up on two legs first); and then the tapestry of human language, which again for generations of our ancestors literally bespoke reason, which itself bespoke a soul—the other thing we had, but animals lacked.

Since then, fables and fabulists from Aesop to George Orwell, from Hans Christian Andersen to Dr. Seuss, have been putting words into animals' mouths, but that's not quite the same as the kinds of conversations we as owners have with the animals who share our lives, one-sided as these may (at first, to the uninitiated) appear to be.

It's this very one-sidedness that keeps us doing it. We just can't bring ourselves to believe that speech of some sort, something that is so central to our experience of life, is not there for the animals with whom we share our lives, and along with speech, comprehension, reason, feelings, and thought. St. Isidore of Seville, who died in 636 AD, was convinced that the horse at least "weeps for man and feels the emotion of grief," while St. Albert the Great in the thirteenth century went even further, believing that all animals shared "knowledge, habits, fear, boldness…desire, wrath and the like…with humans."[17] Anthony Ashley-Cooper, 3rd Earl of Shaftesbury, who died in 1713, believed that dogs had "affections, passions, appetites and antipathies"; the poet and dramatist Samuel Jackson Pratt, who died a century later, echoing William Baldwin and hedging his bets, came up with the maxim that "if animals have not reason, they have *something* that does the business of reason."[18] Friedrich Engels, co–founding father of Marxism, believed that horses and dogs were not only aware of their lack of language but felt deep regret for it, albeit in August 1842 he was writing to his sister Marie, proudly claiming that he had managed to teach his "crazy" spaniel, Namenloser (another dog with no name), to understand one human word at least: "When I say 'Namenloser…there's an aristocrat!' he goes wild with rage and growls hideously at the person I show him."[19] Karl Marx himself also had dogs—three of them—when he was visited by Marian Comyn, who in her *My Recollections of Karl Marx* of 1922 describes them as all named after different types of alcohol and all three of them as being mongrels, "mixes of many breeds," which seems appropriate. Lenin, however, was one of your cat men, as Elizabeth von Arnim might have described him, and as you might expect, cats are very poor subjects for education in any political system whatsoever.[20]

In short, if you think your animal understands you, you are by no means on your own. Even Namenloser, who may not have had the power of speech, was credited by Engels with the power of comprehension—just as, two centuries before, Dr. Johnson had so credited Hodge, appearing famously upset that he might have hurt his cat's feelings. In 1781, Horace Walpole writes of an episode concerning the newest addition to his canine family, Tonton, the dog he inherited from Madame du Deffand. Tonton brought what sounds like a good deal of ancien régime hauteur into Walpole's circle of pets, one of whom retaliated by biting him on the paw. As Walpole's maid, Margaret (whose liking for animals must have been every bit as finely developed as her master's), attempted to comfort Tonton, to Walpole's delight, "she cried 'Poor little thing, he does not understand my language!'"—meaning not that a species separated them but a nationality.[21] We want to make human sense of our relationships with our animals, and that means believing that what matters to us will matter to them, too, and that something as essential to us as language must be something we share.

With dogs in particular, who are so responsive to us in every way, it's particularly hard for us to believe that they don't understand what we are trying to communicate to them. Elizabeth Barrett, in her correspondence with her soon-to-be husband, Robert Browning, describes the point at which she feels Flush has made peace with Browning's presence in her life with the words "So I explained to him...that he ought to be properly ashamed therefore of his past wickedness, and make up his mind to love you and not bite you for the future..."[22] The novelist Henry James was fond enough to attribute not just comprehension but an appreciation of the niceties of etiquette to his dachshund, Max, abandoning all his usual circumlocutions to hail Max as "the best & gentlest & most reasonable & well-mannered as well as most beautiful small animal of his kind," but his brother William (1842–1910), hailed as the "father of American psychology," simply didn't get it at all: "Marvelous as may be the power of my dog," he wrote, "to understand my moods, deathless as is his affection and fidelity, his mental state is as unsolved a mystery to me as it was to my remotest ancestor." To which that 80 percent (at least) of owners today would have to respond: Professor James, you are simply not trying.[23]

And we go on nattering away to them regardless. You can hear Aisholpan in *The Eagle Huntress* doing exactly this with her eagle: "Are you hungry? Do your feet hurt? Are you hot?" And after their first hunt: "Were you afraid, my dear?" When all the time it is Aisholpan herself who was hungry, whose feet hurt, who was afraid. It's this business of projection again. Imagination can fill the dark with monsters, but it can also (almost) make us telepathic. So, remote our ancestors may certainly be, but mystified in their relationships to other species? I doubt it. I would imagine them as negotiating relationships with the animals about them just as we do now, and no doubt using every form of communication they could come up with, physical and verbal, in order to do so. We may still only have our human ways of doing it, but we've all been talking to the animals for centuries.

This ability to imagine the consciousness of another being enters our lives remarkably early—it's been calculated at between seven and nine months old, and as we know, the earlier in our development we learn something, the more fundamental its importance to us.[24] As a species we've been imaginatively entering the experience of other beings since our human history began; as individual infants, tellingly and rather pleasingly, since before we are able to form words themselves. To imagine speech for an animal is, as the historian Tess Cosslett puts it, "to put oneself in its place."[25] This is what Aisholpan was doing, and in so doing she was also giving her eagle a personality—her own.

We may not now be hunting animals in the same way; we may be infinitely more sophisticated in our ways of thinking about them and imagineering, if you like, our relationships to them, but talking to them, whether they comprehend us or not, is part of how we comprehend them. If they have personality, and biography, they make sense to us. Naming is where this creation of personality begins, and talking to them as if the personality we have attributed to them is indeed their own is how we make it part of our narrative of ourselves—how we have it function.

Talking to oneself, which must be how our behavior would appear to many a non-owner, is a thoroughly depressing thing to do; in fact it so lowers mood and self-esteem and enhances confusion and anger that it's linked to mental disorders of all types. Talking to an animal, however, is profoundly mood-enhancing—the description of a minor triumph, the sharing of a personal blow, even the everyday running commentary upon our and our animal's doings, feel *good*; and it does so because of our conviction as owners that the animal both listens and understands; that it enters our experience in turn—and more, that it empathizes with us. "Something to talk to" is still one of the most important reasons given for owning a pet in the first place. Talking to an animal has been likened to the experience of Rogerian therapy, where it's the perceived empathy and non-interventionist behavior of the listener that makes the therapy work. Such "talking" has also been linked to the experience of prayer—another act of faith with no tangible evidence of a comprehending audience, an engaged or interventionist listener at all, but does that stop us from doing it? Hardly.[26]

Children, in particular, talk to their pets as regularly as they might fill a journal. We take it on trust, when we're little, that the animal understands, but it doesn't really matter one way or the other; the animal's role is simply to be that something to talk to. Grace Greenwood wrote in 1853 of how a pet becomes a child's confidante:

For some weeks past we have had with us by the sea-shore a beautiful little Italian girl…who has a remarkable fondness for a pretty little black and white kitten belonging to the house. All day long she will have her pet in her arms, talking to her when she thinks nobody is near; telling her everything; charging her to keep some story to herself as it is a very great secret.[27]

The writer Jenny Diski, a century later, on her many visits to London Zoo, did the same with Guy the Gorilla. "I stood in front of his cage every day," she writes. "I thought we were friends. I loved him and I told him things."[28] Abuwtiyuw's *bow!* or Meone's *meow* is seen as perfectly sufficient for their side of the conversation (and note how we have borrowed and made a language of their "words," as well). Any kind of sound in response to us will do. We can read into it anything we need. I find it most intriguing that when my cats encounter each other, it's with a brief, silent sniff, nose to nose, but when they jump onto my lap it's always with some sound or other, usually a two-note chirrup that I'm going to call a greeting, and a habit that they seem to have acquired from my two-syllable "Hello!"

Now this nudges us up into the very misty territory of anthropomorphism, something the besotted owner has indulged in forever and the scientist is meant to shun with contempt, but the times they are a-changing. Anthropomorphism is at least one way of exploring and interrogating our companion animals and their emotions and sensations.[29] Carl Safina, writer and conservationist, has even called it "our best first guess."[30]

But we need to be realistic in how we use it. Bird, with her friendly creak of welcome, her polysyllabic chirrups, and above all her yowling

"Song of the Mighty Huntress," is an astonishingly vocal cat, but if I read meaning into those sounds as if they were speech, I fall all too thoroughly into the trap of taking them as expressing what I would be feeling if I were she; still me, in other words, just in a little black velvet cat suit—not what she is experiencing and expressing being *her*. Or, as the novelist and proto–animal activist Ouida (Maria Louise Ramé; 1839–1908) put it, "Man, having but one conception of intelligence—his own—does not endeavor to comprehend another which is different and differently exhibited and expressed." I particularly like the way in which Ouida, who at one time was looking after thirty dogs, most of them rescues and strays, on the proceeds of her more that forty novels, manages so cunningly to exclude women from this definition. Anthropomorphism can tell us a great deal about ourselves in our relation to our animals, but it can't be trusted to tell us as much about them.

In particular, once we start putting words into our animals' mouths, it is all too easy to assume they understand them. So the dog digging holes in the garden gets kicked for failing to obey the injunction not to do so, which it must be disobeying willfully; the cat that scratches the sofa is smacked; the hamster that bites is thrown back into its cage. Caring for an animal as a member of the family is good, but relating to an animal purely as if it were human gets us nowhere. Verbal reasoning is not going to work.[31]

At its least worst, anthropomorphism is Jane Loudon assuring her readers that "dogs are…exceedingly sensitive of jealously, and many may be persuaded to eat almost anything by being told that the cat will take it if they do not." Or indeed, Elizabeth Barrett, reasoning with Flush. Or it is us dressing up our animals to celebrate birthdays and bar mitzvahs.[32] But at its most horrible, attributing human judgment of their actions to animals has led to some awful behavior on our part. Medieval Europe saw trials of pigs, bulls, rats, even *weevils*, for disobeying human laws, but before we dismiss this as the cruelty of an ignorant and superstitious age, consider Topsy the elephant, poisoned, strangled, and electrocuted at Luna Park in Coney Island in 1903 in front of an invited crowd—in effect a public execution—because when abused she reacted as an elephant would, rather than as her early twentieth-century audience thought a reasonable elephant-person should.[33] Have we evolved beyond this? Not by much, no. In 2016 a dog in Malaysia had its front legs cut off by a neighbor armed with a sword because it had chewed a pair of his shoes, left out on the street.[34] It's the calculated vindictiveness at work here that leaves me aghast and covering my eyes: *it chewed my shoes, so I'll cut off its legs.* Truly, as Elizabeth von Arnim put it, "to an overworked donkey, to a kicked dog, to a pelted cat, it may well seem that this is a world of devils…a blanket of beauty drawn across horror…if a corner were lifted something so terrible would be seen, such suffering and cruelty, that nobody could ever be at peace again."

But the big mystery, the most fascinating part of the question of animal communication, is not why we talk to them. It's why do they communicate with us? Because the trick here, as Dr. Dolittle knew, is to make the conversation two-way: not merely to "…walk with the animals, talk with the animals/Grunt and squeak and squawk with the animals," but to understand them when they *talk back.*

Hugh Lofting, who originally created Dr. Dolittle, came up with the idea for an animal doctor while serving in the trenches of the First World War, impelled partly by the need to find something to write to his children about other than the horrors of the war, partly by his intense awareness of the injustice in the suffering of the horses and other animals he saw around him. If serving animals, as well as serving soldiers, were to be cared for equally, then communication would have to be possible with them as well. "To give them the same care as the men they served," Lofting reasoned, "to develop a horse surgery... would necessitate a knowledge of horse language. That was the first beginning of the idea"—the notion of the doctor who could "talk to the animals—and *they could talk to me*."[35] Dolittle, predictably, had much in common with Lofting, who seems to have been a restless soul, a little adrift within human society, much more at ease with animals and children than he was with adults, and who took his own children on walks to the same pet shop he had frequented as a boy—a sort of spiritual pilgrimage back to a place where he had himself been happy. How, though, to have his fictional avatar penetrate into the world of animal language? Lofting's solution was to give Dr. Dolittle Polynesia the parrot as interpreter between the world of human speech and that of animal language. Polynesia is fluent in both. "Now listen, Doctor, and I'll tell you something," says Polynesia, at the start of Dolittle's adventures. "Did you know that animals can talk?"[36]

We have always been fascinated by birds that can mimic human speech. "The society which the parrot forms with man is from its use of language much more intimate and pleasing than what the monkey can claim," says William Bingley, sniffily, in *Bingley's Natural History* (1871), blithely assuming that "language" means the same to both bird and man.[37] But then New Zealand Maoris regarded the kaka and the tui, two native birds of the islands, so highly because of their ability to "speak" that they saw them as a link to the world of the spirits. "Speke, Parrot" of circa 1521, another of John Skelton's poetic fancies, presents its hero, an Indian rose-ringed parakeet (the same species now happily colonizing public parks from Brooklyn to Battersea), as a scholar who goes to school with "ladies" and boasts of having mastered seven languages, including Hebrew and Dutch. Again, there is that subversive element—Skelton's parrot mocks Cardinal Wolsey, in a manner that, had it issued from Skelton's own mouth, might well have cost him the power of speech altogether (the Elizabethan punishment for slander was to have your tongue slit in two). But then one of the reasons why we love parrots and crows and mynah birds is because they might, and do, say anything: I still remember the scarlet macaw I encountered taking the air outside its owner's cottage on a country walk in Suffolk that made my day, if not indeed my whole week, by screeching, "You bugger!" at me when I paused to admire it. It's hard for us not to believe that parrots, with their jocular, interrogative expression, and again what looks to us like an animal smile, don't have some inkling that they're breaking the rules and that they don't thoroughly enjoy doing so: J. G. Wood noted with glee that "parrots are just like children in their propensity to say the most dreadful things exactly at the most inconvenient times and to the most fastidious persons."[38] And perhaps most famously of all, there is Alex, the subject of the Avian Learning Experiment of Dr. Irene Pepperberg.

Alex, like Polynesia, was an African Grey. Years before (and here is a bit more of that cultural connective tissue), as the lonely child-owner of a pet bird to whom she talked "endlessly, about anything and everything," Irene Pepperberg had also been captivated and, who knows, maybe even inspired by the story of Dr. Dolittle and Polynesia.[39] And while all parrots are smart, an African Grey is about as smart as a bird can be. Alex had a vocabulary of some one hundred single words and was assessed as having the intelligence of a five-year-old child; what set him apart was the fact that he made use of the concepts represented by those words as a code to communicate his wants and moods pretty much as a five-year-old would as well. This is the breakthrough Alex represented—not simply the mimicking of sounds but their use in a way that certainly looks a whole lot like comprehension in language as we understand it.

Alex is not alone. Washoe, a chimpanzee, had 350 signs in her vocabulary when she died at the age of forty-two in 2007 (sign language is also where the story of Caesar begins, in *Planet of the Apes*). Koko the gorilla, who died in 2018 at the age of forty-six, had, after a lifetime of study with the Gorilla Foundation in Santa Cruz, mastered one thousand signs and reportedly comprehended some two thousand words.[40] Kanzi, a thirty-seven-year-old bonobo at the Language Research Center of Georgia

State University, has mastered the use of some two hundred lexigrams. Nim Chimpsky, a chimpanzee studied at Columbia University, was a fourth, although his grasp of signage, as opposed to language, was less, and frankly his treatment (moved from one environment to another, fostered and abandoned over again), had it been meted out to a human child, reads as if it would have led to a prosecution for abuse. Reducing a living, breathing, feeling creature of any species to the status of a scientific experiment troubles me; but more than that, are any of these experiments really that much more advanced than the efforts of those mob-capped young women in their eighteenth-century parlors, patiently whistling nightingale songs to their canaries? What did those canaries make of the alien sounds issuing from their beaks—did this involve any comprehension on their part of what they were singing, or was their experience the equivalent of an opera singer, who learns a part only phonetically? Is talking about a thirty-year-old parrot as being as "good," whatever that means, in his language skills as a child a sixth his age the way we should be talking and thinking about him? Compared to one of ours, Alex's brain might indeed have been only the size of a walnut, but compared to the size of Alex himself, does the comparison have any usefulness at all? There are, after all, many things a parrot can do that a five-year-old could not (like, you know, *fly*). Is measuring animal intellect against our own an exercise with any value or nothing more than cephalogical hubris? Is teaching apes to sign, or encouraging a killer whale to use its blowhole as a kazoo, a way forward in communication, some sort of stepping-stone—or a dead end?[41] Should we be teaching animals how to communicate with us, or should we focus our efforts and intelligence on learning how communication works for them?

Because it is embarrassing, when you think about it, that with all this expertise and experience in communication behind us (*millennia* of it, for heaven's sake), the language of animals is still such a mystery, and its study such a new science: one of the highest hurdles Irene Pepperberg had to overcome in her quest for a permanent home and permanent funding (along with being female within the scientific establishment, along with the fact she was working with not a great ape but a bird) was simply to get her peers to understand what she was trying to do.[42] We humans have unpacked the mysteries of Sumerian cuneiform and the hieroglyphics of ancient Egypt. We have learned, and taught, binary languages to machines. Why, with all that skill, all that knowledge, have we concentrated on teaching animals a human language, instead of trying to learn theirs?

Somewhere up there, rotating slowly through interstellar space, are two spacecraft, Voyager 1 and Voyager 2. Launched in 1977, each carries a vinyl "golden record" (how antique that technology seems now) loaded with information about our planet. *If* these should ever make their way into the hands of another civilization, *if* they should ever be played, those listening will hear the sounds of the sea, of the wind, and of thunder and the songs of humpback whales. Are these songs language? Are they part of echo location? Are they part of the whales' mating ritual? All that harnessing of the human imagination so characteristic of humankind, all the venturesome technology that went into the creation of the Voyager sisters in the first place, and maybe the most typical of the truths those golden records carry about us is the fact that we sent those songs up there with no idea what they mean, or even why they are sung.

We do so overthink things where animals are concerned. *The Arnolfini Marriage* by Jan van Eyck, in the National Gallery in London, is one of the best-known and best-loved works in its collection, and the little dog standing between the couple in the painting—who may be married or may be only betrothed—has been interpreted as everything from a symbol of lust to a proxy child to an emblem of devotion to a symbol of wealth. Meanwhile, the man may be Giovanni Arnolfini, an Italian merchant in the city of Bruges, or it may be his cousin. The woman may be a wife or fiancée of either. When I was a child, she was interpreted as being pregnant; now she is not. She may even be a ghost—Giovanni's first wife died the year before the painting was signed and dated in 1434. The little dog, therefore, boldly photo-bombing this tranquil interior, could be argued to have more reality than any of the identities put forward for the human figures. And given that the dog may be an early example of a Griffon Bruxellois, a breed known for their sense of self-importance even today, it does seem a bit perverse not to accept that it's simply what it looks like—a pet.

We do the same when it comes to animal language. Take the whine. A whine is a pretty basic sound with a pretty basic message. And when

Daisy whines, as she has just done, my instinct is that it means to her exactly what it would for me, especially as I'm sitting here in a different room from her, typing away: her sister is asleep, her bowl has been emptied, and those darn catnip mice are still refusing to throw themselves up and down the hall. The whine means she's discontented and wants some attention. Bird takes it even further—if she wants something, she uses her whole body to tell me: chirruping to have me follow her, then throwing herself down on the rug on top of their favorite toy, the feather-on-a-stick, which she has already dragged out to the rug to begin with, to tell me she wants me to play. Sometimes Bird runs into the hall and sticks her paws under the rug, as if the feather-on-a-stick were there already. I have no idea if she is still then showing me what she wants or simply connecting paws under rug to the toy being there, but she's getting a message across all the same. An animal behaviorist would call this "embodied communication."[43] Animals are very good at it. "Man himself," declared Charles Darwin, in 1872, "cannot express love and humility by external signs so plainly as does the dog, when with drooping ears, hanging lips, flexuous body and wagging tail he meets his beloved master."[44] Or as Polynesia describes it to Dr. Dolittle: "…animals…talk with their ears, with their feet, with their tails—with everything."

Even my partner's cat, Millie, who is indeed mute, can communicate. If she wants to be picked up, she stands on her hind legs and puts her front paws on the legs of the nearest human, as high as they will go. If she wants to be fed, she comes and walks all over you. If she is content, she lies along the back of the sofa, dead to the world, smiling in her sleep. And if she feels she has been left alone for too long, she pees on the floor. Millie is a very elderly lady now, and stone deaf to go along with the muteness, and we have no idea of her early history at all, although since she is black, and terrified of brooms, my partner has a theory that she was purchased as a kitten as a Halloween prop and literally swept out the door once Halloween was done. Certainly when she was found she was living wild in the woods and shifting for herself, and as many a wild creature has done, learned that making a noise would only attract the attention of any number of other creatures, all of them larger than her and all of them capable of turning her into a snack. So she kept silent and has stayed that way. Many feral cats and dogs have a far smaller repertoire of sounds in their vocabulary—fewer mews and meows, once they are grown, fewer of those expressive yips and whines—than do those who grew up with one of us talking to them, which suggests the possibility that we all somehow learned the many variables of speech-as-sound together, copying and swapping one with the other, as my cats seem to have done with my "Hello."[45] We should put more trust in our own instincts where communication with our animals is concerned. Our instincts are indeed our "best, first guess."

So when on my lap of an evening, Bird sighs what would be (were it me) a sigh of pure happiness, I am going to take it as exactly that. When Daisy bomphs my head or my hand (which both cats quite understandably regard as being an equal organ of communication to my voice), I'm going to take that as a sign of affection as clear as a hug from one of my own species. When Daisy arrives in bed on top of me, like a drunk falling through the door of a bar, with the feather-on-a-stick in her mouth, it's clear to me what she is after, even if in the middle of the night I am not about to comply. And despite his being such a pioneer in the history of the animal's companion, when the Reverend Wood, speaking of the prospective pet to the prospective owner, proclaims, "IT IS DUMB, and has no language to declare its wants or proclaim its injuries," I am going to disagree. Louis Wain, owner of and companion to Peter the Great, would not have agreed, either. "I decline to argue with any critic that ever lived, and repeat, fearlessly and in measured terms, that Peter talked to *me*."[46]

And what we establish between us by this interaction, and the true point of it, is the reiteration and reinforcement of our relationship. The anthropologist Barbara Smuts describes these little bits and pieces of communication, mutually constructed and agreed upon, as being designed to bring owner and animal back in sync.[47] We're checking in with each other. They're an animal poke, if you like, and their purpose is to reassure us both that our status is unchanged and secure, and that "the bond...remains intact." What we're doing is reinforcing an ever stronger mutual trust. This is why even without sharing speech, we can talk to the animals—and why as proof of that, they talk back to us, and it is a big part of how our attachment to each other can become so profound. Speech is a miracle, but you can make the argument that it's too complicated for communication. It gets compromised and traduced and tangled up in itself every time we open our mouths. In a way, animals need the inadequacies of human speech, and we need their lack of it, for this other, more intuitive, immediate, and open form of communication to have come into being. Part of what we look for in a relationship with another human being is that "kinesthetic empathy," as it has been called, where we are so on the same level we can understand each other simply by observing, and where we connect with each other without words of any sort.[48] Completely perversely, with all the tools of verbal and written communication at our disposal, among the relationships we trust the most are those where they play no part at all.

A boy and his chicken, taking the air, from Morris Huberland's "Chicken in the City" series, taken in New York *c.*1940.

CHAPTER SIX

CONNECTING

Some dog to follow, where'er I roam
Some bird to warble my welcome home
Some tame gazelle, or some gentle dove:
Something to love. Oh, something to love!

Thomas Haynes Bayly, *Songs and Ballads*, 1844

A few years ago, I found myself at a publishing conference in Los Angeles. LA was not a city I had ever visited before, so on my first morning I decided to explore it by simply following my nose. But this, it turns out, in LA, is impossible. Within a half mile of my hotel my nose found itself up against a chain-link fence separating me from a six-lane highway, a solid moat of traffic some thirty feet below, which stretched from left to right as far as the eye could see. Never mind that all six lanes were static, an unmoving mosaic of car roofs; clearly this was as far as my nose was going to take me.

Still. The fence also marked the edge of a narrow strip of public park, all very pleasant in the California sun, so I turned about and set myself to stroll through that instead. No sooner had I done so than I saw one of the scariest-looking men I have ever encountered bearing down upon me—literally bearing down, in that he was in a motorized wheelchair.

He was completely intimidating, even so. He had a khaki rag knotted around his forehead; his hair was in a mullet that might have been greased with engine oil; his clothing was combat-style military; his eyes were hidden behind wraparound mirrored shades. His arms (bared—sleeves ripped off the shirt at the shoulder) swelled with muscle and were blurry with tats; even the wheelchair was as if fed upon steroids and designed by Mad Max, with enormous cross-country wheels that lifted its rider way up and some kind of customized joystick surmounted, wouldn't you know it, by a miniature silver skull. Yet as he trundled along the path, the driver was surrounded by a crowd like an entourage, because beside the silver skull, wobbling slightly as the wheelchair moved, there perched a kestrel. An American kestrel, as I later learned, maybe a foot high, with a zebra-striped face, a back barred like tortoise-shell, and gray wings mottled as if with raindrops. It was as delicate and exquisite a creature as its owner was not.

I doubt any of those people crowding around its owner—men looking envious, mothers holding kids by the hand, the wide-eyed children themselves—would have been there had the bird not been there first. In his essay "Why Do People Love Their Pets?" the psychologist John Archer describes how we approach those who have suffered adversity much more willingly if they have an animal with them.[1] The evidence of adversity (wheelchair, white stick) frightens us, as if misfortune were catching, but the presence of an animal reclaims the sufferer in a way that even the presence of a human helper would fail to do. However different such a person may seem from the rest of us, the animal is something we still have in common.

In this case, the social barriers surrounding this particular man (the wheelchair, his wardrobe, his entire staging of himself) disappeared instantly the moment people saw the kestrel, as if that was all they saw: this wild creature, in their midst and, thanks to the man, miraculously accessible. Without it, looking as he did, its owner might have driven the length of the park without one person willingly interacting with him; with the kestrel perched beside him, everybody wanted to do so. It made his company and attention desirable, and it said also that he was an exceptional enough human being to have gained this wild bird's trust and liking; therefore it was safe for the rest of us to interact with him as well.[2] It gave him status, too, a role as the intermediary between the bird and the rest of us. It turned all the negatives in his appearance into unique positives. It made him what Leslie Irvine has described as an "open person...amenable to greeting and conversation."[3]

You would have thought the presence of that many people around it would have thrown the kestrel into a panic, but not at all. It shrugged the feathers around its shoulders and from time to time did a little stress-relieving kestrel two-step, up and down, but otherwise, with the man there, it was calm and still. A kestrel, like any bird of prey, is an intensely charismatic creature, and its trust in its owner—in the seventeenth century, one treatise on falconry advised that a hawk should "love" its owner—made the man one, too.[4] Instead of an outcast, it made him a star.

Animals connect us. They cross all the barriers we erect around ourselves, or between ourselves and those we perceive as being different from us. That they do this literally and spatially is only symbolic of the way they do it emotionally. A grid of animal ley lines surrounds us constantly, whether in the bleak urban spaces of postwar Italy, as in Italo Calvino's story "The Garden of Stubborn Cats":

> . . . a countercity, a negative city, made out of empty cuts between
> walls of minimum distances . . . between the back of one building
> and the back of the next one . . . in a web of dry canals.

or, in what might almost be a bringing to life of Calvino's description, the interconnecting backyards behind L. B. Jefferies's apartment in Hitchcock's *Rear Window*.

The animals in *Rear Window* are almost invisible until you start to look for them, but they're there. Doves and pigeons on the roof above the apartment of Miss Torso, as Jefferies calls her, which fly back and forth across his window, too; a tabby cat that runs up the concrete basement steps; a dog tied to the lamppost at the end of the alley; a canary in a cage, put out on the windowsill in the early morning to take the air, as canaries have been for as long as there have been cages to keep them in; a ginger cat belonging to the sculptress, who is seen petting and feeding it at dusk; a gray poodle, carried into the composer's apartment by its grande dame owner during his soirée; and finally the neighbors' little dog, killed by the villain, Lars Thorwald. (You might argue forward from this that Jefferies himself is the untamed, undomesticated animal, trapped by his broken limb indoors, while Lisa, his Madison Avenue girlfriend, is the ultimate pedigreed indoor pet, who over the course of the movie literally learns how to survive in the hostile, perilous outdoors.) The movie's happy ending is signaled by a replacement puppy for the neighbors, being hoisted aloft to their apartment.

Hitchcock was a pet owner, owning at least four bustling, licorice-eyed Sealyham terriers in his life, two of whom got to share their master's cameo appearances in *The Birds*, and all of whom were given the status of "human" names: Mr. Jenkins, Geoffrey, Stanley, and Sarah.[5] It's worth noting that in *Rear Window* the murder of Thorwald's wife is completely invisible, whereas the discovery of the dog's dead body is a public event, the first to engage every inhabitant of the courtyard, all of them up to that point living their separate lives: "You don't know the meaning of the word 'neighbors!'" screams the dog's heartbroken owner. "Neighbors like each other, speak to each other, care if anybody lives or dies! But none of you do!" And she's right. The inhabitants of L. B. Jefferies's courtyard are completely disconnected from each other. We moved into the cities, away from the kinship groups and support networks of smaller, more rural populations, and the same thing happened to us all. It wasn't animals we lost contact with in doing so. We moved thousands of animals, tens of thousands, into our cities when we first began creating them, because we knew no other way to be—the chicken or rabbit or pig in the backyard for eggs and meat, the cow being milked by the side of the street, the songbird in the parlor, the dog by the door, and the cat in the kitchen. Above all, for centuries pre-1900, there were horses. In 1581, Thomas Wroth counted 2,100 horses in the almost ten miles between the London boroughs of Shoreditch and Enfield, or an average of one horse every eight yards.[6] That's practically the same density as cars today. Even in the nineteenth century, when the cities grew, they still contained vast numbers of animals: six thousand cows in San Francisco; one to every forty-three people on New Orleans; more horses in New Jersey than in Wyoming. In the 1920s Chicago was still home to 55,000 pigs; plus the backyard rabbits, chickens, ducks, and geese, the mice and rats and doves and pigeons, as in Jefferies's backyard, and then you have the cats and dogs as well—as many cats in New York, it was estimated in 1912, as there were voters.[7] No, the creatures we lost touch with when we moved into the cities were each other.

Looking into the backyards of Brooklyn's Park Slope from my partner's kitchen window, the birds and animals variously flying or scrambling over the barriers of walls or fences are the only beings to cross them. The people, when they do appear, all in their separate small gardens, behave as if the backyards abutting theirs and any neighbors in them just weren't there at all. In London my neighbors are no more than muffled noises heard occasionally through the walls. Our isolation from those around us, our pretense that they don't exist, might be seen as the price we pay for the kind of mute cooperation that makes living in cities possible in the first place, but we still have to get that sense of connection from something. It is as necessary to us as air and water. Those animals queuing up for Adam in Genesis 2:19 were there in response to verse 18: "It is not good for man to be alone." No indeed. Loneliness is one of the most excruciating and debilitating disorders we, as animals, can endure; our need to oppose it and the lengths we go to in order to offset it are all about us. You could make a case that the entirety of social media—Facebook, Instagram, Twitter, and all the rest—have come about as synthetic alternatives to community. Of course the Internet is made of cats; cats, dogs, birds—the entire ark of animal-keeping—were part of what we connected with and to and through before the Internet was ever invented. "If all the beasts were gone," Chief Seattle of the Dawlish tribe is supposed to have commented in 1885, "man would die from great loneliness of spirit."

Our need for connection or, as Jessica Pierce puts it, the drive "to tend, to love, to bond" is endless.[8] The balladeer Thomas Haynes Bayly, writing in the middle of the nineteenth century, used it in his poem "Something to Love."[9] "Beloved by none, it is sad to live," says Bayly, in its second stanza. In Paris in the second half of the nineteenth century, as the relentless modernization of the old higgledy-piggledy neighborhoods of the city continued apace, and more and more Parisians found themselves living five or six or seven stories above the pavement, in apartments with no connection, even visually, to their neighbors, this growing isolation of one person from the next was recognized as a new and distinct form of social malaise. It was even suggested that our "unnatural sequestration in cities" might cause the spontaneous generation of rabies, which would be the wild getting its own back with a vengeance.[10] There is a reflection of this in the way that the flaneur, the morally unconnected urban male, and the solitary wandering dogs who figure in so many paintings of this period come to be seen almost as interchangeable—the poet and dramatist Jean Richepin, chronicling Paris in the 1880s and 1890s, even referred to the latter as "boulevardiers."[11] The urban homeless and their animals are seemingly interchangeable as well: unwanted mongrels all, "mean and starved," as Grace Greenwood describes them; feral, unpredictable, and threatening.[12]

Not at all coincidentally, it was during this period that Parisian household dogs, at least those of the bourgeoisie, acquired a sort of canine citizenship, with the first dog tax being introduced in Paris in 1856. Honoré Daumier, printmaker and caricaturist, and a man with whom one suspects Alexandre Dumas would have had much in common, created a lithograph in response to the act, showing a typically stuffy, corseted, snooty-looking Parisienne madame with her spaniel on her lap, holding the dog still as he is immortalized by a down-trodden artist, while the family patriarch makes a face of approval. "Now," Madame is saying, of the dog, "now he is a member of the family, he must have his portrait too."[13] All the humans in the drawing, their pretensions and social status, are skewered mercilessly, but the alert and realistically depicted little dog is not. It gives the subtle message that in her affection for her dog, Madame herself might be humanized. Our need for a sense of connection has not changed one iota since Bayly's or Daumier's day: the sharp-eyed may spot the words of Bayly's poem occurring in the letter John Wick receives from his dead wife in the eponymous 2014 film noir—the same in which she bequeaths to him the beagle puppy, Daisy.

For an animal, inside and out, upstairs and down, are one; to them, our rigidly separated households are interchangeable. Sid, the feline hero of the children's book *Six-Dinner Sid*, has just about every house in Aristotle Street believing he is theirs and theirs alone and can get away with doing so because "no-one talked to their neighbours in Aristotle St." (Sid also has six different names and six different personalities to match his six different lives.)[14] *The Secret Life of Pets* (2016) has every pet in an apartment block in constant contact with one another, while their owners have no contact at all.

We aid and abet in this, what's more. We lock and seal the doors in our homes to members of our own species, but we chop holes in them, or leave boards loose in our fences, or skylights on the latch, to allow our animals to come and go as they please; in particular, our cats. There's a cat flap in Exeter Cathedral, under its famous astrological clock, which dates back as early as the 1600s. The painter J. M. W. Turner, well known to his contemporaries as a cat man, even used one of his own paintings, *Fishing upon the Blythe-Sand* of 1809, as the flap to a hole in a window via which his cats entered and exited his house in Marylebone, London, although in point of fact the half dozen Manx cats with whom Turner shared his home all belonged to his housekeeper and onetime mistress, Hannah Danby. I think you can see Hannah's hand, rather than Turner's, in pinning that canvas into place.[15] Amazingly, the painting survived its treatment and is in the collection of Tate Britain.

But the actions of both the canons of Exeter Cathedral and of Turner pale when set against those of John Harrison of Leeds. Harrison was a notable businessman and philanthropist in Leeds in the seventeenth century and, soon after his marriage in 1603, he set about building himself a grand new house with courtyard, garden, and orchard, and with "holes or passages cut in the doors and ceilings, for the free passage of cats," or so the Leeds antiquarian Ralph Thoresby informs us, adding that Harrison had "as great an affection" for cats as did Dick Whittington.[16] In *Kedi* (also 2016), the award-winning documentary about the street cats of Istanbul, the whole of that city is presented as a mega-version of Harrison's house, with water and food left out for the cats on the street, and holes and runs created for them or left carefully unblocked in every building. You could argue that the unpredictable comings and goings of cats through our lives and our domestic spaces is one of the things that keeps us so in thrall to them. As I write, a dog, if I had one, would be here at my feet. "We cannot stand up under comparison with the dog," wrote Emily Brontë in an essay of 1842. "He is infinitely too good. But the cat…is extremely like us in disposition."[17]

In the past, with domestic spaces so much more hierarchically arranged, the routes our pet animals created around our homes could be said to have connected the inhabitants of its different areas as well. Elizabeth Barrett's spaniel, Flush, might have been the only creature permitted to move, without instruction from a social superior, from stables to garden to kitchen to family rooms to the boudoir of his ailing mistress in the family home in Wimpole Street. Rescuing him, on the three occasions when he was dognapped, physically moved his owner into areas of London where no upper-middle-class woman would otherwise have dreamed of setting foot.

The dog walk is one of the most basic ways in which animals connect us. Fergus's size meant that my walks with him tended to be solitary affairs (although even now, I would cross the road to say hello to another wolfhound), but for most dog owners, the walk through public space, as opposed to the hermetically sealed unit of a private garden, is as social an event for the owner as it is for the dog. My most recent experience was walking Chip in a small park near Highgate Cemetery, on one of those grayish, dampish winter afternoons that in North London in particular is like finding yourself in a John Atkinson Grimshaw painting by daylight; one where even if my human nose couldn't identify them, my human brain could imagine the scents pouring out of the damp black earth, vibrating above the wet grass and leaves, and shimmering on every post and railing. Chip herself—white and tan, with exquisitely expressive ears and a tail like an ostrich plume—has her own intriguing personal geography to add to the mix in this chapter, as she's a rescue dog from Romania, a fact that speaks of another invisible grid, of dog lovers and animal protectors spread around the globe. As yet another layer on top of that, Chip's actual walker, my girlfriend Sally, had connected with Chip via a website where those yearning for dog time in their lives hook up with dog owners who are time-poor and walk the dogs involved in an exchange that can only be described as a win-win *woof.* Here was Chip, chasing after her tennis ball and pausing to swap stares with other dogs she failed to recognize and friendlier, more personal greetings with those she did, while Sally and I did exactly the same—nods to those owners who were strangers and shouted greetings from Sally to those she recognized from previous walks. The non-pet-owning jury may still be out on whether the ownership of a pet is good or bad for one's physical or mental health or whether it makes no difference at all, but there can be no denying: a dog to walk makes a walk a great deal more fun. And you would think, therefore, it disposes you to take rather more of them.[18]

This creation between owners and animals of social spaces in which both animals and people gather can have other, unanticipated, results. In the 1990s, the housing corporation of Starrett City in Brooklyn was sued by its tenants for the right to be allowed to keep pets, and in pursuing their case, the tenants' previous social conflicts, which were all intensely focused around the issue of race, simply fell away.[19] Starrett City is now, sadly and controversially, up for sale.

Animals moving back and forth between us bring individual human beings together, too—a trick used in romantic fiction since Pilot the Newfoundland ran up to Jane Eyre on the lane from Thornfield Hall to Hay. Pub parrots and mynah birds, bodega cats and bookstore pets of all descriptions, welcome you in and immediately fulfill that trick of animal magic of making you feel singled out. "Even if I weren't a pet fanatic," says one bookstore owner, a bookstore pet is a business asset: "it brings in so many people."[20] And no matter how grim your brow (like Rochester's), how alienated you may be from your fellow human beings (like the kestrel man in LA), the presence of an animal beside you overlays you with all sorts of desirable virtues, virtues for which we might perhaps adopt and widen Horace Walpole's term "Dogmanity." If an animal likes and trusts you, odds are it is safe for one of your own species to do so, too.[21] In his *The Animals Among Us*, John Bradshaw speculates that one reason we have pets might be that, historically, carng for an animal would have been a way for young women to advertise their maternal skills to potential mates. Well, possibly. What has been called "the greatest cat painting ever created," an eight-foot-wide feline panoply, commissioned in 1891 by Kate Birdsall Johnson, an American millionaire, was given the unofficial title by her husband of *My Wife's Lovers*, and not entirely jokingly. I can imagine plenty of men who would regard an animal in a woman's life as a rival.[22] But as with Federico Gonzaga, for a man to own a pet suggests a nurturing, caregiving side to his character that might otherwise be completely unsuspected. In the 1997 film *As Good as It Gets*, his sudden responsibility for Verdell, a present-day Griffon Bruxellois, begins the human reclamation of the homophobic, misanthropic Melvin Udall, and as soon as Verdell is in his life, we know he'll get the girl, too.[23] "Guy gets a dog, become a pussy magnet," as James Gandolfini's character, Marvin Stipler, puts it, in *The Drop*.

But cats can serve as witnesses to character, too. I have to admit to a personal bias here, in that my own first chess move, to let my partner know I both liked and was interested in him, was to issue the peremptory request that he should put his cat on Catbook (Facebook for cats) and make her my friend. I put the presence of this animal in my partner's life as a vitally important indicator of his character, which places me right there beside Mark Twain, with his declaration that "when a man loves cats, I am his friend and comrade, without further introduction." But we do trust animals' instincts in such matters, more than, perhaps, we trust our own—the closer connection to a more natural world that we attribute to them means we think, or maybe *suspect* puts it more accurately, that as judges of amiability, they know better than we do—another reason why for so many of us their presence is so acceptable. Also, connection to my partner's cat was a cunning, non-overt way to connect to him. In the park, greeting and patting someone else's dog is a way of greeting and of patting them, and many a beautiful friendship begins with the exchange of a saliva-soaked tennis ball.

Does the ability to connect with an animal, or the animal's willingness to connect with you, in fact say anything about your own ability to connect with others of your own species? There are optimistic studies that suggest a tentative yes; there are those who say such studies are flawed.[24] We're such a complicated species—for every St. Francis, you can guarantee there's a Hitler. There is some recent science to suggest that the ability to enter imaginatively into the experience of another creature, to empathize (that word again) with another being, also varies from individual to individual—so some of us might simply be born better at this than others.[25] Equally, some may be worse. "People who don't love animals don't love people either," says one resident of Istanbul, in *Kedi*. "I know that much." There's a much less-often-quoted second stanza to the poem Percival Stockdale wrote about Dr. Johnson's cat Hodge, in which Stockdale praises Hodge's character thus:

He lived in town, yet ne'er got drunk,
Nor spent one farthing on a punk;
He never filched a single groat,
Nor bilked a taylor of a coat.

"Punk" is used here in its original sense of a whore. By contrast Boswell, Dr. Johnson's biographer, spent many a farthing on many a punk and was a notorious boozehound. Stockdale was a noted and radical abolitionist (as were many of those who in the eighteenth century first campaigned for animal rights, a fascinating connection in itself but one way beyond the scope of this book); Boswell emphatically was not, taking refuge even in the idiotic notion that slaves enjoyed their lot. You wonder if Stockdale might have had Boswell in mind here. Boswell is also in my view a prime example of men who don't like cats not really being at ease with women, either—no matter how many farthings they may spend upon them. I was delighted to find I was perhaps not alone in thinking so: at their 1794 meeting, Boswell recorded this exchange with the philosopher Jean-Jacques Rousseau:

Rousseau: Do you like cats?
Boswell: No.
Rousseau: I was sure of that. It is my test of character. There you have the despotic instinct of men. They do not like cats because the cat is free and will never consent to be a slave.[26]

I rest my case.
The cultural connecting of human with animal is the one that has

the marketing departments of pet food companies rubbing their hands with glee. It says all well-to-do, elderly ladies must have something fluffy and yappy seated upon their laps and speaks of *"man's* best friend," yet "crazy cat *ladies"* and it is solely of our human making. The connecting of women and cats is far and away the most notorious example. The ancient Egyptians are meant to have started it all, with their cat-goddess, Bast, but languorous or devious cats, to the discomfort of every misogynist such as Boswell, have been an emblem of female sensuality ever since. There's a particularly knowing example in Nathaniel Hone's 1765 portrait of the courtesan Kitty Fisher, where Kitty, modestly covering her no doubt delectable breasts with a shawl of Indian tulle, is accessorized by a bowl of goldfish, in which another, smaller black-and-white kitty is fishing, and in which are reflected the faces of the crowd gawping at Kitty just as we are ourselves.[27] A century later, Renoir created a particularly odd example of connection in his *The Boy with the Cat*—the naked adolescent boy, turned away from the artist, is nuzzling and being nuzzled back by a large tabby cat. Renoir at the time was sharing studio space with Frédéric Bazille, who may have been homosexual, and this painting, which is a complete anomaly in Renoir's work, does make one wonder— was the boy Bazille's model, and does the presence of the cat somehow make him, for Renoir, an honorary girl?[28] Most overt of all were the Barrison Sisters, a vaudeville act that toured the United States in the 1890s, whose most famous hit was known as "Do You Want to See My Pussy?" At the end of the song, the sisters would lift their skirts to reveal voluminous frilly bloomers, each with a live kitten in a pouch over the crotch. Truly, there is nothing new under the sun.

And there have always been those whose heroic treatment of an animal indicated nothing whatsoever in their treatment of other members of their own race. Byron risked rabies himself in nursing his Newfoundland Boatswain when Boatswain was dying of that terrifying disease, but when Claire Clairmont, the mother of Byron's daughter Allegra, tried to use his concern for his animals to flatter kinder treatment of herself out of the poet, it had no effect on him at all. Claire wrote to Byron in 1818:

> How kind and gentle you are to children! How good-tempered and considerate toward your servants; how accommodating even to your dogs![29]

And there were plenty of them for Byron to be accommodating to. Visiting him in Italy in 1821 Shelley described his household:

> Lord B.'s establishment consists, beside servants, of ten horses, eight enormous dogs, three monkeys, five cats, an eagle, a crow, and a falcon; and all these, except the horses, walk about the house, which every now and then resounds with their unarbitrated quarrels, as if they were the masters of it...After I have sealed my letter, I find that my enumeration of the animals in this Circean Palace was defective, and that in a material point. I have just met on the grand staircase five peacocks, two guinea hens, and an Egyptian crane.

Byron himself had nonchalantly joined Allegra with those same animal dependents in a letter to his half sister, Augusta Leigh, in November 1820:

> The Child Allegra is well—but the Monkey has got a cough—
> and the tame Crow has lately suffered from the head ache.

By September 1821 the four-year-old Allegra had been packed off to a convent, where she was to die less than a year later. But then you can be offhand and despotic with an animal and get away with it.

At the entire other end of the scale, there is an owner such as Abraham Lincoln. It's almost ridiculous, set against the height of his other achievements, to examine Lincoln as a pet owner, but by contrast to Byron he was a man with a painful empathy for every other creature he encountered. As a farmchild he had a pet pig; his horror when he found it would be slaughtered and his attempts to save it—including running away with it from home—are affecting to read even today. The experience was, said Lincoln, "the beginning of tragedy for me," and even as a grown man he would describe how he could "never see a pig that I do not think of my first pet." The use of that word "pet" is telling: this was a creature carried around, spoken with, confided in, connected to. Numerous stories recount Lincoln's unhesitating concern for animals: how he rescued another pig from a muddy hollow in which it would have drowned, summoned back, as he put it, by the creature's pathetic expression; restored fallen fledglings to their nest ("I could not have slept if I had not restored those little birds to their mother"); and concerned himself with the welfare of a family of abandoned kittens when visiting

Grant's headquarters in Virginia in 1865.[30] But this story about the piglet is particularly illuminating. Lincoln carved a cradle for his piglet, which is about as close to making it a human baby as you can get, and looks very much like what a psychoanalyst would call infantile parentalism, with Lincoln trying to make himself the figure of the mother he had so recently lost.

The connection between pets and children, and pets as children, is another of the most durable and persistent. There are obvious, major differences between a pet and a child—unlike children, Bird and Daisy can happily be left alone all day but then they will also never "grow up" and live independently. If they are transitional objects, like a blankie, they are ones I don't have to give up while we are still breathing. I do pick them up and carry them around, which for them must be one of the oddest aspects of being a pet, and one that they tolerate with great good humor, in my view; while they must have been carried about by the scruff by their actual mother in kittenhood, it's an unnatural part of life as an adult cat. With Bird in particular, because she answers back so readily, I catch myself cycling through her possible wants just as I used to do with my brother's children when they were small, but since she is obviously without spoken language, it's still basically me who gets to decide what she "wants"—although you could say that we achieve communication by mutual agreement, too.

For an actual child, a pet becomes an opposite but equal—an accepting, uncritical ally in the business of negotiating a way through the adult world.[31] For a child, the differences between it and this other being become as smudgy as the outlines round the animals on the walls of the

Chauvet cave.[32] Renoir created a wonderful portrait of exactly this in his 1878 painting of the Charpentier family. One child sits on a chair, the other on the family dog (of course, a long-suffering Newfie), just as if on a parental lap, her hand on the dog's flank, unconsciously. When I was very small indeed, I can remember joining my cat Freddy in a patch of sunlight on the sitting room floor, lying down with him and rolling over when he rolled, and came as close in that moment to understanding what it is to be "cat" as I am ever likely to do.

There's a sort of logic at work here. If you are good at reading people, at constructing and entering into a reliable version of another's reality, then perhaps you can make a better-than-average job of entering into the reality of an animal, too.[33] If you can create a sustained and mutually beneficial relationship with a four-legged creature, doing the same with one who has two legs like you should be a cinch. If you are practiced in doing this by being a pet owner from childhood, then possibly your social skills may indeed be higher, in particular your ability to understand others, when you grow up.[34] But it just doesn't seem to work predictably. The most passionate pet owners can be misfits or outcasts where their own species is concerned; or, like Elizabeth Barrett, they have had their ability to form other relationships curtailed by circumstance. There's a long, long list: Il Sodoma acquired his nickname because he had what we would now call an openly gay lifestyle and "always had about him boys and beardless youths, whom he loved more than was decent."[35] Quite how one managed this in sixteenth-century Florence without being clapped into jail I have no idea; any more than I can fathom how J. R. Ackerley managed it in the Britain of the 1940s and 1950s. Possibly both men were sufficiently charming and well liked—that business of knowing how to read and respond to others again—to create around themselves their own personal microsystems of tolerance, but hats off to them, however they got it done. Frederick II of Prussia, Frederick the Great, was also gay but could be anything other than open about it; coiner of the phrase "a dog is a man's best friend," by the time of his death in 1786, he had so removed himself from affective relationships with the rest of human society that he asked to be buried only with his Italian greyhounds (a highly fashionable breed at the time). The poet William Cowper was persecuted by depression and fears of eternal damnation, paralyzing his interaction with others. J. G. Wood had a childhood marred by ill health and might have suffered from what would now be diagnosed as dyspraxia; certainly as an adult he was notoriously accident-prone. "Seldom was there a man who injured himself more often," said his son, and Wood seems to have suffered from a form of numerical dyslexia, too.[36] Louis Wain found the everyday world impossibly difficult to negotiate and ended his days in an asylum. Irene Pepperberg described her mother as a "refrigerator parent," coldly unemotional and constantly pushing her daughter away. It's not, I think, that those who form passionate attachments to animals prefer these to interactions with members of their own species; it's that even those to whom human relationships are not available, for whatever reason, still need that sense of connectedness to another creature, need it intensely— and an animal is available when their own kind is not. The homeless human being sitting on the pavement, hand extended, has a dog curled up beside them not simply for warmth by any means but much more essentially for companionship, for connection, because being homeless and on the streets is a state of such stultifying boredom and such acute loneliness that the sufferers virtually disappear.

If you are living on the streets, every detail of your existence is made more challenging if you are sharing it with an animal. Finding a bed for the night is impossible unless you can find a shelter that will take in the animal, too. Queuing for assistance within any government building is truly Kafkaesque—what do you do with the animal while you queue? Accessing, let alone paying for, veterinary care is the biggest challenge of all. Yet the pets of the homeless are fed, tended, cared for, loved; in fact sociological research into the attachment between the homeless and their animals, who are indeed in the fullest sense their companions, confirms these relationships of constant contact and constant investigation of each other's needs as being for the animal and the owner both among the highest quality in existence.[37] The dog, wrote Samuel Jackson Pratt back in the eighteenth century, was no more than an indicator of luxury for the rich, but might be "the only thing the poor possess."[38]

There are many arguments as to why relationships with animals can be so much easier, more successful, and less compromised than those with our own species (there is the famous dictum that "a pet won't ask for a divorce"). An animal demands differently from a human partner; their needs have a one-word simplicity (warmth, food, safety, affection) compared to ours, and we can fulfill them more or less entirely. This satisfies us in turn, so in our connection to each other we reach a point of contented equilibrium that in so many human relationships defeats us time and again. (It's maybe the best measure of the need for that sense of connection that even in those human relationships we still keep trying.) And these relationships, once established, are vastly more stable than those with other members of our own species, too. Contrast the steadfast loyalty of James Bowen's relationship with Bob the Street Cat to his unpredictable and erratic connection to the people around him. What an animal requires of us is uninfected by who we are or even where we are, come to that—in nursing home or nursery, hospital or prison, an animal doesn't judge. They are incapable of judging in that way; judging us according to our circumstances would make nonsense, to them, of the whole business of connection. In the most extreme human situations, they are oblivious: Ernst Jünger, pinned down in the trenches at Artois in 1915, recounted the presence of a "white tom-cat... the sole living creature that was on visiting terms with both sides... [It] always made on me an impression of extreme mystery."[39] No wonder. And Bird, sitting here on my notes, has no interest in what I am writing or in anything other than whether I will again perform my part in correct and timely fashion in the ritual of "She does her Chewbacca creak/I stroke her." I do, and apparently perfectly satisfied, she weaves her way around the obstacles on my desk, hops onto the bed, curls up into what my sister-in-law refers to as a kitty-donut, and falls asleep.

We are scared by the misfortunes of others; our instinct with those in distress is to shun. An animal's is not; an animal's instinct is to investigate, which is why when you are in tears, if you own a pet, it will come to see what is wrong. Very conveniently, humans in distress make the kinds of noises animal infants do, but still, the animal comes to see. If you have ever seen an adult in tears on public transport, it is most unlikely any of their human companions in the carriage will do the same (unless you now do so yourself). When Henry Wriothesley, 3rd Earl of Southampton, was imprisoned in the Tower of London from 1600 to 1603, facing personal disgrace and possibly even execution, he was supposedly comforted in his captivity by the presence of a cat. Whether the details of the story are reliable or not, the splendid portrait of Henry, created to celebrate his release, does indeed include a cat. The episode in the Tower is relegated to a tiny vignette over Henry's left shoulder, well behind him, but there on the windowsill right beside him is a splendid tuxedo cat, whose markings parallel Henry's own suit of clothes, of the same chic Jacobean black-and-white. Man and cat gaze down on the viewer with the same calm self-possession: partners not only in, but in overcoming, adversity.

It isn't only in captivity or illness that connection to an animal comforts us. When faced with nigh-on insurmountable disaster, where we are almost powerless to help ourselves, we can still exert some power, some agency, over the situation by helping those creatures even more helpless than we are. We stay in abusive relationships rather than abandon an animal to harm; buy food for them when we can hardly afford to feed ourselves (a mere ten companies produced dog food in the United States at the start of the Great Depression; there were 175 by 1934); bankrupt ourselves rather than have them go without veterinary treatment.[40] It's more evidence of that doubleness that characterizes so many of our dealings with animals—we help them, but that helps us, in turn. Samuel Pepys walking about the still-burning City of London on September 5, 1666 ("the saddest sight of desolation that I ever saw"), on ash and rubble yet hot enough to burn his feet through the leather soles of his boots, he records also how he saw time and effort being given to one small, symbolic rescue: "a poor cat taken out of a hole in the chimney, joyning to the wall of the Exchange; with the hair all burned off the body, and yet alive." Naoto Matsumura, a fifty-five-year-old farmer from the town of Tomioka in Japan, refused to leave when the town was evacuated after the Fukushima nuclear accident in 2011 and became the guardian and caregiver for the town's abandoned animals.[41] As of July 8, 2017, he was still there. The cat man of Aleppo, Mohammad Alaa Jaleel, who looked after abandoned domestic pets as the people of Aleppo fled the city ahead of Syria's civil war, returned to the country to create a new animal sanctuary even after the original was flattened by barrel and cluster bombs.[42] And then there is the tale of Kunkush, a fluffy white tomcat from the Iraqi city of Mosul, who was carried all the way through Turkey by his owner and her five children, only to disappear (in typically ungrateful feline fashion, you may think) after the family had finally reached the island of Lesbos in October 2015.[43] The family went on to a new life as refugees in Norway; but meanwhile behind them volunteers on the island located Kunkush, got him to a local vet, found him a foster home in Berlin, contacted his owner in Norway, flew Kunkush there from Germany, and in February 2016 finally effected a reunion.

Now I am sure there have to be some who would regard Kunkush's rescue as an appalling waste of resources. That is to completely miss the point; just as castigating the hard-up and homeless for wasting their resources on an animal is to miss the point of what they are doing, too.

We cannot solve all the great problems of being human, but we *can* solve the small ones, and in so doing, we retain or repossess our humanity and human dignity, too. It is the most altruistic version possible of the sort of thinking that puts humankind at the head of creation—with responsibility toward the rest.

Woe betide, therefore, the public figure who ignores the laws of connection and appears guilty of overt antipathy toward an animal, in particular if that animal is a public pet, one of those in whom the whole country feels it has a stake. Checkers the spaniel may have single-handedly redeemed Tricky Dicky Nixon during an early awkward moment in 1952, when he allowed Nixon to demonstrate a rare instance of self-awareness and humility (Nixon, running for vice president, had been caught out in what looked like hypocrisy regarding gifts to his campaign funds; his refusal in the "Checkers speech" to give up his cocker spaniel puppy, one such "gift," on the grounds that his children loved it, saved his campaign); in the United Kingdom, the opposite happened in the case of Humphrey, the Downing Street cat.

In May 1997, Tony and Cherie Blair moved into Number 10, and by November, Humphrey, Chief Mouser to the Cabinet Office, was no longer in residence. (The problem of vermin in the buildings of Downing Street was an issue long before the first politicians took up residence.) The popular press in the United Kingdom already had something of a problem with Cherie Blair, who was neither frump nor clotheshorse, and therefore fitted neither of the existing categories for a politician's wife; now it appeared that as a woman who disliked cats, who had banished Humphrey (or possibly worse), she was positively unnatural in other ways, too. So fierce did speculation become that before the end of the month, Downing Street was forced to issue a photograph of Humphrey posing in his retirement home with the day's newspaper, like a kidnap victim with proof of life. Even so, the idea of Cherie Blair as cold-hearted persisted; and the initial response from Downing Street, so tone-deaf to public opinion and so full of injured feeling, did nothing to dispel it.

The public pet, as Kunkush's story made him, as Humphrey's apparent disappearance made him too, belongs to everybody. A public pet creates a community, a coming together (the porters at Billingsgate Fish Market, for example, regard the seal that occasionally disports itself outside my front window as "theirs," and vie to feed it). The public pet has done so since the days of Hanno the elephant, presented to Pope Leo X in 1514. Hanno was so celebrated that he even joined the pope in civic processions. Much the same thing happened in Paris in 1827, when the entire city fell in love with a giraffe, presented to the French king, Charles X, by Muhammad Ali, ruler of Egypt. The giraffe became a source of such civic pride that hairstyles, spotted fabrics, and a color ("belly of giraffe") were named in her honor. Cecil the lion is another whose death made him public property; then there was the London whale, a juvenile bottlenose who swam into the Thames in 2006 and died as she was being taken by barge out to the North Sea to be released. Londoners crowded the bridges over the Thames to watch the rescue attempt and will it to be a success, and when the news broke that the whale had died of heart failure, the entire city felt we had failed her. Public grief at her death was extraordinary. In other words, we cared.

"Yes, I came back. I always come back."

CHAPTER SEVEN

CARING

The caressing regard of a dog, the sweet touch of a cat, the rhythmic modulations of a bird in a cage, the triumphant trills of a canary, have they not, on occasion, chased away our melancholic thoughts?

—Laure Desvernays, *Les Animaux d'Agrément*, 1913

T here is our care for them, and there is their care for us, and the two meet somewhere in the middle. "Why does the lamb love Mary so?" her schoolmates ask in Sarah Josepha Hale's poem. "Why, Mary loves the lamb, you know," the teacher replies. Jane Loudon, invoking the same sense of partnership, begins *Domestic Pets* with a tableau of domesticity that both woman and animals have an equal share in creating, even if only one of them can put it into words:

I have taken up the subject...with my favourite dog lying at my feet, a cat purring at my side, and two gold fish swimming merrily about in a vase before me...[1]

A description that I read lying on the sofa with one cat on my shoulder, there as if pinned like a prom-night corsage, and the other under my raised knees, both with purr set to a gentle simmer, and as far as I could tell, a sense of perfect content suffusing us all.

Such Garden of Eden moments, of mutual quiet content, when the animal-companion boundary almost dissolves itself, are to the owner one of the very best rewards of having an animal in your life—in fact if you should find a member of your own species with whom such amiable, undemanding happiness is possible, you should probably marry them. Kay Milton (she who talks to her cats) makes the point in her 2005 essay that people engaged in similar activities tend to reach similar understandings of the world.[2] Perhaps that's true for our animals as well—the dog being walked, the cat being played with, the animal quietly keeping company with you just as you are with it: we're sharing the same experience and the same responses to it, simply from different sides. We certainly gain the same benefits. When you stroke an animal, its blood pressure reduces and its stress levels go down, as well as yours. "She loves it when you pet her," says the self-appointed guardian of Bengü, one of Istanbul's street cats. "She almost passes out."[3] "Companionship and love," wrote the artist Carolee Schneemann in 2015, "is as precious to the pet as it has been to you."[4] It's good, in other words, to care. Maybe these are the moments of ideal caring for our animals, too.

Care itself is simple and instinctive. Faced with the ordeal of their first Russian winter in the Crimea, "the misery of which you can hardly realize," as Lieutenant Temple Godman put it in a letter home to Park Hatch, he and the redoubtable Kilburn dig out a sort of sunken stable for his three horses, despite the fact that Godman describes himself by this point as being "so weak I could hardly cut a flea in half." When the chestnut has his rug stolen, very much more likely by some desperate frostbitten sentry rather than for another horse, Godman goes cold in the horse's stead: "I was obliged to give him the waterproof rug off my bed in consequence," he writes.[5] In Istanbul again, walking through the Grand Bazaar, I came across a bone-thin street cat stretched out asleep on the dusty ground under the window of a jeweler's shop. Below the waterfalls of semi-strung pearls, the rainbow glitter of jewels, and the links of gold chain, someone, presumably the jeweler, had laid out a square of carpet for the cat to sleep on.

Let that image sit with you a moment, because it symbolizes what you might call, for the owner, the contradiction of caring. Here's another example: there once lived, in third-century Carthage, near what is now the port of Tunis, an elderly lapdog, another Maltese type, who was literally economically worthless, suffering from not only arthritis and a dislocated hip but with so few teeth left that its food would have had to have been a soft mush, specially prepared.[6] Nonetheless, so carefully tended was this dog that when it died (and was buried with its owner, another mark of the affection in which it was held), it was at least fifteen years old, which compares very favorably with the age a Maltese dog might reach today. There is the emotional value an owner ascribes to a pet—even an elderly, nigh-on toothless dog, even a little street cat—that is based purely on sentiment and where the care displayed toward the animal can be almost without limit; and then there is the actual, economic value of the pet to anyone other than the owner, which is something very different. In the same way, there are the Garden of Eden moments, which to the owner are priceless and which you might argue are what we put ourselves through everything else involved in the care of an animal for, and then there is the everything else itself, which has been monetized to the hilt.

Let's start with the food and toys and litter, with even Fuller's earth having expanded into an industry now worth $2 billion a year in the United States alone.[7] Then there are the dog beds and cat baskets and the cages for their smaller furry cousins. There are the coats and collars. There are the obedience and training classes and the professional dog walkers, who don't come cheap and never have—King John (bad King John, über-villain of all those tales of Robin Hood) awarded the entire manor of Bari-cote in Warwickshire to the servant who looked after one of his favorite dogs for a year, which makes the amount paid to dog walkers today seem paltry.[8] Obedience boarding school in New York in 2017, perhaps the near-est we have today to the care given to King John's "white bitch with red ears," might cost $2,500. And if you want to explore serious money in pet care today (and we will), there are, above all, the vet's bills.

Then there are all those costs about which the owner can do little more than shrug—the once-prized scarf or sweater, adopted by your adoptee, which now plumps up the dog bed or cat basket, treasured still but in a completely different way by its new user. Think of the ornate yet also well-chewed slippers behind Bachelier's Havanese. I've watched my oldest nieces tussling over who owns what in their wardrobe, and all I can say is, the argument that "I took it because it smells of you" got the one using it nowhere. I ask myself sometimes how much the quality of those Garden of Eden moments of content stem from the fact that we are capable of being so much more tolerant and forbearing toward our animals than we are to one another; and how much of that is the result of what seems to put them at a disadvantage (they're smaller, helpless, mute) actually working in their favor?

Because if we're talking forbearance, if we're in that area, along with the possessions annexed and destroyed, the never-ending interruptions to our routine should we vary from theirs, the solicitations for attention even if we don't, there are all those other aspects of caring for an animal that are, frankly, disgusting—the hairballs to be picked off the rug, the fleas and ticks to be tackled, the upchuck to be removed, hopefully before it has been trodden in, the half-eaten prey to be disposed of, and the cleaning to be undertaken when the carefully purchased litter tray has been missed or forgotten about entirely. Every owner has been there, from the earliest to the present day. Samuel Pepys was struck positively philosophical when one of Charles II's little dogs pooped in the royal barge—it made him think "that a King and all that belong to him are but as others are," but as we've seen, was vastly less amused when Fancy did the same in Pepys's own house; and this at a period when from

Hampton Court to Versailles, courtier and courtier's dog were both equally likely to be found relieving themselves in some empty corridor.[9] Even the makers of those early Irish law books must list in weary detail and with a sigh that is still almost palpable the measures required should a favorite hound misbehave, or to make good the damage should Little Meow disgrace herself on a perfectly good floor covering of fresh rushes.[10] Fictional pets are no better: Tom, in *The Life and Adventures of a Cat*, retires "into the coalhole for reasons we do not think decent to mention," which is one of those tiny historical details that in this case illuminates as if with a floodlight all the unconsidered indignities of being a scullery maid: it's dark, it's secluded, and the material is friable— of course that's where cats went, and then the wretched, put-upon skivvy was sent down there to fill up the coal scuttle.[11]

Even nastier, in terms of historical evidence of all the horrors our animals have inflicted upon us, was the discovery made by a fifteenth-century monk in Deventer in the Netherlands, who left the manuscript he was working on open on his desk overnight, and on the page he found himself forced to leave unused the next day, inscribed the following:

> Here is nothing missing, but a cat peed on this page during the night. Cursed be the pest of a cat that peed on this book during the night in Deventer and because of it, many others too. And beware not to leave books open at night where cats can get at them.

Both urine stain and quick sketch-portrait of the offender survive.[12]

And all us owners today have a great deal for which to thank Edward Lowe, the man who first thought to use Fuller's earth as cat litter in 1947.

Likewise, young James Spratt, who began life as a lightning-rod salesman, of all things, and ended it in charge of the first and one of the largest pet food companies on the planet. According to the creation myth, if one may call it that, of Spratts (now Spillers), James Spratt's moment of inspiration came on a visit to London in 1860, when he watched stray dogs gorging themselves on the hardtack biscuits that sailors threw away with relief the moment they came ashore—and so the dog biscuit, and the entire pet food industry, was born.

The point to take away from these highlights in the history of the pet owner is how immensely more convenient and less time-consuming they made the practical side of caring for a pet. If there are more companion animals living with us than in the past, if the percentage of us who share our lives with them has indeed increased (68 percent of all households in the United States were sharing their home with a pet in 2017, and roughly 50 percent were doing so in the United Kingdom), then part of the reason why is no doubt the ease of looking after them.[13] Pre–Edward Lowe, if litter was needed, which it certainly would have been once we all began living like the neighbors in *Rear Window*, in those apartments in the air, it was earth or paper or ashes, which you provided your animal with yourself, while food for a pet would have been scraps and guts husbanded from the human table. Or at least, that's what it was supposed to be, and most commonly, so the historical sources would have us believe, bread, plain and simple, the commonest means of keeping body and soul together for man or beast. Alexandre

Dumas's Mysouff is regularly offered a bowl of bread and milk; Louis Wain's Peter has his in a Crown Derby dish, while for Christmas 1833, the then Princess Victoria gives Dash a "basin of bread and milk, three Indian-rubber balls and two bits of gingerbread," not all of them for consumption, obviously.[14]

The Latin for bread, *pane*, is where our word "companion" comes from—which itself in the Oxford Dictionary today is defined as "a person *or animal* with whom one spends a lot of time" (my italics). Having an animal accept food from you is as significant as having it accept a caress, and to be responsible for another creature's sustenance is highly symbolic. If you take that on, it is very difficult not to feel responsible for them in every other way as well. You also have to bear in mind that historically meat would have been far rarer in most owners' diets as well; but is all this business of bread and milk to be believed?

I rather suspect not. In fact, I suspect that asking an owner in the past what they truly fed their pet would be like asking one today to be honest about their consumption of units of alcohol. And the reason behind this is once again the dichotomy between emotional worth and economic value.

Emotional worth is invisible. As early as 1588 the lawyer William Lambarde was declaring that "to take dogs, apes, parats, singing birds and such like is no felonie; because these latter be but for pleasure only and are not of any value."[15] Two centuries later and this was still the view: Sir William Blackstone, writing in 1760, decreed that the value of a pet is "depending only on the caprice of the owner."[16] Hence the example of Dr. Johnson going out to buy oysters for an elderly and toothless

Hodge, and the sedative valerian to make his cat's last days more comfortable. Yes, both are famous examples of care, but Johnson undertook these errands himself because the value of the animal they were for, while obvious to his owner, would be completely inexplicable to his servants, who, Johnson feared, could well have seen such an errand for an elderly and economically worthless cat as demeaning and insulting.[17]

Hence also the apoplectic rantings in 1756 of the traveler and pamphletist Jonas Hanway—surely the last person any pet owner would have wanted to find themselves stuck inside a mail coach with. "We may sometimes see a fine lady act as if she thought the DOG, which happens to be under her precious care, is incomparably of more value, in her eyes, than a HUMAN creature," Hanway shrieks. The pamphlet might be described as the eighteenth century's version of Twitter, and sure enough, Hanway breaks into full caps to give his indignation full vent. "The costly chicken is ordered for the CAT or DOG, by her who never thinks of giving a morsel of bread to relieve the hunger of a MAN."[18]

Oh, come on, you may think, how costly could that chicken be? It so happens that we have an estimate from one of Hanway's near-contemporaries, the agriculturalist Charles Varlo, who in 1775 calculated that a lady's lapdog, fed on bread, butter, a pound of meat a day, and, rather surprisingly, "tea," cost four pounds, eleven shillings, and threepence a year to maintain. That could equate to as much as a whopping £6,000, or $8,000, today, if you had to go out and earn it.[19] Now I am as indulgent an owner, I hope, as two little rescue cats could ask for, but I doubt mine cost me even a third of that amount a year. The great difference between then and now is that then as owner you were meant to feel guilty if you were feeding your pet too well; now, thanks to the overflowing cornucopia of pet food products inspired by Mr. Spratt, you are meant to be anxious that you are not feeding them well enough. When as an owner I am offered "Gourmet Soup" for cats at £1 per forty-gram sachet (roughly $1.30 for one and a half ounces) by an industry worth £4.6 billion in 2017 in the United Kingdom, and no less than $69.5 billion in the United States, I find I can become quite Hanwayish myself.

But if an animal has that quality of emotional worth to you, on you go indulging it regardless. Adriaen van Ostade depicted a ramshackle peasant's cottage in 1668, one where even basic economic survival would have been hand-to-mouth, yet beside the small child eating his supper there is a small dog, waiting expectantly at the joint stool that serves both as a table. Renoir paints a later interior in his study of *Mother Anthony's Tavern*, of 1866—there is Mother Anthony, clearing one of the tables in her tavern in the forest of Fontainebleau, where Renoir and his friends often met, and beneath the chair of the artist Alfred Sisley on the right lies her dog, confidently waiting for the leftovers.

At the other end of the social order, Islay, a Scotch terrier who joined Queen Victoria's dog pack in March 1839, seems to have become something of a favorite with Lord Melbourne, who a few months later in September is caught out in the luncheon room, feeding him bones.[20] Dickens, in *David Copperfield*, has Dora's little lapdog Jip enjoying not only his own *niche de chien* but a mutton chop every day at noon to gnaw within it; and one can imagine all too easily what Hanway or Varlo would have had to say to that.

And overindulgence brought the same results in the past as it does today. Obesity is not quite what George Bernard Shaw meant when he wrote that animals "bear more than their natural burden of human love," but it is certainly part of the picture.[21] Jane Carlyle's Nero was pronounced a victim of "high living" in August 1851 and is to be found taking the equivalent of the "water-cure," then being followed by Jane's husband, Thomas—Nero "is to be cured by boluses and reduced diet (say the Authorities)," Thomas writes to his mother.[22] Grace Greenwood, writing in 1853, faced a different moral dilemma—much like the vegetarian or vegan owner today, she was greatly troubled by her hawk Toby's determined hunting of mice and songbirds, so attempted to convert him to a non-meat diet. The attempt was not successful; she and Toby compromised on a diet, for him, of frogs.[23] On we go—turning a blind eye to their behavior, buying them possessions to chew their way through, toys to bat under the furniture, and gourmet food that they scuff over as if it were indeed fit only for the coal hole. And still, in the midst of all the sophisticated marketing of the pet care industry and the vast amounts of money it now involves, what we treasure most highly in our relationships with our animals are those same moments as in Jane Loudon's drawing room—an animal's involvement in our life, and the affectionate response to ours in theirs. "Keep Love Strong," as IAMS pet food cannily put it in their 2012 marketing campaign.

For every one of us, there is something our animal does that makes it special and precious and better, frankly, than any other animal in creation. For the owners of Pearl, another much-loved lapdog of the classical world, who was born in Gaul in the first or second century AD, it was her habit of quietly cuddling on their laps—

> *I used to lie on the soft lap of my master and mistress*
> *and knew to go to bed when tired on my spread mattress*
> *and I did not speak more than allowed as a dog, given a silent mouth.*
> *No-one was scared by my barking.*

as her epitaph, now preserved in the British Museum, describes her.[24] For Martial, praising Issa, the little white dog owned by Publius, governor of Malta in the first century AD, it was the fact that she asked when she wanted to go outside:

> *…with her sweet paw she nudges (you) and from the couch*
> *forewarns (you) that she needs to be put down and asks to be lifted*
> *up.*[25]

For Lady Wentworth, it was being groomed by Pug, as if she were her monkey's responsibility, rather than the other way around. There is a theory that the reason we so enjoy stroking animals is because it compensates for the grooming we no longer get to give our unfurred selves, but that doesn't stop them—here is Lady Wentworth, describing Pug's antics in 1710: "She has now got upon my shoulder, pulled off all my head clothes and [is] busy looking [at] my head."[26] For an elderly lady in 1710, that might have meant Pug removing artificial flowers, ribbons, combs, lace cap, and wig from her owner. Does the owner complain?

She does not: she sounds beguiled and delighted. For Jane Carlyle, immured in a difficult marriage and suffering from all the quotidian ailments such an unhappy situation could produce, it was the attention her dog, rather than her husband, bestowed on her: "Really Nero makes a capital little nurse!" she wrote to the latter in October 1851, after she had been felled by "a raging headache." Nero "never left me for an instant…he warmed my feet and my back by turns…"[27] For Mary Ansell, perhaps revealing rather more of her own needs than she may have realized, it was her dogs' absolute devotion to "me, me, me, me": "When the dogs loved me, they did it without forethought or after-thought, because they couldn't help it…they just loved me, me, me, me with passion and warmth, without thinking about it."[28] For Elizabeth von Arnim it was everything: when one of her dogs "is so obliging as to show its trust by snuggling," she writes, echoing Pearl's owners, two thousand years before; or it was the ecstatic canine greeting of her dachshund, Cordelia, coming up to her with "her whole body…one great wag of welcome."[29] Or it was the "protective paw" that Coco, her Saint Bernard, too big to get into her lap, always placed over her ankle. For me it is Daisy climbing up onto my shoulder to bomph my face, or Bird luring me up from my desk and into the hallway, to collapse beside the feather-on-a-stick that has mysteriously found its way onto the rug as well. It's all the little evidences of affection that make us feel they care for us and prize our company just as we care for them and prize theirs. Another ancient term for the way we relate to our animals was the Greek word "storge,"[30] meaning an instinctive affection, such as siblings feel, something equal on each side.

It must be said, cats do have an advantage here, because they have the purr. Dogs may wag their tails, show us their grin, turn turtle for a belly rub; the cockatoo bobs delightedly on its perch; the house rabbit comes lolloping up the hall to say hello; but cats have the purr. Thomas de Cantimpré, who with a little license you might describe as a thirteenth-century naturalist, calls it "their own form of singing"; while Edward Topsell, in 1658, came up with the term "whurleth."[31] We still don't quite know how cats purr (although they are not the only animal capable of it, by any means; guinea pigs and even gorillas produce a sound of contentment like a purr); nor do we quite know why—as a steady internal oscillation, it may promote healing or it may help prevent loss of bone density in an animal with all a cat's skills as Rip van Winkle, but it has entranced us from the first. Charles Baudelaire made his cat's purr a sort of higher form of communication:

It lulls to sleep the sharpest pains,
Contains all ecstasies;
To say the longest sentences,
It has no need of words[32]

Even Elizabeth von Arnim, who was very much more dog than cat, admitted that "purrs are enchanting. I used to long to have one myself." Purrs please us as much as they do, perhaps, because they are the sound of our care working. The *Corpus Iuris Hibernici* lists a cat as worth three cows if it could guard the barn and mill from mice and purr, and worth only one and a half cows if purring was its only skill, but even so—that's no mean worth, for a purr, and must be one of the very few times in Western history when a cat was assessed at a higher economic value than a cow. It does underline, however, how high that emotional worth can run, how much such evidence of reciprocal caring on the animal's part counts for with us.[33]

It takes us by surprise, how much we come to care ourselves. "I love him," Elizabeth Barrett would write of Flush, in 1842, "as far as dog love can go—& that is farther than I supposed possible before I had knowledge of him."[34] And it can change us, this bond with an animal. For the poet William Cowper, caring for his three pet hares made him virulently anti–blood sports. In *The Task*, his high-flown epic of 1785, he addresses one of his pet hares directly:

Yes—thou mayst eat thy bread, and lick the hand
That feeds thee; thou may'st frolic on the floor
At evening, and at night retire secure
To thy straw-couch, and slumber unalarm'd.
For I have gain'd thy confidence, have pledg'd
All that is human in me, to protect
Thine unsuspecting gratitude and love.[35]

Ignore the archaic poetical language; look instead at the emotion set down here and how it leaves no doubt but that the care in the relationship is seen as being on both sides. J. R. Ackerley would find himself reflecting how much his relationship with Queenie had changed him: having spent just about the whole of his life in search of the "ideal [human] friend," he came to realize that perhaps the ideal was Queenie herself, with her "constant, single-hearted incorruptible uncritical devotion which it is the nature of dogs to offer."[36] He was certainly far likelier to find that with a dog than with a member of his own species, you may think, with all our conflicted, unreliable passions. The revelation came to Ackerley when he and Queenie were walking in the country, Queenie sniffing out rabbits and Ackerley cursing the workmen whose noise was frightening the rabbits away. It suddenly occurred to him that at any previous point in his life, he would have been down on the road with the workmen, seeing if by any chance he could pick one of them up.[37] During Queenie's final illness, Ackerley too found he had become virulently anti-hunting.

It's the reliability in an animal's response that makes caring for them so different from caring for one of our own. Animals are such obsessive little sticklers for routine. The ball will always be chased, the stick brought back; the purr is always there in readiness, as is the gambol of delight when the leash comes off the coatrack. The lap will always be filled, the welcome will always be genuine. The relationship with an animal is "constant, rather than contingent," as Leslie Irvine describes it, and in that constancy and its effects, it differs from those you may form with any of your own species.[38] James Serpell, who was one of the first to study human-animal interactions on this level, counted this as one of the key qualities (for us) of a pet: "their special combination of human and unhuman traits—their uncritical friendliness and willingness to interact."[39] A relationship with an animal reaches a bandwidth, if you like, of mutual comprehension and appreciation, uncritical and unforced, and it stays there, reinforcing itself by the repetition of those little bits of business day by day by day, but basically stable and unchanging.

In the 1740s, the Reverend William Stukeley, who has been described as the father of English archeology, was living in Stamford in Lincolnshire, together with his second wife and his cat, whom William had rather endearingly named Tit. Maybe she was a chirruper, too. Every evening, after his none-too-onerous duties as a clergyman and his researches for the local antiquarian society were done, Stukeley would retire into the garden for a smoke. And every evening, Tit would accompany him. She was, said her owner, with all an owner's shameless bias, "a most uncommon creature and of all I ever knew, the most sensible, most loving... [she] had such inimitable ways of testifying her love to her master and mistress, that she was as a companion, especially so when to me according to my custom I smoak'd my contemplative pipe in the evening at 6 o'clock." Stukeley's house at 9 Barn Hill still survives in this most picturesque of English market towns (so picturesque that it has done service in films from *Pride and Prejudice* to *The Da Vinci Code*). The house gives the impression of hiding something far older behind its crisply cut, golden limestone façade, and you would not be surprised in its garden to catch a whiff of pipe smoke still, with Stukeley's affable shade contemplating the day and his cat beside him, purring; and both of them taking the same quiet pleasure in the presence of the other—an image of companionship that is both ideal and eternal.

They are our ears if we are deaf, our eyes if we are blind, our proxies for the testing of everything from vaccines for Ebola to bath salts. They saved our lives down coal mines. They kept wolves, literally, from the door. They plowed and manured our fields. Chief Seattle understated the case when he said that without them we would die of loneliness. Without them we would have been dead long before that. What do we do in return for all of this? We take them to the vet.

Until around 150 years ago, there was no such thing as a vet's bill for the owner of the domestic pet. There was no such thing as a vet. The veterinary surgeon was reserved for horses and cattle, for those animals Charles Varlo would have recognized as having visible, economic worth. The clue, again, is in the name—its root is in the Latin *veterinae*, or "working animals" (I always feel "worked" would be more accurate). For an ailing cat or dog or canary bird, their recovery would have been the charge of the woman in whose chamber or outhouse they found themselves. Nursing those of invisible, emotional worth was women's work. Thus Samuel Pepys, writing his diary entry for August 18, 1660: "leaving my wife to look after her little bitch, which was just now a-whelping, I to bed." The next day, the number of mouths in the Pepys household had increased by four. "The little puppies…" Pepys writes approvingly, "are very pretty ones."[40]

Medical care was as hit-and-miss for an animal as it was for our human ancestors, a mash-up of a more or less inaccurate understanding of physiology, a lot of superstition, and some folk medicine that with luck might do more good than harm. There is a bit of an irony here, in that for all those centuries when the status of the companion animal was supposedly so low compared to now, it was judged by the same laws, fed the same food, and physicked with exactly the same medicines we used for ourselves and assumed to suffer from the same maladies, too: Olina, for example, informs his readers that the goldfinch was prone to vertigo, epilepsy, consumption, and (hardly surprisingly, given that list) melancholy.[41]

Not until more than two centuries later does the professional "dog-doctor" make an appearance, so that Jane Loudon, writing in 1851, can even cite the advice of one of the first, William Youatt, by name. By 1868 Alexandre Dumas could place his Scotch pointer Pritchard in the care of a "veterinary" at Sainte-Germain for three weeks after he is shot by a fellow hunter, while Flora, his other favorite, is placed under the care of a veterinary surgeon at Sainte-Ouen after she is bitten by a viper. Mother Anthony's dog, under the table in her tavern, was remembered by Renoir as having at some point been fitted with a wooden leg.[42] But Dumas and dogs such as Mother Anthony's were the exception. For most owners and animals alike, veterinary knowledge was whatever you could come by, and nursing was still done at home.

The experience of a seriously sick or injured animal was as heartbreaking then as now. "At night was brought home our poor Fancy, which to my great grief continues lame still, so I wish she had not been brought home ever again, for it troubles me to see her," writes Pepys in August

1664, remorselessly honest as ever, although Fancy was to be part of the Pepys household for another four years. We know the emotional upset Tonton's mishap caused Walpole's maid; even more traumatic was Jane Carlyle's experience with Nero, who in October 1859 was flattened by a cart while out with her maid, Charlotte, and was brought home

all crumpled together like a crushed spider, and his poor little eyes protruding, and fixedly staring in his head!

Jane mastered her horror and did what she could:

I put him in a warm bath—and afterwards wrapt him warmly and laid him on a pillow—and left him; without much hope of finding him alive in the morning.

But Nero amazed them all by surviving the night, and then a second night, and then a third:

…in the morning he still breathed, tho' incapable of any movement: but he swallowed some warm milk that I put into his mouth—About midday I was saying aloud "poor dog—poor little Nero!," when I saw the bit tail trying to wag itself!—And after that, I had good hopes—In another day he could raise his head to lap the milk himself—And so by little and little, he recovered the use of himself—but it was ten days before he was able to raise *a bark*—his first attempt was like the *scream* of an infant![43]

In all this, and despite what would turn out to be the mortal nature of Nero's injuries, the nursing is no more than might have been offered to a sick child—wrap them up, put them to bed, offer the universal panacea of warm milk. The Carlyles were fairly well-to-do, and Nero was loved to a fault, but this basic nursing was Jane's only recourse. There was simply hope and prayer, and doing what one could—or taking the animal to a domestic Good Samaritan such as Mrs. Rosalia Goodman, who, according to *Frank Leslie's Illustrated Family Almanac* for 1876, ran a "private hospital" for cats in her three-story home at 170 Division Street, New York:

> Besides many pets, who for years have been kindly cared for, the family is constantly being increased by the addition of unfortunate tabbies whose wants are brought to the notice of the worthy woman. Lean and hungry cats…cats who bear the scars received by having bootjacks, crockery ware etc thrown at them…cats who come out with broken limbs and disordered fur from the ordeal of an interview with naughty little boys, and all cats hungry and in distress, when brought to this asylum receive the tenderest care.[44]

How very different this aspect of "caring" has become today.

The British broadcaster Evan Davis owns a whippet, Mr. Whippy, a charmingly mild-mannered-looking creature, as all whippets are, with that typical whippet expression of spinsterly anxiety and fur the soft shade between gray and fawn that used to be referred to as "Isabella." What brings Mr. Whippy into this book is the fact that at an early age, Mr. Whippy managed to break a leg, and Evan Davis, who broadcasts as a commentator on economics, went on the record with the amount it cost to have the leg mended—some £4,000.[45]

Mr. Whippy had insurance—private health care in the small-animal world. Miss Puss did not. Her eczema, and mine, were treated with steroids, which in her case had the eventual and most undesirable side effect of her developing diabetes, and as an even nastier pendant to that, ketoacidosis. A sudden scrabbling noise from the corner of the room, and there was my eccentric little cat, clearly with no idea of where she was or what was happening to her and possibly even struck suddenly blind, trying to dig her way through the wall with the awful persistence of a remote-controlled toy. The fact that she was purring frantically throughout the whole episode only made it more horrifically bizarre.

Of course this had to happen late on a Saturday night, when our usual vet had shut up shop for the day. Of course the emergency vet had to be a lengthy taxi ride away. We arrived in their reception area, Miss Puss by then leaking urine and as inert in my arms as if she were made of Jell-O, to be greeted by crisply uniformed nursing staff and a swath of silk tenting over the reception desk. If our usual vet, just up the road, was the ER on a Saturday night, this was the world of the private wing in the state-of-the-art hospital, and my first thought as I carried this limp, soggy little body into the examination room was

Jean-Jacques Bachelier, *A Dog of the Havana Breed*, 1768.

William Hogarth, *The Painter and His Pug*, 1745. Tate Gallery, London.

Jan van Eyck, *The Arnolfini Portrait*, 1434.

— Puisque maintenant il est de la famille,il faut aussi qu'il ait son portrait .

Daumier's cartoon: "Now he's one of the family, he needs his portrait too,"
which appeared in the illustrated magazine *Le Charivari* in January 1856.

Carl Kahler, *My Wife's Lovers*, 1891. Kate Birdsall Johnson, who commissioned the painting, reportedly owned 350 cats; just 42 are depicted here, including, in pride of place at the center of the composition, Sultan.

The Barrison Sisters in the 1890s and their most risqué number. They advertised themselves in the United States as "The Wickedest Girls in the World."

Auguste Renoir, *Madame Georges Charpentier and Her Children*, 1878.
Georgette-Berthe is seated on the family dog, her brother Paul-Émile-Charles
is seated next to their mother.

Johann de Critz, *Henry Wriothesley, 3rd Earl of Southampton,* 1603.

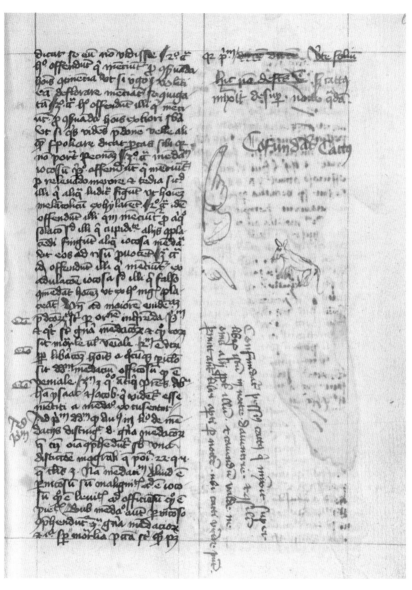

The perils of cats in the scriptorium—the 15th-century manuscript from Deventer bearing a monk's tale of woe.

Auguste Renoir, *Mother Antony's Tavern*, 1866.

Jacques Callot, *A Blind Man with a Dog*, 1622.

Mark Gertler, *Gilbert Cannan at His Mill*, 1916. Luath is on the right; Sammy on the left.

The grave of Fanny the dog in Sir John Soane's Museum, Lincoln's Inn Fields, London, *c*.1813. The inscription reads "Alas poor Fanny."

The funeral procession of King Edward VII in 1910. The unknown photographer captured both Caesar and the King's horse as mourners in the cortège.

The Basse-Yutz Flagons, 450–400 BC, detail of the lid.

Franz Marc, *The White Dog* (also known as *My Dog Before the World*), 1912.

that we could forget the new sofa we had been saving for—this was going to cost a fortune.

Evan Davis, interviewed by the BBC with Mr. Whippy on his lap, had drawn the analogy between a damaged pet and a broken watch: if the repair would cost more than the watch was worth, said he, wearing his economist's hat, you threw it away and bought a new one—"Only once you've got the dog, you don't think like that." Of course you don't. As a pet owner, you deal in worth that is completely irreducible to bare economics. In her "biography" of Elizabeth Barrett Browning's spaniel, Flush, Virginia Woolf, also a dog owner, describes him as being to his mistress "of that rare order of objects that cannot be associated with money." Exactly. When the dog tax was first introduced in Paris, you can't help suspect that for many bourgeois households, it was a tax on worth that was incalculable—which is no doubt exactly why it would be paid.

The cost, in the end, to bring Miss Puss through, was £3,000. If you had asked me before, I would have said that was more money than we had in the world. At one point, a day or so into her treatment, with my cat still hanging on in there but no more than that, the vet rang to ask if I wanted them to open another £600 vial of drugs to continue flushing the excess glucose out of her system. It was a rational question from a conscientious professional, but there was no logic or rationality in my response at all; my answer came straight from the gut: obviously I wanted them to open that new vial. If my cat was hanging on, I wasn't going to take the chance of recovery away from her. Miss Puss's economic worth was so small as to be barely calculable—as a kitten, her food bowl had cost more than she did—but her emotional value to me was far beyond any vet's bill. So you could say that I was spending that money on me; but so was the value, I imagine, to her, of seven more summers, which was what we had her for, rolling around in the sun in the garden, or her nightly creeping into bed with me, or her daily party piece of winding her way up through the rails of the towel rack in the bathroom like Nadia Comaneci on the parallel bars. In effect, the vet was asking me to come up with a figure for something whose ticket price was tiny but whose emotional, sentimental value immense. In either case, she was most definitely worth more to me than a new piece of furniture.

Sentiment, like anthropomorphism, is one of those words that used to be said out the corner of the mouth. John Hogg, who created the five hundred–odd page *Parlour Menagerie* in 1878, would write of giving his pet nightingale a kiss and feel he had to add afterward, "I am not ashamed to say so." This aspect of our dealings with our companion animals has changed completely. Where there was Hogg's self-conscious justification, now there is Carolee Schneemann's "Infinity Kisses," a nine-minute video from 2008 of her and her cat, Vesper, kissing (and in bed). The soundtrack to this is a sonorous cello and Vesper's own deep and happy purr. What changed here? How did the once-invisible emotional worth of our companion animals become not simply visible but paramount?

First of all, the animals themselves changed. The number of sheep, pigs, cattle, and horses for the veterinary surgeon to attend became fewer and fewer; the number of cats and dogs, rabbits and guinea pigs, ferrets and hamsters, snakes and lizards, more and more. But it wasn't simply the patients who changed; the vets did, too. "If pets become patients," wailed an editorial of 1915, "we may soon expect to see advertisements of our veterinary colleges in the ladies magazines," thus aligning the second of these developments together with the first with an accuracy and prescience that would no doubt have appalled the writer.[46] When women entered the medical profession, they had done so by tending to other women and their children. When they entered the veterinary profession (and the animal welfare and the anti-vivisection movements), it was as the granddaughters of those who had had the invisible animals, those domestic pets of purely emotional worth, under their care for generations, and the attitude that these animals mattered *too* was imported into the veterinary profession with them. The small dog nuzzled in your lap, which once might have been justified simply as a convenient means of getting rid of your own human vermin ("small ladyes poppes that bere awaye the flees," as the *Boke of St. Albans* of 1486 describes them), or as a living hot water bottle and "comforter," as John Caius dismisses them in the case of menstrual cramps, could now sit there for no better reason (and what better reason can there be?) than that it was loved, and because it loved back, in turn, and the entire veterinary industry was transformed as a result. Which in the United Kingdom, as of November 2017, was into something worth £3 billion. There is, it turns out, a price to be put on caring, and you can pretty much name it yourself. And Mrs. Rosalia Goodman is the ancestor of the four-figure vet bill—astounded as I am sure she would have been to discover it.

There is a final aspect of caring to be considered, and that is the animal's role in caring for us, as our eyes, our ears, and our lifesavers. It's a long, long history. Those Neolithic hunting dogs tracking across the snowfields of the Ardèche with us were assistance animals, let's not forget, as were the mousers padding around the barns and mills of ancient Babylon. According to the earliest ABCs, before A was an apple and B was a ball, "A was an archer and shot at a frog," while "B was a blind man, led by a dog"—another reminder of quite how much we are in the dog's debt. Even the lapdog had responsibilities—the Irish law books detail its role as a watcher by the pillow of women in labor, to keep the little people away, lest they try to harm mother or child. And should some mishap befall the animal before its duties were completed, the law books go on to say, in a wonderfully Irish blend of pragmatism and mysticism, whoever was responsible for the loss of said lapdog would not only have to pay a fine, but as a makeshift must provide a priest as a fairy-watching lapdog substitute.[47]

There's the eye of newt and toe of frog aspect of animals in human medicine (and yes, we may laugh, but are those repulsive-sounding potions really any more primitive or ridiculous than testing lipstick on a rabbit?), but much more significantly, there has been their role in benefiting human mental health, in indeed chasing away our melancholic thoughts. The Quaker philanthropist William Tuke created his revolutionary York Retreat in the 1790s, for those who were suffering mental affliction of all types, and as Tuke's grandson Samuel explained in his

Description of the Retreat, his grandfather believed that the retreat could "awaken the social and benevolent feelings...by attachment to some of the inferior animals."[48] You can now add to animals' care for us their presence in nursing homes, retirement homes, long-stay geriatric wards, and high-security prisons. Louis Wain, writing as president of the National Cat Club in 1898, was another early believer in the value of animals as human therapy, writing that "all people who keep cats...do not suffer from those petty ailments which all flesh is heir to...All lovers of 'pussy,'" he declared, "are of the sweetest temperament."[49] So now we know.

Today, where the miners of the Harz Mountains had their sentinel canaries, we have assistance animals that warn of impending diabetic collapse or epileptic fits; we have the much-abused, in fact at times downright exploited "emotional support animal," we have the OncoMouse, and because we have been living with them for so long and share so many pathogens with them, scientific research suggests that dogs might hold the key to finding cures for illnesses from diabetes to hemophilia.[50]

I have skin in this game, quite literally. Every year in the United Kingdom, some ten thousand women under fifty are diagnosed with breast cancer, and in 2011 one of them was me. In the mind-mangling way that cancer specializes in, what could have killed me might help save another woman, so little bits of me are now in research labs up and down the country—together, of course, with the animals on whom some of the drugs used to treat me will have been tested. The spiraling ethical complexities of this bring sweat to one's brow. For example: I have never had a rat as a pet, but my friend Jane has three. She takes treats back home for them in her napkin when we dine out together. So what is a test specimen for the researchers creating the next generation of Tamoxifen and (before I was put in the situation of having to think about it) some nebulous animal resource for me, for her are companions treasured just as much as I treasure Bird and Daisy. My permission was requested for the use of my tissues; that of the rats and dogs and other creatures involved in past and future medical research was not and will not be. I don't want any animal to suffer for my health, any more than I want them to suffer for the cause of longer-lasting bloody lipstick, but I would also far sooner not be dead.

But if there is no absolute solution to this dilemma, perhaps there is a reachable point of balance, achievable if the process of scientific investigation can place the inevitable suffering involved on those who will also benefit from the results—human and animal alike.[51] Because Olina was right, in a way. Animals suffer for us, but they also suffer like us. They too are scarred by stress and trauma, sink under diseases such as diabetes and cancer, develop dodgy hearts, lose sight and hearing. If you have deep pockets or good insurance (another unwelcome parallel with human health care), some of the same treatments for you as owner are already available for your pet. But we're deep in the ethical forest, even so. The animal still can't give permission—not to receive the donor kidney (certainly not to agree to donate it), not to have the operation, take the drugs, acquiesce to cloning. It has almost no agency in the treatments we may decide on for it, and the danger here is that the more we love them, the more we care, the more weight is placed on an animal's emotional importance to us and the more we want for them the same care options available to us—the more we want to treat them as human, in other words—the more invisible as animals they once again become. One of the biggest issues in our care for them today is where to draw the line, and one of the biggest challenges we ever have to face as owners is the granting of death to something we love.

The artist Dante Gabriel Rossetti lamenting the death of his wombat, 1869.

CHAPTER EIGHT

LOSING

Where there is grief, there was love.

—Barbara J. King, *How Animals Grieve*, 2014

I f by some chance you should ever find yourself driving near the village of Loxhill in the southeast of England, you may well start to suspect that you are traveling through the landscape version of a detective story. Here, for instance, is a stretch of boundary wall, just visible from the leafy road—well built, still solid with self-importance; there a run of railings, so old it has rusted a purplish dark. Now you pass what was clearly once an entrance of some importance, complete with gatehouse; and behind it trees dotted across the landscape that show the unmistakable signs of having had livestock browsing beneath them since they were planted maybe two centuries ago, and which now all branch at the same level, just a little higher than sheep or cow can comfortably reach. But where's the mansion that would make sense of all of this, looking down on the road from one of those tree-crowned hills—and why, in that field beside the road, with nothing around it but trees and rough grass, should there be, rather creepily, a tombstone?

Toward the end of her biography-by-dog, Elizabeth von Arnim writes, "This story, like life, as it goes on, is becoming dotted with graves," and I am afraid this chapter is going to be the same.[1] If you have an animal in your life, you can't get away from the fact that in almost every case, you will outlive them. It's as true for the tiniest as it is for the biggest and most brave—even the Earl, whose grave here in this Surrey field is now all that remains of Park Hatch and of those who lived there, who very likely had no more serious notion of their own passing from this landscape than did the Earl himself. "HERE LIES 'THE EARL,'" the stone declares:

HE WAS CHARGER TO R.T.GODMAN IN THE 5TH DRA-GOON GUARDS FOR 19 YEARS SERVED THROUGH THE RUSSIAN WAR IN TURKEY AND CRIMEA 1854–6

And here is how he met his end:

SHOT IN CONSEQUENCE OF AN ACCIDENT ON 26TH DEC. 1868 WHEN STILL IN FULL VIGOUR

There's some comfort in that. No slow descent into decrepitude, just a tragic mishap on what sounds to have been a Boxing Day hunt, and a bullet, presumably where he lay (and where he lies still), but even so. The Earl was not simply a companion animal. Like soldiers and their service dogs in Iraq and Afghanistan, Godman and his horse were brothers-in-arms. They had passed together through experiences that set their relationship apart. You can imagine how much Godman must have grieved.

It is quite stunning, as an owner, how much it can hurt to lose a pet. When Sir Walter Scott's favorite, a bull terrier named Camp, died in 1809, Scott's only comfort was that the loss was not more painful: "If we suffer so in losing a dog after an acquaintance of ten or twelve years, what would it be if they were to live double that time?"[2] According to Scott's daughter, Sophie, at Camp's burial the whole family stood around the grave in tears, while Scott himself smoothed the turf where Camp lay as if it were a substitute for and as close as he could now come to stroking the dog itself.[3] It sounds like a Victorian version of the final scene in the movie *Marley and Me*, which in itself is saying something about the universality of the experience and how desolating it can be. The death of a pet can be agonizing to a degree where even as bereaved owner you're asking yourself how it is possible for it to hurt quite so much. Joachim du Bellay was asking himself this very thing circa 1558, three days after the death of his cat:

> *I cannot speak, or write*
> *Or even think of what*
> *Belaud, my small grey cat,*
> *Meant to me, tiny creature…*

How indeed, we quiz ourselves, can the loss of something so small create a pain so immense? "Incomprehensible" was how Jane Carlyle described her sorrow, after Nero finally succumbed to his injuries in February 1860, and at once set about memorializing him in mourning jewelry, much as another woman of her age and class might have commissioned the same for a lost spouse—or child. Indeed, Jane drew the parallel herself: "My little dog is buried at the top of the garden," she wrote to Mary Russell in February 1860, "and I grieve for him as if he had been my human child."4 She was also as vicious as a woman of her age and class might ever have felt herself free to be with those who failed to comprehend the depth of her grief—which, true enough, can be as baffling to the outsider as it is to the owner. "All my other visitors," she wrote to Lady Ashburton, "have spoken odiously on what they call my 'little bereavement.'"

> They don't conceive what pain they give me. Three several men, the only men I am intimate with here, offered one after another to "give me *another little dog*." And two women, of the sort called "full of sensibility," inquired if I had "had him *stuffed*?" "I wonder you didn't" said one of them plaintively, "he would have looked *so* pretty in a glass case in your room, and still been quite a companion to you." Merciful Heavens! If one lived in what Mr. Carlyle calls "a sincere age of the world," wouldn't one take such a Comforter as *that* by the neck and pitch her out the window?5

Nothing "little" about such bereavement at all. When Linky, Edith Wharton's final Pekingese, had to be put to sleep in April 1937, her death had so great an effect upon the seventy-five-year-old writer that it seems to have played a part in severing Wharton's own last ties with the world as well. In her diary Wharton writes of Linky's ghost standing at the front of all those others she had lost, human as well as canine. After that, the flow of words in the diary she had kept for decades stutters to a halt. Four months later, Wharton herself was dead.

The taxidermy that her visitor was rash enough to suggest to Jane Carlyle—to keep her companion with her in some way, as well as, you could argue, the cloning of pets today—is a measure of how extreme the reaction can be to their loss and how much we dread it. There is a particularly nasty (and, thankfully, rare) syndrome, an acute response to grief, known medically as takotsubo cardiomyopathy—a bulging outward of one chamber of the heart, in response to intense stress, so that the whole heart takes on the shape of a Japanese *tako tsubo*, or octopus pot.[6] It causes the sensation that the heart is indeed about to burst, or break, and physical pain extreme and similar enough to an actual heart attack to send one to the emergency room. A recent case involved a sixty-two-year-old woman in Texas. There were other stresses in her life, but it was the death of her dog that finally precipitated the physical crisis. Why is the loss of a non-human animal felt so cruelly? What is it that makes the death of such a companion being an experience this profound?

You have to begin with the living relationship to answer that question, and sometimes it is only the end of it, the severing of the bond, that reveals how exceptional it had become. It was the death of Alex, her Avian Learning Experiment, that showed Irene Pepperberg how much more he had become to her than that. She describes how "his passing taught me the true depth of our shared connection," and most tellingly, she uses the language of human bereavement ("passing") to do so.[7] When Scott spoke of Camp's death, it was as that of a "dear old friend."[8] Even Pepys, for all he might protest in his relationship with Fancy, was not immune. When in September 1668 he learned of her death "big with puppies" in a letter from his father in the country, to whom the pregnant Fancy had presumably been sent for her confinement (another parallel with the human world), he describes her in his diary as "one of my oldest acquaintances and servants"—not as a dog but as a human equal. Or possibly as even more than that. Sociological studies aplenty support the idea that in our family groups we see the animal members as being more reliable allies and steadier friends than the human ones. Never mind if they truly are or not—the baroque inner wiring of our emotions places such value on this perception that these companion animals end up being literally invaluable to us.[9] Sigmund Freud, whose consulting room in the 1930s smelled at least as strongly of Chow, those "stodgy teddy bears," as it did of Freud's own cigars, believed this was because animals offered, in his famous phrase, "affection without ambivalence... an intimate affinity...an undisputed solidarity." So in contrast to the much more challenging and changeable (and more compromised) relationships we have with the other humans around us, there is this steady, reliable, unchanging alliance—and then with the animal's death, all that emotional stability and security is suddenly removed as well. Even being reminded of the loss can be painful beyond bearing. "Dyed our favourite Cat, Tit," William Stukeley writes sorrowfully in his memoirs for August 31, 1720, and then adds, revealingly, "my gardner buryd her in Rosamunds bower the pleasantest part of my garden, wh. gave me great distaste to it."[10] The very language of death where a pet is concerned is all about physical sundering—we pick them up and carry them about in life, but in their death, we "put them down." Of course our mourning is going to be unambivalent and unalloyed.

But are we allowed to make it public? Perhaps this is another reason why pet death hurts so much and so disproportionately—the fact that unlike other bereavements there's societal pressure to keep it low-key. Isabella d'Este, on the death of Aura in 1511, might make no secret among her circle of the fact that she expected fully worked-up poetic elegies for her favorite dog, and receive them, including three from the scholar Carlo Agnelli alone, but this was Isabella d'Este.[11] For the garden-variety owner, much as they might howl in anguish in private, descriptions of their grief nearly always have an apologetic coloring. Two hundred years after Isabella, Lady Wentworth felt she must beg God's forgiveness for being "more than I ought concerned" about her dog Fub's death, although the grieving was heartfelt and still took place. When (an even greater blow) Pug, her monkey, died in 1712, again she wrote, "God forgive me, there is some that bears the name of Christian, that I could have rather had died." When her son offers her a replacement, she declines on the grounds that she herself is "so great a fool" ("fool" being the term she also uses for her animals) and so "foolishly fond" that such relationships are simply too much for her in her old age.

She also speaks of how she forced herself to go about in society, even as she grieved, for appearance's sake.[12] Walpole nursed Rosette, Tonton's predecessor, for many weeks in 1773 and divided his friends into those with "Dogmanity," who would understand and empathize with his distress, and those who would not. When Rosette died, he wrote his own elegy for her ("Sweetest rose of the year") and sent it to one of the former, disclaiming any literary merit for it but saying that "it came from the heart…therefore your Dogmanity will not dislike it."[13] Move on by another hundred years, and Grace Greenwood, who had a small necropolis coming into being in a quiet corner of her family garden, records how she had to add to it the pitiful corpse of Jack the drake, who in the course of a singularly accident-prone life had been trapped in a cistern, run into the fire, sustained a broken leg in a rattrap, and who ultimately drowned in a millrace. Grace writes shamefacedly, "It may seem very odd and ridiculous but I really grieved for my dead pet."[14] What's foolish or ridiculous about it? We love, we lose, we mourn. It shouldn't take us by surprise; it certainly shouldn't be something we feel the need to apologize for.

There is evidence of a change in the general attitude toward pet death, which seems to back up the emergent status of pets being publicly accepted as overt members of the family, as opposed to their being so for their owners alone. In 2016, a number of newspaper reports appeared, listing those companies that elected to give employees time off to mourn an animal's death.[15] Many owners still feel diffident about asking for such leave, which is understandable—this has been a private grief for centuries—but the fact that now it needn't be so reflects an increased general acceptance of what for the owner, I believe, has always been the case: losing an animal hurts, and the way you deal with that hurt, as with any other loss, is to grieve and to have that grief recognized. This change in attitude might also be an inevitable result of the increased numbers of pets we are supposed, now, to have living with us. If indeed many more of us encounter this situation, many more of us will know how excruciating it can be.

And just to make the death of a pet even more agonizing, it is so often we who have to be responsible for it. That's bad enough now, but consider how much more difficult and horrible it would have been to euthanize a pet before the lethal injection from the vet was available. As if Jack the drake's loss had not been enough, Grace also records how she lost her cat, Kitty, who had her back broken in a bit of roughhousing by Grace's beloved older brother, and for whom there was no other means to hand to put her out of her agony than beheading by the straw-cutter in the barn. Kitty's owner hides in her closet and stops her ears (that vivid little detail) "until it is all over."

Far better, if you had to, if you could, to find a coup de grâce for a pet via a local farmer with a shotgun. This was the fate of Luath, "not ill, only grown old and worn out," as Mary Ansell offhandedly describes him. Mary had by this time left J. M. Barrie and was living with the poet Gilbert Cannan in a converted mill, where Cannan and their two dogs were painted by Mark Gertler. Luath is on the right; the other dog is Sammy, who according to Mary sat every day on Luath's grave until he too died, thus displaying, you may well think, rather more distress than Mary herself. And a bullet was all very well if the person holding the gun knew what they were doing, but many did not—thus the American Humane Education Association's edition of *Black Beauty* of 1904, which, with the sort of horrid benumbed pragmatism that has to characterize this area of our dealings with our animals, included instructions for shooting both horses and dogs.[16]

Otherwise the only quick, sure death was by poison. Louis Wain's Peter encounters a neighbor who has nine cats, plus the tombstones of five more in his garden, all of them finished off with prussic acid, which would be cyanide to you and me. Nero's death, in her maid Charlotte's arms (Jane could not stand to witness it, any more than Ackerley could with Queenie), came about in this way, thanks to the intervention of Jane's own doctor. Prussic acid or chloroform remained the agents of choice until the 1880s, when a lethal gas chamber using carbonic acid was created at Battersea by Sir Benjamin Ward Richardson (1828–96). Richardson did much to advance human anesthesiology, too, which does at least suggest his heart was in the right place when it came to sparing living creatures pain. Luath's predecessor, Porthos, was sent to Battersea Dogs Home once "it became impossible to have him any longer about the house," as Mary euphemistically puts it, "and in that lethal chamber he was peacefully put to sleep," or at least so one hopes, but as Mary could hardly have entered the chamber with the poor dog, you have to ask, how would she know? It took just twenty years before the suggestion was made that the same means might remove "defectives" from among the human population. It's as heartening as it is heartbreaking, after all that, to read Jessica Pierce's 2012 account in *The Last Walk* of her struggles with her aging dog, Ody, to find him "a good end"; to put herself, with him, through all the indignities and infirmities of old age for as long as he has enough quality of life left for there to be good moments among the bad—and then when she senses that this balance has been lost, to acknowledge that the good end has been reached, that to extend Ody's life would not be good any longer, not at all, and to act, at once.

Of course what that "good end" might be, our animals cannot articulate for us—but then many of us will be unable to do so, either, when the time comes. The questions of human and animal death brush up against each other, with the death of a pet animal being both a rehearsal for and a lesson in our own. My father, at ninety, and increasingly incapacitated by a series of microstrokes, could not have said what he wanted his death to be, either, but our inability to describe what our own "good end" might be doesn't mean we won't know it when we reach it. The difference is that with an animal, the decision so often must be ours, not theirs. And that's a terrible place for an owner to be. As Ackerley put it, writing of Queenie's final trip to the vet, "She knew nothing that happened to her; it is I who knows too much."[17]

There is an emotional equivalent, I think, to *takotsubo*, in making the decision to end a pet's life: the same sense of bulging agony, only mental this time. The psychiatric term for this is "cognitive dissonance," when we are placed in a situation where the only thing we can do is so counter to what we want to do that the mind feels ready to explode; yet the thing cannot be escaped, and must still be done. As a historian, Thomas

Carlyle appealed to Jane's sense of "Roman Virtue" to end Nero's suffering, but to no avail—it was only when her doctor convinced her that all the dog's pain would only end in death in any case that she could be brought to the decision. It's still the worst dilemma for any owner, and not only of domestic animals—in his studies of farmers on the island of Zakynthos, the anthropologist Dimitrios Theodossopoulos found that even they had to come up with rationales to make the act of killing acceptable. In the farmers' case, they saw the animals' rendering up of their meat as payment for the care the farmer had taken of them during life.[18] For the animal's companion, a merciful death at our behest can be seen as payment for the love the animal has shown us during its life, and our grief at losing them is the price we have to pay for having loved them in turn.

But it is still such a terrible decision to have to make—all the more so because you can't consult with the creature you are making the decision for. John Archer describes it as demanding "the ultimate in unconditional love" but points out also the guilt involved and the way in which all the circumstances in which we're acting remind us of our own impotence and mortality; and there is very little the human spirit finds harder to think its way through than that. Even now, years after all the drama, it's not the scars that set us survivors of cancer apart; it's the fact that death is no longer something that happens to other people, it's something we know now—we *know*—will happen to us; that one day the world will be carrying on, and we won't be a part of it anymore. It's the most extraordinary knowledge to carry within you, and it changes everything.

It's also one of the very good reasons why life is lived best and most easily oblivious to its ending—and again why losing a pet is so difficult, because the death of a beloved animal is our own, writ small. When her cat Vesper was run over, Carolee Schneemann wrote how her helplessness at this event encompassed "not only the constant terrible spacelessness, loss of my own past as we carry it between us, but my present which shatters constantly into glittering splinters covering, cutting, this moment into those past."[19] Louis Wain, cat man extraordinaire, having traced Peter's adventures from kittenhood, couldn't bear to end the story with Peter's death, even though when his "tale" was published, Peter would have been coming up on twelve years old—a splendid age for a Victorian cat. So Wain ends the story with Peter in philosophical old age, "heavy for mouse-hunting...and more critical in the quality of his dinner than he was in days gone by." A pet animal has so little agency in our world that its death (sometimes even a fictional death) must always have some taint of betrayal to it, even when we know it is the right and only thing to do. Even if the death, as with Vesper, is none of our doing, it still leaves a painfully deep scar. In her memoirs, the pioneering woman scientist Mary Somerville was still bitterly angry at the recollection of her pet goldfinch's death at the hands of her family's servants, who casually let the bird starve while she was on holiday, even though this had happened in 1797, and her memoirs were published in 1873. We care for and protect them in every other way, but in this extremity, when they need us most, we cannot but fail. It's maybe not that we have to usurp the role of God at the end;

it's that in every way up to that point, we have been God to them—yet saving them is as far beyond us as it is to save ourselves.

We lost Millie as I was working on this chapter. Her kidneys were failing, there was some kind of mass in her stomach, her leaking thyroid had left her almost weightless—quills for bones and thistledown for fur, a delicate fetish where there had been a cat. For months she had been losing substance, then within a week everything accelerated; and within a further day and a half the vet was updating us hourly. With perfect timing, she turned her back on the world just ahead of the needle. Miss Puss was the same. That first hospitalization she had hobbled on three legs up to the front of her cage (the fourth was encased in a sort of paw-shaped boxing glove, through which that £600-a-vial drug was being dribbled into her bloodstream), yowling with delight at seeing me. The last, years later, infinitely slowly and unmistakably in pain, she got herself to the front of the cage again, close enough to sniff my fingers, then even more slowly turned herself about and lay down with her back to me. My suspicion is that vets get better training for these end-of-life scenarios than do human doctors, where the death of a patient is still seen as a failure, even if an unavoidable one; and I think Miss Puss's vet had anticipated a far harder task in convincing me to let my cat go, but as soon as I saw her turn her back, I knew: this was the end of the thread. I held her as the vet gave her the injection; I felt her go; and then we brought her body home; my ex made a last sketch of her, curled up with her blanket in a cardboard box; we put her favorite toys into the box with her; and then we buried her in the garden, under a catnip plant and in her favorite spot for rolling about in the sun.

These are the non-human members of our family, and just to prove it, we create around them new versions of human rites and rituals (burning incense, for example, as well as the burial with grave goods), memorializing them as we would each other and burying them close by because we want to keep them near us even in death—and because again, we only have our human way and our human models to guide us.[20] No matter how self-conscious the Roman pet owner may have felt about doing so ("Do not laugh, I beg you, you passing by, because it is a mere dog's grave," reads the inscription on one), they created graves for their pets just as we do.[21] Pearl had one, so did Helena, as we have seen; there were animal burials within Roman houses, in the marketplace, by the roadside, and in human graves, such as the elderly dog buried near Carthage.[22]

And we have gone on burying them close by ever since—what else would we do? Lady Wentworth buried Pug in her garden, just as Jane Carlyle did Nero (and I Miss Puss), and had two portraits painted of Pug, one in miniature, exactly as did Jane Carlyle and presumably like Jane, to wear as personal jewelry—to keep close, even in death.[23] Flush too was buried at home, "in the vaults of Casa Guidi," where he had no doubt hunted many a rat in life and where presumably his bones lie still, while those of Elizabeth Barrett and of Robert Browning are separated, lying in the English Cemetery in Florence and in Westminster Abbey, respectively—which as the end to such a famous love match seems completely wrong, but must be one of infinite examples, like the Earl, where the remains of a pet lie within the footprint of a house or its lands, while the family that laid them there are long, long gone from the place. (And since Flush was not castrated, his genes might run about the piazzas of Florence still.) Even Tom-Cat, after all his adventures, is "decently interred in the garden," as is Peter's grandfather Lear, strongly suggesting that indeed for most pet owners, this was simply what you did, without thinking about it at all.

And you memorialize them. Sir John Soane (1753–1837), architect of the Bank of England, raised a memorial to his wife's dog Fanny in the "Monk's Yard" (so-called) of his extraordinary maze of a house in Lincoln's Inn Fields, London, which is so somber, so imposing, that visitors are sometimes heard pointing it out to one another as the grave of Mrs. Soane herself. Tonton also has a statue, at Strawberry Hill, Walpole's house in West London, where he is shown clutching his owner's escutcheon as if declaring his right to membership of the family. Byron raised a tomb to Boatswain in the gardens of Newstead Abbey in 1808, complete with epitaph that would have satisfied even Isabella d'Este: "Near this Spot," it begins, in a preamble supplied by his friend John Hobhouse, "are deposited the Remains of one/ who possessed Beauty without Vanity,/Strength without Insolence,/Courage without Ferocity,/and all the virtues of Man without his Vices," and goes on to fulminate against the injustice of how "The poor Dog, in life the firmest friend," might be "Denied in heaven the Soul he held on earth."

But what if you lived in one of those apartments in the air, with no access to a garden of your own? It was more than a little shocking to learn, as what were clearly the last few months of Millie's life approached, that the official guidelines for disposing of her body, if she died at home, included simply wrapping it up and putting it in the trash: "The remains must be placed in a heavy-duty black plastic bag or double plastic bag and a note should be taped to the bag stating its contents ('dead dog' or 'dead cat,' the instructions state bluntly)."[24] In the event, it was her ashes that came back to us, complete with small clay paw print. Neither of us was particularly comforted by the idea of Millie's little dead paw being pressed into cold, wet clay by a stranger, nor were we consoled by the card in which we could insert her photograph; nor did we like the idea of depositing her in the pet cemetery sixty miles away, let alone in the section referred to as "Kitty Korner." Millie had attacked every other cat she'd ever met. What helped was swapping our stories of Millie, our cat, whose presence-in-absence along the top of the sofa is now as much a thing in the apartment as the box of her ashes on the mantelpiece to which in life she constantly aspired to climb.

Millie was my first black cat; Bird is only my second. We owners of black cats, so I discovered, gang together, many of us via social media within such groups as the Black Cat Appreciation Society (because, as we all know, black cats are different). It has been a revelation, given what social media usually seems to bring out in people unconnected and unaccountable geographically, how kind these many strangers are to each other, when one of our number loses a pet—the sympathy, the shared tales of loss, the urging that the heartache will fade—the very conversations my partner and I were having. One post from a bereaved owner included a photograph of the cat itself, wrapped in a blanket, but limp and eyes closed and obviously after that final visit to the vet, and for a moment I was shocked. But is this so very different from Lady

Wentworth and Jane Carlyle, with their portraits of their pets in miniature, small enough to wear pinned at the throat or over the heart?
This—recorded and treasured within the core of our lives and families—
is where our animals belong and where we remember them.

And when we bury them, if it can't be close by in our gardens, and if
we don't have gardens, it most certainly is not going to be in the trash.
Hence the urban pet cemetery.

One of the first, if not the first, in Britain, was set up informally in
1881 behind Hyde Park by the parkkeeper. In the United States the first
was Hartsdale, in Westchester County, New York, again set up informally, this time in an apple orchard owned by a local vet. Owners can
have their ashes buried here as well (and as of 2016, in New York State
at least, your pet's ashes can also now be interred with you in a human
cemetery). The Cimetière des Chiens et Autres Animaux Domestiques
was founded in northwest Paris in 1899 precisely to stop owners depositing dead bodies in the trash or, worse, in the Seine. Londoners, according to John Stow's *Survay* of 1603, had been doing the same thing in the
Thames tributary of Hounds Ditch for centuries, thus giving what is
now a street its name, but you do wonder—casting bodies into water, to
travel to the next world, has been a feature of religion in the British Isles
and beyond since the Celts. Is there a trace of ceremony, even here?

And we don't simply bury them, when we do. We bury them with
grave goods. A dog in fourth century BC Athens, presumably one rather
less courageous than Fergus when it came to padding through the dark,
was buried with a beef bone and a miniature lamp.[25] Early and pre-
medieval burials in Scandinavia and Germany have horses and dogs

buried as grave goods themselves, with the human deceased, but while this certainly witnesses the animal's importance in the next world, it can't tell us much about the affection in which they may have been held in this. In Peru, however, in its southern Ilo valley, between the tenth and fourteenth centuries, the Chiribaya people were burying their dogs with food and blankets to keep them warm and fed until (presumably) their owners could join them, because what burying an animal with grave goods says is that we believe they have an afterlife, just as we may believe this for ourselves—and what's more, we intend meeting up with them in it.

Sometime in October 2009, two churches in Beulah, Kentucky, got into what the *Independent Catholic News* referred to as a "barking match." The churches and their reader boards were positioned (or so one imagined) within sight of each other, catty-corner in this small Southern town. One is Cumberland Presbyterian, and the other, Our Lady of Martyrs, is Catholic. Our Lady of Martyrs had supposedly announced on its reader board:

ALL DOGS GO TO HEAVEN

to which the Presbyterian Beulahians had apparently responded, on theirs:

ONLY HUMANS GO TO HEAVEN / READ THE BIBLE

The exchange continued:

> Our Lady of Martyrs: GOD LOVES ALL HIS CREATIONS/ DOGS INCLUDED
>
> Cumberland Presbyterian: DOGS DON'T HAVE SOULS/ THIS IS NOT OPEN FOR DEBATE
>
> Our Lady of Martyrs: CATHOLIC DOGS GO TO HEAVEN / PRESBYTERIAN DOGS CAN TALK TO THEIR PASTOR
>
> Cumberland Presbyterian: CONVERTING TO CATHOL- ICISM DOES NOT MAGICALLY GRANT YOUR DOG A SOUL
>
> Our Lady of Martyrs: FREE DOG SOULS WITH CON- VERSION
>
> Cumberland Presbyterian: DOGS ARE ANIMALS/ THERE AREN'T ANY ROCKS IN HEAVEN EITHER
>
> Our Lady of Martyrs: ALL ROCKS GO TO HEAVEN

Game, set, and match, one might conclude.

As we all know, the only true guarantee of immortality is to be given an existence somewhere on the Internet, and sure enough, in 2013, the exchange appeared in the feed on my Facebook page.

What made the Beulah churches' spat stand out for me was that it was such a recent and public chapter in a debate that has been going on for centuries. What made it even more notable is the fact that it was fake, from beginning to end.[26] There are no two such churches in Beulah, Kentucky; they had no such reader board face-off. All that human ingenuity, and the website wizardry that brought it into being, not to mention the pantheistic theological leap by its (presumably) Catholic author, and where are we on the question of animal souls and an animal afterlife? Just about exactly where we have always been—only, possibly, even more confused.

If we are to believe the written evidence (*if*), all our ancestors confidently believed in God, or in a God, of some similar appearance and character to their own, but on this matter of an animal afterlife, some very human doubts appear. Mrs. Thrale, musing over her copy of Isaac Watts's *Philosophical Essays*, annotated it with the reflection that "their souls are of an inferior order, but souls they are…it is with the greatest difficulty I can persuade myself that my dear favourite dog or horse is wholly dead and dead for ever." Jane Carlyle went still further, asking herself on Nero's death

what *is* become of that beautiful, engaging little *life*, with its *"manifold undeniable virtues"* (as Mr. C. said)? Could these be extinguished, abolished, annihilated by some drops of Prussic Acid? Is *that* credible? Is Prussic Acid more powerful than qualities which, found in a *Human Being*, the self same qualities—we call *divine, immortal?* "I cannot make myself believe that," I said.

Jane uttered this gentle heresy in conversation with Lady William Russell, and it's refreshing to read Lady Russell's reply: "But why *should* you make yourself believe it, my good Lady? Who does believe it? *I* don't."

Jane's bafflement at Nero's not-being reflects exactly the questions we ask ourselves when faced with human loss—where, on death, does it all go?

Even J. G. Wood, an ordained churchman, writing during the period when the Anglican church held sway over the thinking of its human flock as rarely before and certainly never since, rejected orthodox teaching on this point, declaring himself a "firm believer in the immortality of animals."

> ...although I do not claim for them the slightest equality with man, I do claim for them a higher status in creation than is generally attributed to them. I do claim for them a future life in which they can be compensated for the suffering so many of them have to undergo in this world...due to the habit of considering them as mere machines.

You can blame the seventeenth-century philosopher René Descartes (or perhaps it is more accurate to say you can blame a specific reading of his works) for the notion of animals as unfeeling automata. Opposing this is the attitude expressed by Byron on Boatswain's behalf, and by every owner before and since, that animals surpass us in all the qualities we most esteem, and to put it bluntly, if we get an afterlife, then they deserve one, too. In other words Lord Byron and the Reverend J. G. Wood are both on the same page here, and both on the side of the angels. The Maori peoples of New Zealand had no doubt about animal immortality, believing that their dogs went to the same place after death as their human owners, albeit by a different route—a variant on the Rainbow Bridge, perhaps. Animals in ancient Egypt, from cats to crocodiles to dung beetles, were mummified in the thousands for an afterlife incomplete without them. Medieval lords and ladies lie piously side by side in churches scattered across northern Europe—and there, nestled in the folds of the lady's gown, or at her feet, there also lies a little lapdog, sometimes with collar, occasionally even with a name.[27] It's one of the paradoxes of the modern age that as society's religious faith has wavered, the individual owner's belief in an animal afterlife seems to have grown stronger and stronger, to the point where, reflecting on life after death (and echoing Lady Wentworth), one of the contributors to the documentary *Kedi* would declare of a favorite street cat, "If there is an afterlife, I want to meet her again, not my grandmother." It's maybe time to look here at another instance of doubleness, and of how the experience of being an animal mirrors our own, because they lose us, too.

This is a particular problem for owners of parrots, those birds who "live forever, mostly," as Long John Silver described his parrot, Captain Flint. A parrot's life span can easily match if not exceed ours. But it's a dilemma for any owner who feels themselves likely to underlive their pet. Who will look after our animals, if we, their companions, are gone? Madame du Deffand began petitioning Walpole to take Tonton six years before her own death, and Walpole himself, after Tonton's death, refused another pet. "I am too old and should only breed it up to be unhappy, when I am gone."[28] Walpole and William Stukeley shared a friend in John, 2nd Duke of Montagu, a great-hearted soul who kept a retirement paddock for elderly cattle and horses on his estate in Northamptonshire, and who, like Hogarth, supported Coram's Foundling Hospital in London. The 2nd Duke (great-grandson, incidentally, of Henry Wriothesley, 3rd Earl of Southampton—he of the portrait with the tuxedo cat) also funded the education of the freed slave Ignatius Sancho. Walpole describes the duke settling the codicils to his will in his study at Boughton House in 1749 when "one of his cats jumped on his knee. 'What,' says he, 'have you a mind to be a witness too? You can't for you are a party concerned.'" And a codicil to the duke's will did indeed make sure that after his death, his animals' well-being was safeguarded. But not all owners have such resources to draw upon after death. Elizabeth von Arnim could do no other in her will but leave pathetically precise instructions as to how "all my dogs are to be put to sleep... the greatest care being taken that the dogs should suffer neither fear nor pain."[29]

Fear nor pain, no, and no mourning for their owner, either. I always hated the story of Greyfriars Bobby, a Skye terrier who is supposed to have spent fourteen years sleeping every night beside his owner's grave in Greyfriars Kirkyard in Edinburgh. It was so unremittingly maudlin, and what did the lonely little dog get in return for all that faithfulness? I was much comforted to discover quite how many doubts have been cast upon the tale, and that Bobby might have been no more than an enterprising local stray who frequented the churchyard because there he was pitied and fed. But the story of Hachiko, who for more than nine years went down to Shibuya Station near Tokyo to await his dead master's arrival, is absolutely authentic. Keeper followed Emily Brontë's coffin, as King Edward VII's disreputable little terrier, Caesar, did his. In bloodier times Charles I's spaniel Rogue is supposed to have attempted to follow its master to the scaffold; and Mary, Queen of Scots' little dog, another Skye terrier, perhaps, is meant to have been discovered under her skirts at her execution, and then to have sat between its mistress's body and her head, howling with misery.

Do animals experience loss? Do they comprehend death, and do they grieve, too? Miss Puss certainly seemed to do so. Miss Puss's boon companion for the first few years of her life was a fluffball ginger tom, a softer, 1990s, metrosexual version of Freddy, the cat I grew up with, who for some reason we named Widget. Having survived with no difficulty living in a cul-de-sac solid with cars, Widget died biffed by a vehicle in a quiet country lane outside my parents' garden. My parents buried him and broke the news, and back we went, full of misery, to London, and as soon as we arrived home, Miss Puss went around the house howling. She kept that up for days. She developed eczema and all the symptoms of a stressed and most unhappy cat within a week. I don't know if you could describe what she felt as being the same as human grief, but it had every appearance of bewilderment and loneliness, and she and I made this wretched mournful pair for weeks, given to explosively sudden fits of weeping (me) and bursts of this heartbroken calling out (her). We had let Miss Puss and Widget have one litter of kittens (with homes assured for them all, I hasten to add) before we had her spayed and him castrated, and were extremely proud of her when she produced six kittens, all lively and active and feeding, but I was much distressed the next morning when only five were still alive. Miss Puss, however, was not perturbed at all. The stiff, cold body of the dead kitten, really not much bigger than my thumb, was unceremoniously shoved out of the basket where she lay nursing its living siblings. Yet alone in the house, without her feline companion, there was this positively Victorian heartbreak and decline.

It may be that owners, in attributing emotions such as affection and contentment and its opposite to their pets, are a little ahead of the biologists here. The field of animal emotion is very new, and very contested, but one suggestion is that for animals who seem to be registering loss, and suffering under it, what matters to them is understanding what has happened.[30] Animals know what death is, so the dead kitten was of no interest or importance at all—it was sniffed at and then ignored; but from my cat's point of view, it must have seemed as if her animal companion had simply disappeared. There had been no dead body to nose, no change in him to recognize: he was simply gone. And echoing Grace Greenwood, and ridiculous as this may appear in turn, it was the memory of the aching sense of loss that not saying goodbye to our cat had caused in me too that a good decade later still had enough force left in it to send me into the room at the undertakers' where my father's body lay. I remember, I put one hand on his forehead, and it was like laying it against a marble wall, and my father, wherever he had gone, was on one side of that wall, and I was here on the other, and the change was so complete there was no possible response other than, in this dim, instinctive manner, to accept it. In such ways do we learn, and sometimes all we can do is make the best peace with the business of losing that we can.

This chapter began at Park Hatch, and it's going to end there. The original mansion, with its shade trees and ghosts of the butlers and the housemaids, was demolished in the 1950s (the fate of so many country houses in that decade), and by the 1990s, the site boasted no more than a bungalow. A family from Holland was living there. When the site was redeveloped again, in 2012, the father of the family supplied the new owners with the following story from an earlier visit to the site in 2010:

the most likely new owner, I was given to understand [would be] a filthy-rich Russian Mafioso...My all-time favourite dog Bas...laid buried in the grounds. Visiting requests [were] likely to be met with a curt "Njet," a hail of bullets, or the jaws of a hungry Rottweiler. I dug Bas's remains up, transported them, plus the heavy granite gravestone...and re-interred him...Never done so weird an undertaking. At the first sight of animal remains, buried deeper than I'd thought (though vividly remembering the hard work at the time), I started talking to him, almost involuntarily. But his ghost cannot have been there: the "obolon," the small coin I'd pressed under his tongue when burying him, was untraceable—whilst all the other "imperishables" were there. So he must have paid the mythical Ferryman to be transported to the Elysian Fields, and deservedly so.[31]

For those of us who would or have done exactly the same—the unburying, the re-interment, the talking to the animal although long gone, even the coin to pay the ferryman—it is no more possible to imagine an afterlife without animals than it would be to imagine the Garden of Eden without them; and Paradise will be a poor sort of place altogether if they do not share it with us.

The Stanwick Horse Mask, *c.*50 BC–AD 100

CHAPTER NINE

IMAGINING

"Ah sir," said an 18th-century ostler, "considering that I have lived thirteen years in a stable, tis surprising to think how little I knows of a horse."

—Keith Thomas, *Man and the Natural World,* 1983

T he Stanwick Horse Mask was discovered in 1843, at Stanwick in North Yorkshire. It's part of the Stanwick Horde, a find of dozens of random metal bits and pieces unearthed at this enormous site that, two thousand years ago, was one of the largest native British hill forts in existence. The mask is just under ten centimeters or four inches long, although it's also in that rare category of objects that you always remember as being bigger than they are. It's also rather confusingly named, in that it's a mask not *for* a horse but *of* one.

The horse mask was cut from a thin sheet of copper alloy, shaped and worked in low relief, and was probably intended as no more than a little bit of ornamentation to some utilitarian wooden object such as a bucket—maybe even a bucket for watering horses. There's a cultural tradition associating metalworking with men, but the horse mask is so small and the sheet from which it was made so lightweight—no thicker than a piece of card—that there's no physical necessity for it having been made by a man. Whoever created it, one thing about them is certain: they must have been living with and observing horses all their life, must have been as familiar with their temperament and conformation as one could get, to be able to create such a perfect simulacrum of a horse's face on something so small, and with such simplicity—two curves for the shape of the skull, two open circles for the nostrils, and two almost-closed for the eyes. How many horses do you have to have looked at to be able to reduce their essence down to this?

And to be able to give it a personality, too. This is a jocular horse. To quote the Book of Job, this is a horse that, like the Earl, sayeth among the trumpets, ha-ha! This is a horse with both wisdom and humor and a wry take on the whole business of beingness as it applies to horses; and that, as my personal response to the Stanwick Horse Mask (an object that has enchanted me ever since I first came across it twenty years ago), is as good an example as you could wish for of how our human imagination and our notion of being intersect with and color our relationships with those other creatures with whom we share our personal worlds. You will have your own response, which will color yours. Maybe to you those narrowed eyes look tired or ill. Perhaps with the flared nostrils they suggest to you a horse at full gallop. Perhaps to you they summon up something else altogether. We see a face, and in our imagination, we construct a creature and an identity behind it. We simply cannot stop ourselves. And this is merely for a metal artifact. How much more against all the grain there is in human nature not to do so for living beings? "Anthropomorphize Owl…" says William Service, in his memoir, "it is going to be impossible not to."[1]

At my all-girls school in Suffolk, deep in farming country, you could always spot those among my fellow pupils who had horses or ponies of their own, whose lives revolved around pony club or gymkhanas, not by their conversation but in the art studio. They lived with horses and they loved them, to a degree, sometimes, that the horse or pony became a substitute first boyfriend, so intense were the feelings they poured into these relationships; but because of this, they knew how to draw them. They had taken them in, in the smallest details, almost without knowing they were doing so. They knew how the hairs of the mane rose from the muscle of the neck, how the insanely elegant concave of a horse's back legs should be curved and where, how front legs connected to shoulder, and how long or short the head. They had not only looked; you might say that in their imagination they had inhabited.

You find this kind of looking throughout Celtic art. The British Museum, where the Horse Mask lives, also contains the Holcombe Mirror, contemporary with the Horse Mask and again made of copper, and where handle meets mirror, if you were to turn it upside down, you'd see a cat's face with prominent pincushion cheeks, a grinning cat's face, a Celtic Cheshire cat. Cats tend to their appearance constantly—as every owner knows, "When in doubt, wash" is a dictum of cat lore—so in this case, feline behavior is being used to poke fun at human vanity. Did the maker of the mirror own a cat? Did the high-status woman (or man) it was perhaps made for? If you think of the human imagination as a watering hole, we gather those on four legs around it just as often as we go to it ourselves. Most entertaining of all are the Basse-Yutz Flagons, again in the British Museum, and from about five hundred years earlier. At the tip of the spout of each flagon there sits a dinky and completely daft-looking little duck, blithely paddling along and wholly oblivious to the three dogs charging toward it across the lid of the flagon, or what (playing the flagons' game) I suppose we should think of as the duck's liquid element; the largest of which, forming the handle and chained to the lid, is a veritable slaughter hound, a sort of Celtic Black Shuck.

Here's the point of all this art. These works are not only portraits of their subjects but in the way in which they inform us of the attitudes and imaginations of the individuals doing the depiction, they are also records—the offset portraits, if you like—of the people who made them. They tell us about their notion of beauty, their responses to the world around them, and what they prioritized in their own surroundings; their individual readings of the world. This is just as true for the Stanwick Horse Mask as it is for the sketches in a student's school portfolio, and as it is for the artists of the Chauvet cave. Their imaginations are what they have left us of themselves.

We're in a strange situation, in relation to the other species on this planet. We are so uniquely unlike them, yet they are still all we have by which to measure ourselves. No wonder the thinkers, like Montaigne and Derrida, "look" endlessly, drilling down, as if trying to find the bedrock, the layer where we all—cat, dog, duck, horse, you, me—connect, and then somewhere above that, the layer where we separate, and we become us, and they remain them.

So far as we know, animals don't use their imaginations in the same way as we do. They anticipate, certainly, they project in order to predict, but what our imaginations enable us to do differs from that. The Qoobo therapeutic robot, "A Tailed Cushion That Heals Your Heart," as its marketing describes it, would be no more than a cushion to a cat or dog, but to the poor, pet-deprived human stroking it on their lap and watching its tail start to wag, it is a living creature (of whatever chimera-species a Qoobo is supposed to represent), animated and individualized by the owner's imagination. Without which, "the comforting communication that warms your heart the way animals do" just would not happen. What Qoobo's marketing is selling is something that happens not on our laps but in our heads.

We would not have pets without imagination. We could have beasts of burden, we could have animals as food, but we would not have pets. And while this might indeed all stem from our endless human insecurity, our condition as "a fragile bubble," as Carl Linnaeus described it more than two hundred years ago, this desire to reach down into also stems from our need to understand and to relate to, which says different things about us, and rather better ones. The artist Franz Marc, who was one of the best advocates in art for the animal world it has ever had, and who died far too young during the Battle of Verdun in 1916, described this when he wrote: "I try to sense pantheistically the shiver and flow of 'blood' in nature, in the trees, in the animals, in the air..."[2] and was in no doubt of the importance of doing so: "Animals with their virginal sense of life awakened all that is good in me."[3] Marc grew up with his dog Schlick and had dogs (and tame deer) on the farm he bought as an adult in Upper Bavaria, and in 1912 created a portrait of one of his dogs that might be called the embodiment of this kind of imaginative comprehension.

Originally titled *This Is How My Dog Sees the World*, it shows his white dog gazing out across a landscape of trees, hills, rocks, and sky, all rendered in Marc's brightly colored Expressionist palette, while the dog itself is hardly tinted with color at all. It's as if the dog exists only in response to his surroundings, and as if his reactions to these surroundings flow out from him and color them continually. Marc also wrote of the "wretched and soulless...convention of placing animals in a landscape that belongs to our eyes, instead of immersing ourselves in the soul of the animal in order to imagine how he sees." Perhaps that too is part of what we're after, as owners—the privilege of immersing ourselves, even if only for a moment, in the world as another being experiences it. Linnaeus believed that our sense of our own fragility was one of the things that defined us as human, but some bioethicists suggest that our ability to imagine ourselves into the lives of other creatures is a definition of being human as well; part, it has been said, of an inner biological heritage.[4] Very appropriate, therefore, that Walt Whitman's famous poem "I Think I Could Turn and Live with Animals" (which J. R. Ackerley wanted inscribed on his tombstone, by the way), with its much-quoted line "They bring me tokens of myself," came into being not as a work in its own right but within and as part of the poet's *Song of Myself.*

Animals are our constant mirror, an ever-present reminder of the business of beingness as it applies to human.

And they do bring us tokens of ourselves. Bird and Daisy, as I write this, with a springtime breeze flowing through the flat, are engaged in a mad game of chase up and down the hall, with much polysyllabic, hyper-excited meowing, those bubbly kookaburra callings back and forth that stop when the chase stops, and then apparently start it up again. I have no idea what has set them off, but it happens most mornings at this season of the year and reminds me every time of my own joyous capering, as a child, around my mother as she hung out the washing in the Suffolk garden where I grew up, and in exactly this kind of weather, too—sun and wind, and a blue sky, and clouds of both gray and white speeding across it. Freddy, the cat I grew up with, used to catch the madness, too, and would go hurtling across the lawn in sympathy. "Wind up the tail," my mother called it, in a phrase I thought was unique to our family, yet have since discovered to be one of those spontaneously generated memes celebrating exactly this behavior in felines and small children alike—clearly, millions of cats welcome spring in this way. It makes perfect sense to me to see my cats' response to a long-delayed, much-yearned-for new season to be exactly the same as mine. I may no longer be capering under a clothesline to express it, but looking out of the window here at the clouds and the sky and with the breeze on my face, I still feel that effervescence in the blood—why not believe they feel it, too?

Our human imagination is a two-edged sword and can distort the world for us as much as it reveals it, with us perceiving it most forcefully in ways that reinforce what we already believe. Even Humphrey, the

Downing Street cat, had political opinions ascribed to him.[5] But without this other side to our imagination there would be no anthropomorphism, either. Last night on UK television the mirage-animals of our imagination included dogs selling air fresheners and washable paint; a chameleon offering soluble Vitamin C; in the United States, via a gecko, they might have been selling me car insurance; and in newspaper cartoons fat cats too numerous to count exploit one economy after another. Anthropomorphism tells us our companion animals require weddings and bar mitzvahs and makes possible movies such as *Zootopia* and the character of Blue in *Jurassic World*. I loved both movies; I am fascinated by the creation of Blue; and I don't see anything in the way of actual harm to animal or human in doggie weddings and horse bar mitzvahs, either, but they do make me ponder whether another reason for our companion animals is that they bring us back to a truer shared reality. They force us to consider the world, and create a way for us to see it from a different viewpoint, and thus perhaps as it more truly is. They help us triangulate our own reality. I am surprised to find myself quoting Mary Ansell here, but what she had to say is apposite, and you may be surprised to find yourself agreeing with her: "An animal is so helplessly itself [and] I become one with them, I too become helplessly myself. They never withhold themselves from me…."[6]

Nor do they. Another suggestion from the field of bioethics: that the animal and its companion should be seen as a cultural unity, which is very much the case that the people of Starrett City were making with such conviction.[7] Now that would make for a very intriguing future for both parties involved.

"Animal rights," wrote Adrian Franklin, back in 1999, "is a social construct, an issue about what it is to be properly human and how to behave in the world." And as you would expect, it is thus as confusing and contradictory (and overthought) as every other issue involved in the business of trying to decide how to be properly human. But not so for the animal's companion, with whom, you might claim, society as a whole is finally beginning to catch up. In 1792 Mary Wollstonecraft published *A Vindication of the Rights of Women* to a predictably polarized reception, including, in refutation of Mary's arguments, a satire entitled *A Vindication of the Rights of Brutes* by one Thomas Taylor, translator of the works of Aristotle and Plato. Taylor's strategy was to ridicule the idea of rights for women by claiming them for animals. I've read Taylor's *Vindication*, and believe me, I took one for the team in doing so; but which of those two writers appears the more ridiculous now? What was once, in its demand for equality and respect, the cutting edge of social change is now a given across most of the planet (and will get all the way there, too); rights for "brutes" is following in its wake. We are coming to recognize that we cannot claim rights without also granting them; not insist upon them for ourselves without acknowledging them for others.

"Before man's arrival," wrote William Service, "eagle and bear and horned owl and the like had things much their own way. Now we are all of us in the deepest kind of trouble." And so we are. Small point in the most perfectly worked-through ethical argument if the environment we live in is so damaged it will no longer support any of us. The increase in our animal keeping and owning today (if increase there has truly been, from the days when every cottage had a dog, horses were to be encountered on the road as frequently as cars, and every household was a home to a half dozen cats) has been put forward as a response to all the ways in which the natural world is so imperiled; insurance by biomass, if you like. Certainly our more openly affective relationships with our animals and our determination in claiming rights for them have increased in parallel with our fears for the world where we originally found them, as have the arguments for "good" anthropomorphism, and for the validity of sentiment and value of imagination in our dealings with them. Far from being an evolutionary problem, you could make a case that being capable of such a relationship with a being from another species *is* evolution. But if I imagine an ideal future for myself and for the animals who are my companions, it's one where the differences between us are still honored. We lose something of them if we think of them as being simply alternative versions of what we are. And we also lose a means of thinking of and understanding ourselves.

There's a moment in *Kedi* when one of the contributors to the documentary suggests that "maybe we solve our problems as we solve theirs." That's an ideal, but maybe it's also a pointer as to how the next chapter in our long mutual companionship will work out. We could not be human if we had not been animals first, and we could not be human now without that point somewhere in prehistory when some creature more like us than it was not encountered some other creature less like it, and crouched down, and reached out toward this other creature in an attempt to understand it; and stood up with a better understanding of itself as a result.

Acknowledgments

Thanks first and foremost to all the many animals' companions who shared with me the stories of their animals while I was writing this book or directed me toward this little gem of information here or that illuminating anecdote there, in particular Jan Beatty, Virginia Blackburn, Jon Drori, Grace Eagle, Tom Keymer, Leah Kharibian, Michael Park, Lee Ripley, Pru Robey, Gwen Roginsky, Eve Sinaiko, and Maureen Winter.

Thanks again to JP, to Becky Koh for her support and endless patience, to Rachel DeCesario (picture research maven), to Kara Thornton, Melanie Gold, Ruiko Tokunaga, to Becky Maines (especially for the Porgs), proofreaders Andrea Monagle and Stephanie Finnegan, to Katie Benezra for solving the conundrum of the cover, and to Betsy Hulsebosch. And at Fox and Howard thanks to Chelsey and Charlotte.

To the staff of the British Library, who answered all queries, inane and insane, with perfect good humor, and to my colleagues at the Royal Collection Trust for the same; to the Celia Hammond Animal Trust for Bird and Daisy, and in the spirit of gratitude to all the other animals along the way who enriched my world with theirs.

To my family—my favorite animals. And to Mark, my perfect companion, always and again.

Reading for *The Animal's Companion*

The literature on this subject is enormous, but those works I found myself making most extensive use of are cited here, and their titles given in shortened form if they are also cited in the endnotes. Other works, no less illuminating but on specific points, are cited at the relevant note in full.

Ackerley, J. R. *My Dog Tulip.* New York: Poseidon Press, 1965

Adams, Maureen. *Shaggy Muses: The Dogs Who Inspired Virginia Woolf, Emily Dickinson, Elizabeth Barrett Browning, Edith Wharton, and Emily Brönte.* New York: Ballantine Books, 2007, Kindle edition

Ansell, Mary. *Dogs and Men.* New York: Scribner's, 1924

Archer, John. "Why Do People Love Their Pets?" *Evolution & Human Behavior* 18, no. 4 (July 1997): 237–59

Baker, Steve. *Picturing the Beast.* Manchester: Manchester University Press, 1993

Beck, Alan M., and Aaron Katcher. *Between Pets and People: The Importance of Animal Companionship.* West Lafayette, IN: Purdue University Press, 1996

Belozerskaya, Marina. *The Medici Giraffe: And Other Tales of Exotic Animals and Power.* London: Little Brown, 2006

Benes, Peter, and Jane Montague Benes. *New England's Creatures.* Boston: Boston University, 1995

Birkhead, Tim. *The Red Canary.* London: Bloomsbury, 2014

Boehrer, Bruce Thomas. *Parrot Culture: Our 2,500 Year-Long Fascination with the World's Most Talkative Bird.* Philadelphia: University of Pennsylvania Press, 2004, Kindle edition

Boland, Bridget. *The Lisle Letters: An Abridgment,* from the original edition edited by Muriel St. Clare Byrne. Chicago: University of Chicago Press, 1983

Bradshaw, John. *The Animals Among Us: The New Science of Anthrozoology.* London: Allen Lane, 2017

Braitman, Laurel. "Dog Complex: Analyzing Freud's Relationship with His Pets." www.fastcompany.com. Accessed August 20, 2018.

Burt, Jonathan. *Animals in Film.* London: Reaktion Books, 2002

The Carlyle Letters.
Carlyleletters.dukeupress.edu

Carroll, Michael P. "What's in a Name,"
American Ethnologist 7, no. 1 (February
1980): 182–84

Carson, James P. "Scott and the
Romantic Dog," *Journal for Eighteenth-
Century Studies* 33, no. 4 (December
2010): 647–661

Darwin, Charles. *The Expression of the
Emotions in Man and Animals.* London:
John Murray, 1872, Darwin-online.org.
UK online edition

Davenport, Emma. *Live Toys.* London:
Griffith and Farran, 1862

DeMello, Margo. *Animals and Society: An
Introduction to Human-Animal Studies.*
New York: Columbia University Press,
2012, Kindle edition

Donald, Diana. *Picturing Animals in
Britain c.1750–1850.* New Haven, CT:
Yale University Press, 2008

Dugatkin, Lee Alan, and Lyudmila Trut.
*How to Tame a Fox (and Build a Dog):
Visionary Scientists and a Siberian Tale of
Jump-Started Evolution.* Chicago:
University of Chicago Press, 2017,
Kindle edition

Dumas, Alexandre. *My Pets,* translated by
Alfred Allinson. London: Methuen and
Co., 1909. See archive.org online edition.

Feeke, Stephen. *Hounds in Leash.* Leeds,
UK: Henry Moore Institute, 2000,
exhibition catalog

Fogle, Bruce, ed. *Interrelations between
People and Pets.* Springfield, IL:
Charles C. Thomas Ltd., 1981

Franklin, Adrian. *Animals and Modern
Cultures: A Sociology of Human-Animal
Relations in Modernity.* Thousand Oaks,
CA: Sage, 1999

Fudge, Erica. *Pets (The Art of Living).*
London: Routledge, 2008

Greenwood, Grace. *History of My Pets.*
Boston: Ticknor, Reed and Fields, 1851.
See Google Books edition.

Gilhus, Ingvild Saelid. *Animals, Gods and
Humans.* Abington, UK: Routledge,
2006

Grier, Katherine C. *Pets in America: A
History.* Chapel Hill: University of North
Carolina Press, 2006

Grimm, David. *Citizen Canine: Our
Evolving Relationship with Cats and
Dogs.* New York: Public Affairs,
2014

Gunter, Barrie. *Pets and People.* London:
Whurr Publishers, 1999

Hill-Curth, Louise. *The Care of Brute
Beasts.* Leiden, Netherlands: Brill
Publishers, 2010

Hobgood-Oster, Laura. "The Ancient
Art of Burying Your Dog." www.salon
.com. Accessed August 20, 2018.

Hogg, John. *The Parlour Menagerie.*
London, John Hogg, 1878. See archive
.org online edition.

Horowitz, Alexandra. *Inside of a Dog, What Dogs See, Smell, and Know.* New York: Scribner, 2009, Kindle edition

Howell, Philip. *At Home and Astray: The Domestic Dog in Victorian Britain.* Charlottesville: University of Virginia Press, 2015

Irvine. Leslie *If You Tame Me.* Philadelphia: Temple University, 2004

———. *My Dog Always Eats First: Homeless People and Their Animals.* Boulder, CO: Lynne Reiner Publishers, 2015

Kelly, Fergus. *Early Irish Farming.* Dublin: Dublin Institute for Advanced Studies, 1997, reprinted 2000

Kete, Kathleen. *The Beast in the Boudoir, Petkeeping in Nineteenth-Century Paris,* Berkeley: University of California Press, 1994

King, Barbara J. *How Animals Grieve.* Chicago: University of Chicago Press, 2013

Lobell, Jarrett A., and Eric Powell. *Constant Companions.* Archive. archaeology.org

Loudon, Jane. *Domestic Pets: Their Habits and Management.* London: Grant and Griffith, 1851, Google Books edition

Mithen, Steven. *The Prehistory of the Mind.* London: Thames and Hudson, 1999

Montague, Jeanne. *Touching: The Human Significance of Skin.* New York: Harper and Row, 1978

Mowl, Timothy. *Horace Walpole: The Great Outsider.* London: Faber & Faber, 1996

Olina, Giovanni Petro. *Pasta for Nightingales: A 17th-Century Handbook of Bird-Care and Folklore.* London: Royal Collection Trust, 2018

Pampered Pets. St. Louis, MO: The Dog Museum of America, 1984, exhibition catalog

Pepys, Samuel. www.pepysdiary.com

Pepperberg, Irene M. *Alex and Me.* Victoria, Canada: Scribe Publications, 2008, Kindle edition

Pierce, Jessica. *The Last Walk.* Chicago: University of Chicago Press, 2012

———. *Run, Spot, Run: The Ethics of Keeping Pets.* Chicago: University of Chicago Press, 2016, Kindle edition

Podberscek, Anthony L., Elizabeth S. Paul, and James A. Serpell, editors. *Companion Animals & Us: Exploring the Relationships Between People & Pets.* Cambridge: Cambridge University Press, 2005

Redman, David. "Holy Bonsai Wolves," *International Journal of Cultural Studies* 17, no. 1 (2014): 93–109

Ritvo, Harriet. *The Animal Estate: The English and Other Creatures in the Victorian Age.* London: Penguin Books, 1987

Robbins, Louise E. *Elephant Slaves & Pampered Parrots: Exotic Animals in*

Eighteenth-Century Paris. Baltimore: Johns Hopkins University Press, 2002

Room, Adrian. *The Naming of Animals: An Appellative Reference to Domestic, Work and Show Animals Real and Fictional.* Jefferson, NC: McFarland Publishers, 1993

Rosenblum, Robert. *The Dog in Art.* New York: Harry N. Abrams, 1988

Schwartz, Marion. *A History of Dogs in the Early Americas.* New Haven, CT: Yale University Press, 1997

Serpell, James. *In the Company of Animals.* Cambridge: University of Cambridge Press, 1996; digital edition 2003

Service, William. *Owl.* New York: Alfred A. Knopf, 1972

Stukeley, William. *The Family Memoirs of the Rev. William Stukeley, M.D.* Northumbria, UK: Publications of the Surtees Society, 1882, archive.org edition

Swarbrick, Nancy. *Creature Comforts: New Zealanders and Their Pets.* Dunedin, New Zealand: Otago University Press, 2015

Tague, Ingrid H. *Animal Companions: Pets and Social Change in Eighteenth-Century Britain.* Philadelphia: Pennsylvania State University Press, 2015

Thomas, Keith. *Man and the Natural World: A History of Modern Sensibility.* New York: Pantheon Books, 1983

Thomson, Richard. "Les Quat' Pattes: The Image of the Dog in Late Nineteenth-Century French Art," *Art History* 5, no. 3 (September 1980): 323–337

Tuan, Yi-Fu. *Dominance and Affection: The Making of Pets.* New Haven, CT: Yale University Press, 1984

Vigne, Jean-Denis, Isabelle Carrière, François Biois, and Jean Guilaine. "The Early Process of Mammal Domestication in the Near East," *Current Anthropology* 52, no. S4 (October 2011): 255–271, www.jstor.org

von Arnim, Elizabeth. *All the Dogs of My Life.* London: Virago Press, 1995. First published 1936.

Wain, Louis, and Charles Morley. *Peter, A Cat o' One Tail.* New York: G. P. Putnam, 1892, babel.hathitrust.org

Walker-Meikle, Kathleen. *Medieval Pets.* Woodbridge, UK: Boydell Press, 2012

Walpole, Horace. *Letters from the Hon. Horace Walpole.* London: Ridwell and Martin, 1818, Google Books edition

Warner, Philip. *A Cavalryman in the Crimea.* Barnesley, UK: Pen and Sword, 2010

White, Gilbert. *The Natural History of Selborne,* Project Gutenberg edition

Wood, J. G. *Our Domestic Pets.* London: George Routledge and Sons, (1870?), Google Books edition

———. *Man and Beast, Here and Hereafter.* New York: Harper Brothers Publishers, 1875, babel.hathitrust.org

NOTES

INTRODUCTION: REGARDING

[1] Grier: 4

[2] Quoted in Adams, Kindle edition

[3] von Arnim: 1

[4] Think too of Paolo Uccello's *St. George and the Dragon* of *c.*1470, now in the National Gallery, London, where the ferocious dragon is tethered to the princess by the flimsiest of leads. In both cases the implication is that the holiness of the woman has enslaved the dragon and made it her pet.

[5] https://en.wikipedia.org/wiki/2013 _horse_meat_scandal. Pope Gregory III outlawed the eating of horse meat in 732, so this is a taboo that in Europe has significant history. Even more outrageous than the fraud behind the scandal was the grotesque length of the chain of supply it revealed, with horses and horse meat being shipped virtually from one end of the continent to the other.

[6] For the story of Temple Godman in the Crimea, see chapters 4 and 7 of this book.

[7] "House cats" crop up in Gilbert White's correspondence, too. See for example White: Letter XXIX, May 12, 1770.

[8] See the TED talks: Laurel Braitman, "Depressed Dogs..." and especially Carl Safina, "What Are Animals Thinking and Feeling?," as well as others.

[9] Pepys: April 8, 1663. For those of you, like me, who would worry about this kind of thing, the Pepyses and their dog were all reunited once again in nearby Greenwich Park.

[10] Gainsborough's first known work, of 1745, is a portrait not of some land-owning grandee but of Bumper, a singularly rough-and-ready-looking white terrier belonging to the Reverend Henry Hill, who was indeed a patron, just in this very specific, dog-centric way. On the back of Bumper's portrait are to be found the words "a most Remarkable sagacious Cur," scribbled there by the artist.

[11] Carson: 647

[12] Podberscek et al: 33

[13] Michel de Montaigne, "The Language of Animals," in *The Works of Michel de Montaigne*, 1865, translated by William Hazlitt. http://www.animal-rights -library.com/texts-c/montaigne01.htm. Accessed August 19, 2018.

[14] https://www.kickstarter.com/ projects/1477302345/qoobo; for the Pet Rock fad of the 1970s, see https:// en.wikipedia.org/wiki/Pet_Rock.

[15] The term "companion animal" has had dictionary definition since the 1980s, and legal definition at least in New York State since 2006.

[16] Kete: 88

[17] Erick L. Laurent, "Children, 'Insects' and Play in Japan," in Podberscek et al: 83

[18] Yi-Fu Tuan gives an elegantly expressed and comprehensive account of this particular conundrum in his *Dominance and Affection.*

[19] The gravestone itself is in the Getty Museum in Malibu, California, and includes a carved likeness of Helena, who is shown to have been short of snout, short of leg, and somewhat barrel-bodied—and without a doubt much loved as well.

[20] Podberscek et al: 33

[21] Grimm: 98ff. And it's appalling that Hurricane Harvey, twelve years later, revealed so many animals still being abandoned to their fate.

[22] "It is incredible, if their account is to be depended upon, what a prodigious number of those creatures were destroyed. I think they talked of forty thousand dogs, and five times as many cats; few houses being without a cat, some having several, sometimes five or six in a house." Defoe was born in 1660, so his account of the events of 1665, which was published in 1722, is thought to rely on the experiences of Defoe's uncle as a primary source. See Daniel Defoe, *A Journal of the Plague Year,* Project Gutenberg online edition. The register of dogs in New Romney is cited in Thomas: 105.

[23] William Blake, "Auguries of Innocence" 1803. "The Beggars Dog & Widows Cat / Feed them & thou wilt grow fat," writes Blake, in his poem of paradoxes in praise of both human and animal rights.

CHAPTER 1: FINDING

[1] The dating of the art in the Chauvet cave is a matter of much debate, and the dates I give here are the widest possible. The paintings themselves may have been created thousands of years apart. Werner Herzog, no less, made an enthralling documentary about Chauvet, in *Cave of Forgotten Dreams* (2010); there are also numerous books on the subject. See Jean Clottes, *Chauvet Cave: The Art of Earliest Times,* translated by Paul G. Bahn, Salt Lake City: University of Utah Press, 2003.

[2] For an extensive and one of the most recent discussions (at the time of writing) of the ramifications of "thinking animal," see Bradshaw.

[3] Black Shuck has been part of Suffolk folklore for centuries, and alarmingly for those of us with fertile imaginations, the skeleton of a giant dog was indeed discovered in the medieval ruins of Leiston Abbey in Suffolk in 2014. http://www.ibtimes.co.uk/bones-7ft-hound-hell-black-shuck-discovered-suffolk-countryside-1448864. Accessed May 19, 2017. For Ingraban see von Arnim: 38.

[4] The importance of this, the cat's original purpose as far as our ancestors was concerned, is borne out by the fact that different versions of the Dick

Whittington story, of cats saving communities by killing the mice that plagued them, exist in no fewer than twenty-six countries around the world. See Katharine M. Rogers, *Cat*, London: Reaktion Books, 2006.

[5] After dogs and cats, in the trinity of pet prehistory, the largest came last. Horses had certainly been domesticated by the late Bronze Age, the epoch of the Uffington White Horse in Oxfordshire in England, all 110 meters of it, cut into the chalky soil of a hillside a mere 3,000 years ago; and wild horses may have been tamed by tribes on the steppes of central Asia (enough to be mounted and ridden, at any rate, even if not selectively bred and individually cherished) a couple of thousand years before that.

[6] https://en.wikipedia.org/wiki/ Spotted_hyenas_in_Harar; http:// articles.latimes.com/2010/jul/31/world/ la-fg-harar-hyenas-20100731; http:// thechive.com/2009/09/14/african -pets-by-pieter-hugo-17-photos/. Accessed June 3, 2017.

[7] For a fuller discussion see Room: 20ff. The single syllable "mi" is another such near-universal. In ancient Egypt, the word for "cat" was "miw," or "mii." Whether as "Minou" in French, or "Mitzi" in German, or "Micino" in Italian, it's always understood as embodying littleness and thus cuteness and has done time-honored service in the naming of pets. In Swedish, one word for "kiss" itself is "puss."

[8] Fogle: 152

[9] In *Animals, Gods and Humans*, Ingvild Saelid Gilhus describes the way animals give "emotional value and impetus to anything they are linked with," while the cultural historian Norine Dresser believes there is "something uplifting" in interacting with another species. See Norine Dresser, "The Horse *Bar Mitzvah*..." Podberscek et al, 90ff.

[10] Boland: xv

[11] Archer: 82

[12] See Philippe Erikson's essay "The Social Significance of Pet-Keeping among Amazonian Indians," in Podberscek et al: 7ff; but also John Bradshaw's detailed exploration of pet keeping in tribal societies in *The Animals Among Us*: 27ff.

[13] William E. Deal, *Handbook of Life in Medieval and Early Modern Japan*, Oxford, Oxford University Press, 2007: 355

[14] Giorgio Vasari, *Lives of the Most Excellent Painters, Sculptors and Architects*, Project Gutenberg online edition. First published in 1550, Vasari's *Lives* has hardly been out of print since. The quote from Vasari's life of Giovanni Bazzi, aka Il Sodoma, comes from the same source.

[15] Liliane Bodson, "Motivations for Pet-Keeping in Ancient Greece and Rome: A Preliminary Survey," in Podberscek et al: 27ff

[16] Walker-Meikle: 51; and for the translation of the *cantiga*, Kathleen Kulp-Hill, *Songs of Holy Mary of Alfonso X*, ACMRS, 2000. There's some

confusion as to whether Alfonso's pet was a weasel or a ferret, but I favor the former—a ferret cage would surely be too big to carry comfortably on horseback, and a weasel might just, with a bit of divine intervention, be small enough to emerge unharmed from under a horse's hoof.

[17] White, Letter XII, July 2, 1769

[18] In Twain's *Roughing It* (1872) and Conan Doyle's *The Adventure of the Lion's Mane* (1926), respectively

[19] Wood: 84ff

[20] George Jennison, *Animals for Show and Pleasure in Ancient Rome*, Manchester, Manchester University Press, 1937: 18

[21] The saying "Turtles all the way down" is referenced by Stephen Hawking in Chapter 1 of *A Brief History of Time* as an example of the problem of infinite regress. "A well-known scientist (some say it was Bertrand Russell) once gave a public lecture on astronomy. He described how the earth orbits around the sun and how the sun, in turn, orbits around the center of a vast collection of stars called our galaxy. At the end of the lecture, a little old lady at the back of the room got up and said: 'What you have told us is rubbish. The world is really a flat plate supported on the back of a giant tortoise.' The scientist gave a superior smile before replying, 'What is the tortoise standing on?' 'You're very clever, young man, very clever,' said the old lady. 'But it's turtles all the way down!'" See https://en.wikipedia.org/wiki/Turtles_all_the_way_down.

[22] Podberscek et al: 48

[23] Marvin Harris, *Good to Eat*, London, Allen & Unwin, 1986: 188-89

Chapter 2: Choosing

[1] William Cowper, "Epitaph on a Hare." The edition of Cowper's *Poetical Works*, edited by the Reverend H. F. Cary and published in 1839, includes Cowper's "Account of the Treatment of His Hares" first published in *The Gentleman's Magazine*. It makes clear the very different temperaments of Tiney and Puss. See Google Books.

[2] Dugatkin and Trut: Chapter 3 in particular

[3] Robert A. Hinde and L. A. Barden, "The Evolution of the Teddy Bear," *Animal Behaviour* 33, no. 4 (November 1985):1371–73. As part of the history of the tabby in our lives, one of the earliest soft toys was the Ithaca Kitty tabby cat, produced by the Atticus company in 1892. See https://en.wikipedia.org/wiki/Ithaca_Kitty.

[4] Simon J. M. Davis and François R. Valla, "Evidence for the Domestication of the Dog 12,000 Years Ago in the Natufian of Israel," *Nature* 276, no. 7 (December 1978): 608–10

[5] The poem was probably composed in Reichenau Abbey on Lake Constance in southern Germany; we don't know if Pangur made the journey from Ireland with his owner, but his name might

suggest that this was so. This translation of the poem is by Robin Flower.

⁶ When movable type took over from monk and quill, the connection was still preserved—printers were great keepers of cats in the pre-Industrial age. See Robert Darnton, *The Great Cat Massacre...* London, Allen Lane, 1984: 75ff.

⁷ Kate Andries, "Curious Cat Walks Over Medieval Manuscript," *National Geographic.* https://news.national geographic.com/news/2013/03/ 130326-animals-medieval-manuscript -books-cats-history. Accessed January 9, 2018.

⁸ Henry Mayhew, *London Labour and the London Poor,* Vol. 3, "Jack Black," Tufts Digital Library. Accessed January 9, 2018. https://dl.tufts.edu/catalog/tei/tufts: UA069.005.DO.00079/chapter/c1s5

⁹ For a detailed discussion of the consequences of domestication, see Serpell.

¹⁰ Gunter: 3

¹¹ Wood 1870?: 25

¹² Antoine de Saint-Exupéry, *The Little Prince.* First published in 1943, *The Little Prince* now exists in 300 different languages and dialects, and editions too numerous to count. It's a thought-provoking meditation on many things, the responsibilities of taming and of trust being only one.

¹³ Paul Webster, *Antoine de Saint-Exupéry: The Life and Death of the Little Prince,* New York: Macmillan, 1993: 133

¹⁴ A fundamental human tendency, which as you would expect, is discussed very widely in this field. See for example Archer; Erica Fudge, *Pets*; Grimm; Thomas; among many others.

¹⁵ http://under-these-restless-skies. blogspot.com/2013/09/anne-boleyns -pets.html says "some sources" suggest this, but doesn't specify them.

¹⁶ "A pleasurable and excited state of mind, associated with affection, is exhibited by some dogs in a very peculiar manner; namely, by grinning... Sir W. Scott's famous Scotch greyhound, Maida, had this habit..." Darwin: 120

¹⁷ Mowl: 242

¹⁸ See Horowitz in particular for how dogs "read" us.

¹⁹ For a detailed discussion of this phenomenon, see Irvine 2004: 109ff.

²⁰ Pepperberg, Kindle edition

²¹ www.queenvictoriasjournals.org, November 18, 1835

²² Sir Roy Strong, *Diaries,* London, Weidenfeld & Nicholson, 1997: 288

²³ Dumas: 65

²⁴James Serpell's essay can be found in Podberscek et al: 178; DeMello: 160

²⁵ Pepys, February 12, 1659/60

²⁶ White, Letter XIII, April 12, 1772

[27] Sarah Tytler, *Landseer's Dogs*, London: Marcus Ward and Co., 1877: 133

[28] Shirley Jackson, *Raising Demons*, New York: Penguin, 1957, reissued 2015, Kindle edition

[29] The song on Twindog's introductory video includes the line "Teach me how to be your best friend," which rather charmingly puts animal and owner on exactly the same level of emotional availability.

CHAPTER 3: FASHIONING

[1] For a detailed examination of the relationship between owners and dogs in portraiture in particular, see Feeke. In Federico's case, you can't help but suspect, with its silky coat and supplicating raised paw, that the dog depicted here isn't at least partly a stand-in for Margherita herself, a pointer as to what Federico would expect of her, too.

[2] Gunter: 28

[3] Elizabeth S. Paul essay in Podberscek et al

[4] Serpell: xiv

[5] Werner Muensterberger, *Collecting: An Unruly Passion*, Princeton: Princeton University Press, 1994: 8

[6] Oliver Lawson Dick, ed., *Aubrey's Brief Lives*, Boston: David R. Godine, 1999. Gallipots were the little earthenware pots used by the thousands by apothecaries at the time, and the only examples I have seen have been either sandy yellow or a ruddy brown, but presumably there must have been others that were glazed bluish-gray as well. D'Hondecoeter's painting came up for auction in 2017, and can be found online here: https://www.lempertz.com/en/catalogues/lot/1087-1/1032-gillis-claesz-de-hondecoeter.html. For a full account of Isabella's quest for her kitten, see Walker-Meikle: 28ff.

[7] Casey Smith, "Cats Domesticated Themselves," *National Geographic*. http://news.nationalgeographic.com/2017/06/domesticated-cats-dna-genetics-pets-science. Accessed August 18, 2018. The connection of the tabby cat with the Middle East is also there in the fact that the "M" above the nose of every tabby, which in the West is supposed to commemorate the fact that the Virgin Mary petted such a cat, is in the Islamic world said to celebrate the fact that a tabby cat was the pet of the prophet Mohammed.

[8] Robbins: 25

[9] Davenport: 18

[10] Wood 1870?: 244

[11] Robbins: 26

[12] "Frances Teresa Stuart," Duchess of Richmond, Westminster Abbey. http://www.westminster-abbey.org/our-history/people/frances-teresa-stuart. Accessed July 4, 2017.

[13] Christopher Plumb, "Exotic Animals in Eighteenth-Century Britain" (thesis), 43–54. https://christopherplumb .files.wordpress.com/2011/05/ plumbthesis2010.pdf

[14] Tague: 42

[15] Tague: 101; Tuan: 105

[16] In her *The First Lady of Fleet Street...* (2012), Eilat Negev recounts how in 1896 Mr. W. R. Brown clipped the entire family crest of Frederick and Rachel Beer into the coat of their poodle, Zulu.

[17] Kete: 87

[18] https://www.huffingtonpost.co .uk/2015/10/05/dying-your-dogs-hair -animal-cruelty_n_8245390.html?guc counter=1. "Neuticles" feature in Peter Haldeman's "The Secret Price of Pets," *New York Times* online. Accessed August 18, 2018. And in January 2018, the *Guardian* reported that twelve contestants had been disqualified from Saudi Arabia's annual camel beauty contest because their lips and noses had been injected with Botox. See Matthew Weaver, "Twelve Camels Disqualified from Saudi Beauty Contest after 'Botox' Row," theguardian.com, January 24, 2018. Accessed August 19, 2018.

[19] "14 Ridiculously Expensive Pet Products," Incredible Things. http:// incredible things.com/lists/14 -ridiculously-expensive-pet-products/. Accessed August 19, 2018.

[20] Wain: 71

[21] Such birds and their equally delicate female owners become something of a meme—think of Beth March's canary, Pip, in *Little Women* (1868–9). For the nineteenth-century reader, Pip's death would have been an obvious prefiguring of Beth's own.

[22] Where the bird ultimately gave its name to the city's soccer team.

[23] Birkhead: 27

[24] Birkhead: 112

[25] Wood 1875: 154

[26] Walker-Meikle: 28; see also Emmanuel Vidal, *The History and Methods of the Paris Bourse*, Washington, DC: GPO, 1910: 117. https:// searchworks.stanford.edu/view /10367151. Accessed August 19, 2018.

[27] Grier: 241ff. An especially useful account.

[28] Discussed in Grier: chapter 2 in particular.

[29] Peter Haldeman, "The Secret Price of Pets," *The New York Times*, July 4, 2018. https://www.nytimes.com/2018/07/04/ style/how-to-pamper-your-pet.html. Accessed July 6, 2018.

[30] Pepys, March 23, 1663/64. A later attempt was less happy: "I was vexed to have a dog brought to my house to line our little bitch, which they make him do in all their sights, which, God forgive me, do stir my jealousy again, though of

itself the thing is a very immodest sight." Pepys had that same day spent the afternoon with his mistress Betty Martin and seems to have been squirming under Mrs. Pepys's suspicions, the parallels with his own behavior, and the rebellion of his own conscience.

31 Thomson: 324; Tuan: 107

32 https://www.telegraph.co.uk/ science/2017/10/13/extreme-horse -breeding-leaves-animals-looking-like -cartoons. Accessed August 19, 2018.

33 Thomson: 324

34 http://www.redfactorafricangreys .com/babies-4-sale.html. Accessed July 4, 2017.

35 Hester Lynch Piozzi, *Observations and Reflections Made in the Course of a Journey through France*. London, 1789: 148. See archive.org online edition.

CHAPTER 4: NAMING

1 https://www.biblegateway.com/ passage/?search=Genesis+1. New International Version

2 *Donna Haraway, When Species Meet*, Minneapolis: University of Minnesota Press, 2008: *11*

3 Mary T. Phillips, "Proper Names and the Social Construction of Biography: The Negative Case of Laboratory Animals," *Qualitative Sociology* 17, no. 2 (1994): 132

4 https://en.wikipedia.org/wiki/ Ham_(chimpanzee)

5 Room: 117

6 Meanwhile the Horniman Museum in London has its own totem animal in the form of a century-old taxidermied walrus, mistakenly stuffed as tight in its skin by the taxidermist as a cigar in its wrapper. See https://www.horniman.ac.uk/ collections/stories/horniman -highlights-tour.

7 It's the formula used for Mickey Mouse, for example, and on *TV-AM* in Britain in the 1980s, the ubiquitous Roland Rat.

8 George A. Reisner, "The Dog Which Was Honored by the King of Upper and Lower Egypt," *Bulletin of the Museum of Fine Arts* 34, no. 206 (December 1936): 96–99. We have neither Abuwtiyuw's mummy nor his grave, but his name was preserved on a white limestone plaque.

9 Kelly: 123

10 Walker-Meikle: 17

11 In Act II, scene 3, lines 4-11

12 DeMello: 49

13 Schwartz: 32; Podberscek et al: 8

14 See Franklin in particular for a discussion of the differences it makes in

our attitudes when we bring an animal into our human space.

15 If you want to deep-dive into the ingenuity displayed by us as owners in our naming of pets, I heartily recommend Adrian Room's *The Naming of Animals.*

16 Irvine 2015: 116

17 Although one can't be categorical about this. Research from 2013 suggests that dolphins may have individual call-names for themselves as well, although we have no idea how they come by them or decide upon them or use them, or indeed what, to a dolphin, such a name might mean. See https://news.nationalgeographic.com/news/2013/07/130722-dolphins-whistle-names-identity-animals-science.

18 The family who bred Maida and gave her to Scott had a family connection to the battle that obviously they wished to preserve.

19 Dumas: 70

20 There's a rather lovely double portrait of the poet and what may have been one of the Bounces, dated to about 1718 and attributed to Jonathan Richardson. https://www.pbslearningmedia.org/resource/bal72319eng/alexander-pope-and-his-dog-bounce-c1718-bal72319-eng

21 Quoted in Lisa Berglund, "Oysters for Hodge..." *Journal for Eighteenth-Century Studies,* 33, no. 4 (December 2010): 638

22 See https://en.wikipedia.org/wiki/Hodge_(cat) and http://mrswoffington.

blogspot.com/2009/03/elegy-on-death-of-dr-johnsons-favourite.html. Accessed August 19, 2018.

23 Helen Macdonald, *H Is for Hawk,* London: Penguin Books, 2014, Kindle edition

24 Warner: Godman's first letter was written while still en route, on board the *Himalaya,* on May 30, 1854.

25 Warner: letter of August 24, 1854

26 Radio 4, *Word of Mouth,* February 7, 2017

27 http://jezebel.com/this-is-how-you-name-a-bunch-of-shelter-cats-1640762509. As Angela Speed of the Wisconsin Humane Society was well aware, in response to my query, "Names are powerful, and we do find that animals whose names are unique or surprising can attract more attention—especially on social media—than animals with standard pet names..." It was also fun for the staff at the shelter to create the names. Email communication, March 12, 2017.

28 Quoted in Phillips, op.cit.: 130. The phrase comes from a review by Michiko Kakutani that appeared in the *New York Times* in 1989.

CHAPTER 5: COMMUNICATING

1 Nancy C. Carlisle, "The Chewed Chair Leg," in Peter Benes, ed., *New England's Creatures,* Boston: Boston University Press, 1995: 13

² Graham Robb, *Victor Hugo*, New York: W. W. Norton & Co., 1998: 361

³ For a brief account of the strands of medieval carols and folklore that came together to create the legend, see http://mentalfloss.com/article/72843/how-talking-animals-became-christmas-legend. Accessed August 27, 2017.

⁴ Francis Klingender, *Animals in Art and Thought to the End of the Middle Ages*, Boston: MIT Press, 1971: 12

⁵ http://www.presscom.co.uk/halliwell/baldwin/baldwin_cat.html provides the text of the five variant editions of *Beware the Cat*. There is more information at https://en.wikipedia.org/wiki/Beware_the_Cat.

⁶ The record for this is instead held by her neighbor and co-accused, Agnes Waterhouse, who also claimed co-ownership of Satan. Elizabeth followed Agnes to the gallows after a second accusation of witchcraft, some years later.

⁷ Quoted in Tess Cosslett, *Talking Animals in British Children's Fiction 1786–1914*, Farnham: Ashgate Publishing, 2006: 36.

⁸ Norman R. Shapiro, *Fe-Lines: French Cat Poems through the Ages* (translated edition), Champaign: University of Illinois Press, 2015: 29

⁹ In real life Cochon belonged to the Duc de Vivonne (1636-88), the brother of Louis XIV's mistress the Marquise de Montespan.

¹⁰ Rashleigh Holt-White, ed., *The Life and Letters of Gilbert White of Selborne*, Cambridge: Cambridge University Press, 1901; digital edition 2015: 128

¹¹ Tague: 19

¹² Adams: Kindle edition

¹³ Archer: 251

¹⁴ Kay Milton, "Anthropomorphis or Egomorphism," in John Knight, ed., *Animals in Person, Cultural Perspectives on Human/Animal Intimacy*, Oxford: Berg, 2005: 257

¹⁵ Archer: 237–59

¹⁶ Mithen: 208

¹⁷ Quoted in Hill-Curth: 115

¹⁸ Tague: 180

¹⁹ Thomas: 97; https://communistswithdogs.tumblr.com. Accessed August 10, 2017.

²⁰ von Arnim: 8. Elizabeth describes herself as "subsisting" on cats between her first and second dogs. "One of your cat men" was her description of her father.

²¹ Walpole to Henry Seymour Conway, May 6-8, 1781, quoted in Tague: 225

²² Virginia Woolf, *Flush: A Biography*, 1933, Kindle edition

²³ But then I once found myself lunching with a highly respected psychoanalyst on

New York's Upper West Side, who recounted with complete candor how on a visit to his daughter, her cat had come to sit beside him, and when he placed his hand on its head, it began (as he thought) "growling" at him. He had never encountered a cat's purr before.

[24] Irvine 2004: 153

[25] Cosslett: 42

[26] Fogle: Chapter 3; Beck and Katcher: 44

[27] Greenwood: 12

[28] Jenny Diski, *What I Don't Know About Animals*, New Haven, CT: Yale University Press, 2011, Kindle edition

[29] Michael Fox, "Relationships between human and non-human animals," Fogle, Chapter 2

[30] TED talk

[31] As Victoria Voith, one of the investigators into the human-animal bond, has put it, in relation to her work with dogs and their owners, "It has been amazing to me how many people talk to the dog, discuss the situation with it, and try to use verbal reasoning to get the dog to change its behavior." See Fogle, 284.

[32] Norine Dresser, "Horse *Bar Mitzvah*," in Podberscek et al: 106

[33] Part of Topsy's fame, or the fame of her dying, stems from the fact that the ghastly event was filmed by the Edison film company and is still viewable. Nor was she alone in her suffering: another elephant, Mary, was hanged and eventually strangled to death in a horribly botched execution in Tennessee in 1916, while Chunee, a "public pet" in nineteenth-century London, was put to death by firing squad and died in a welter of bullets and gore (and public outrage) in 1826.

[34] Sasha-Lee Yates and Riyah Collins, "Dog Who Had Legs Cut Off for Chewing Neighbour's Shoes Walks Again Thanks to Prosthetics," *The Mirror*, http://www.mirror.co.uk/news/uk-news/dog-who-legs-cut-chewing-8652111. Accessed August 12, 2017.

[35] Gary D. Schmidt, *Hugh Lofting*, New York: Twayne Publishers, 1992: 6

[36] Hugh Lofting, *The Story of Doctor Dolittle*, New York: Frederick A. Stokes Company, 1920

[37] Rev. W. Bingley, *Bingley's Natural History*, Cincinnati and New York: C. F. Vent, 1871: 504

[38] Wood: 246

[39] Pepperberg: Kindle edition

[40] During her lifetime "adopted" five kittens as "pets." See https://en.wikipedia.org/wiki/Koko_(gorilla). Accessed July 2018.

[41] http://www.independent.co.uk/news/science/killer-whale-learns-imitate-human-speech-dolphin-voice-a8185931.html

⁴² One of the newest discoveries in this area is that whales from different areas of the ocean employ different dialects. This opens up the possibility that breeds of the same animal from different parts of the world do the same, that when I wake up in Italy and the cockerels all sound as if they have laryngitis, and are unmistakably *not* English birds, I'm not imagining the difference, and that Walpole's maid Margaret spoke truer than she knew. https://www.livescience.com/512-whales-speak-dialects.html

⁴³ Lorne Campbell, *The Fifteenth Century Netherlandish Paintings*, London: National Gallery, 1998. Lorne Campbell is another who believes the dog in the painting is, purely and simply, a pet.

Barbara Smuts, "Embodied communication in nonhuman animals," in A. Fogel, B. King, & S. Shanker (Eds.), *Human Development in the Twenty-First Century: Visionary Ideas from Systems Scientists*, Cambridge: Cambridge University Press, 2008: 136-46

⁴⁴ Darwin: 63

⁴⁵ Suggested by Jessica Pierce, for one. See Pierce, 2016, Kindle edition.

⁴⁶ Wood 1875: 338; Wain: 15

⁴⁷ Barbara Smuts, "Embodied Communication in Non-Human Animals," in Fogel King and Shanker, eds, *Human Development in the 21st Century* (Cambridge: Cambridge University Press, 2008): 137

⁴⁸ See Margo DeMello: 18; quoting Ken Shapiro's 1990 coining of the phrase.

CHAPTER 6: CONNECTING

¹ See Archer in particular for a discussion of how the presence of an animal creates and modifies how we connect to each other.

² Archer: 150ff

³ Irvine 2004: 21

⁴ Quoted in Thomas: 101

⁵ The scene from *The Birds* is illustrated here: http://www.spellboundbymovies.com/2012/05/16/for-the-love-of-film-blogathon-alfred-hitchcock-his-terriers. Accessed September 29, 2017. Hitchcock thought so highly of Sealyham terriers that he gave one to Tallulah Bankhead as a thank-you for having gamely struggled on through the filming of *Lifeboat* while she was suffering from pneumonia. She named it Hitchcock.

⁶ Thomas: 101

⁷ See Susan D. Jones, *Valuing Animals: Veterinarians and Their Patients in Modern America*, Baltimore: Johns Hopkins University Press, 2003:18–22.

⁸ Pierce 2016: 15

⁹ Bayly also, poignantly, coined the phrase "Absence makes the heart grow fonder." His *Songs and Ballads* were

published in 1844, five years after his death in 1839.

[10] Kete: Chapter 6 in particular

[11] Thompson: 331

[12] Greenwood: 42

[13] James Rubin, *Impressionist Cats & Dogs*, New Haven, CT: Yale University Press, 2003: 8. Twenty years before, Daumier had also created a day in the life of bachelor, M. Coquelet, who promenades his self-satisfied way about Paris with his dog, Azor, as his companion by day, and at night comes home to Minette, his cat. This, in nineteenth-century Paris, was a family.

[14] Inga Moore, *Six-Dinner Sid*, London: Hodder and Stoughton, 2004

[15] James Hamilton, *Turner, A Life*, London: Hodder and Stoughton, 1997: 304

[16] https://www.yorkshireeveningpost .co.uk/yourleeds/nostalgia/leeds -nostalgia-of-murderedkings-and-cat- flaps-from-1715-1-7154691. Accessed September 29, 2018.

[17] Emily's remarks come from one of a series of essays penned by her and her sister Charlotte in 1842 as exercises in French composition. See Sue Lonoff (ed. and trans.), *The Belgian Essays*, New Haven, CT: Yale University Press, 1996. Emily Brontë's Keeper, another bodyguard of a dog, trudged the moors with his mistress and accompanied her down into Haworth on her errands, but unlike any other soul she would have encountered in either place, also bounded upstairs to the bedrooms of the Brontë parsonage— and despite the views put forward in her 1842 essay, was beaten mercilessly for it. See Adams, Kindle edition.

[18] For a levelheaded discussion on this topic, see Bradshaw: Chapter 3.

[19] https://www.academia.edu/403301/ Petropolis_The_Social_History_of _Urban_Animal_Companions

[20] http://www.bookweb.org/news/ furry-faces-bookselling-bookstore -pets-34439

[21] Gunter: 5, 25ff

[22] https://news.artnet.com/market/cat -painting-sothebys-carl -kahler-355508

[23] *As Good as It Gets* is another example of how being in company with an animal changes the way those around you react to you; it is another trope we are so comfortable with that it can play a part in a movie plot.

[24] Gunter: 25, but it's a belief with a long history. Isabella d'Este was noted as "liberal and magnanimous," for example. See George R. Marek, *The Bed and the Throne: A Life of Isabella d'Este*, New York: Harper and Row, 1976.

[25] Bradshaw: 110–17

[26] David Lay Williams, *Rousseau's Social Contract: An Introduction*, Cambridge: Cambridge University Press, 2014: 29

[27] Now in the National Portrait Gallery, London (NPG 2354)

[28] Now in the Musée d'Orsay (RF 1992 409)

[29] Quoted in Peter Cochran, *Byron and Italy*, Cambridge: Cambridge Scholars Press, 2012: 176–7.

[30] Matthew Algeo, *Abe and Fido* (Chicago: Chicago Review Press, 2015) is a highly readable account of this aspect of the sixteenth president's character.

[31] Gunter: 92. "Having no ego for the child to meet, [it] can accept the child for what he or she is, not for what they might be or ought to be."

[32] DeMello: 328; and think of Jenny Diski and Guy the Gorilla.

[33] See Podberscek et al, in particular James Serpell's essay (Chapter 7).

[34] Gunter: 25

[35] http://members.efn.org/~acd/vite/VasariSodoma.html. Accessed October 27, 2017.

[36] Theodore Wood, *The Reverend J. G. Wood*, Cambridge: Cambridge University Press, 1890; digital edition 2014: 12

[37] Irvine 2015: 10

[38] Tague: 139

[39] From Ernst Jünger, *Storm of Steel…*, quoted in Feeke: 56

[40] I slightly suspect the demand might have been partly the result of poverty-stricken humans attempting to keep body and soul together on dog food, but could that explain quite so huge an increase? Susan D. Jones makes no mention of the possibility, what's more. See also John Knight, ed., *Animals in Person: Cultural Perspectives on Human-Animal Intimacies*, London: Bloomsbury, 2005: 109: "People who can least afford to pay costly veterinary treatments are often the ones who wish to proceed with them."

[41] https://www.aol.com/article/2015/10/12/the-worlds-most-radioactive-man-spends-his-days-taking-care-of/21244627

[42] https://www.thedodo.com/aleppo-syria-cat-sanctuary-reopens-2288368832.html

[43] https://www.theguardian.com/world/video/2016/feb/19/refugee-family-who-fled-iraq-are-reunited-with-cat-video. Kunkush's adventures have also become the subject of a children's book.

CHAPTER 7: CARING

[1] Loudon: ii

[2] Kay Milton, "Anthropomorphism or Egomorphism," in John Knight, ed.,

Animals in Person, Cultural Perspectives on Human/Animal Intimacy, Oxford: Berg, 2005

3 The *Kedi* documentary can be found here: https://www.youtube.com/watch?v=PpGOz-npFIY

4 Thyrza Nichols Goodeve, "'The Cat Is My Medium': Notes on the Writing and Art of Carolee Schneemann"; http://artjournal.collegeart.org/?p=6381. Accessed August 18, 2018.

5 Warner, letter of January 18, 1855

6 Michael MacKinnon and Kyle Belanger, "'Sick as a dog': Zooarchaeological evidence for pet dog health and welfare in the Roman world," *World Archaeology,* 42, No. 2 (June 2010): 290-309; and Lynn M. Snyder and Elizabeth A. Moore, eds., in *Dogs and People in Social, Working, Economic or Symbolic Interaction,* Oxford: Oxbow Books, 2016

7 https://www.washingtonpost.com/national/health-science/you-wont-believe-how-old-that-kitty-litter-is/2015/02/02/9ecac9ea-a1b4-11e4-903f-9f2faf7cd9fe_story.html?utm_term=.627b329a6e65

8 Podberscek et al: 52. https://www.theguardian.com/money/shortcuts/2015/may/26/dog-walkers-do-they-really-earn-more-than-average-salary

9 Pepys: May 25, 1660

10 Kelly: 144

11 Henry Fielding(?) and William Guthrie, *The Life and Adventures of a Cat,* London: John Seymour, 1760, Google Books online edition: 182

12 https://medievalfragments.wordpress.com/2013/02/22/paws-pee-and-mice-cats-among-medieval-manuscripts

13 https://www.pfma.org.uk/pet-population-2017

14 http://www.queenvictoriasjournals.org. Entry for December 24, 1833

15 Walker-Meikle: 2

16 Richard J. Goldstone (foreword), *The Commentaries of Sir William Blackstone, Knight...,* Chicago: ABA Classics, 2009: 230

17 Lisa Berglund, "Oysters for Hodge..." *Journal for Eighteenth-Century Studies* 33, no. 4 (December 2010): 631-45

18 Jonas Hanway, *A Journal of Eight Days Journey from Portsmouth to Kingston upon Thames,* Letter XXV, "Remarks on Lap-Dogs," London: Henry Woodfall, 1757

19 Tague: 37

20 www.queenvictoriasjournals.org. Entry for September 4, 1839

21 Serpell: 32

22 Carlyle: Letter of August 23, 1851

23 Greenwood: 25

24 www.britishmuseum.org, "epitaph plaque," 1756,0101.1126

25 Issa was either carefully house-trained or a remarkably accommodating little fluffy white dog indeed. The poem can be found at http://www.usu.edu/ markdamen/Latin1000/Readings/ 1020B/29Martial22.pdf.

26 Tague: 175; for the theory of human "grooming," see Bradshaw: 216.

27 Carlyle, letter of October 1, 1851

28 Ansell: 11

29 von Arnim: 23ff

30 For the use of the term "storge," see Liliane Bodson, "Motivations for Pet- Keeping in Ancient Greece and Rome: A Preliminary Survey" in Podberscek et al: 35

31 Walker-Meikle: 11

32 https://fleursdumal.org/poem/146

33 Kelly: 122

34 http://www.browningscorrespondence .com/correspondence/1080/

35 http://www.eighteenthcenturypoetry. org/works/o3795-w0030.shtml

36 J. R. Ackerley, *My Father and Myself,* New York: New York Review Books, 1968: 216–17: Google Books online edition

37 Peter Parker, *Ackerley: The Life of J. R. Ackerley,* New York: Farrar, Straus and Giroux, 1990: 261

38 Irvine 2015: 51

39 Podberscek et al: 109

40 Pepys: August 18, 1660

41 Olina: 63

42 Dumas: 260. For Mother Antony's dog and its wooden leg, see James Henry Rubin, *Impressionist Cats & Dogs: Pets in the Painting of Modern Life,* New Haven, CT: Yale University Press, 2003: 38

43 Carlyle: Letter of October 26, 1859

44 https://catalog.hathitrust.org /Record/012284048. Accessed November 11, 2017.

45 http://www.telegraph.co.uk/news/ uknews/12142148/Evan-Davis-reveals -he-sent-his-dog-for-hydrotherapy.html. Accessed November 7, 2017.

46 Susan D. Jones, *Valuing Animals: Veterinarians and the Patients in Early Modern America,* Baltimore: Johns Hopkins University Press, 2003: 12

47 Kelly: 120

48 Samuel Tuke, *Description of the Retreat, an Institution near York, for Insane Persons of the Society of Friends: Containing an Account of Its Origin and Progress, the Modes of Treatment, and a Statement of Cases,* Philadelphia: Isaac Pierce, 1813: 63, 87.

49 Louis Wain, letter to *The Idler,* 1896; quoted in *Louis Wain,* exhibition catalog, Chris Beetles Gallery, 1989

[50] "The Secret Life of the Dog," BBC *Horizon*, December 14, 2016

[51] Donna J. Haraway, *When Species Meet*, Minneapolis: University of Minnesota Press, 2008: 61

CHAPTER 8: LOSING

[1] von Arnim: 204. See also for Elizabeth von Arnim's will and the instructions about her dogs, Jennifer Walker, *Elizabeth of the German Garden: A Literary Journey*, Sussex, UK: Book Guild Publishing, 2013

[2] Carson: 647

[3] http://www.walterscott.lib.ed.ac.uk/portraits/miscellaneous/camp.html

[4] Carlyle: Letter of February 24, 1860

[5] Carlyle: Letter of February 12, 1860

[6] http://www.telegraph.co.uk/news/2017/10/24/woman-diagnosed-broken-heart-syndrome-death-dog

[7] Pepperberg, Kindle edition

[8] http://www.walterscott.lib.ed.ac.uk/portraits/miscellaneous/camp.html. Accessed March 18, 2018.

[9] It's one of the questions explored most thoroughly in *Companion Animals and Us*. For studies up to 2012, see http://ro.ecu.edu.au/theses_hons/85.

[10] Stuart Piggott, *William Stukeley*, London: Thames and Hudson, 1985: 124

[11] Walker-Meikle: 106

[12] Tague: 175

[13] Mowl: 242; Tague: 224

[14] Greenwood: 20

[15] https://www.theguardian.com/commentisfree/2016/apr/26/paid-time-off-care-pet-pet-ernity-leave

[16] Grier: 104

[17] Peter Parker, *Ackerley: The Life of J.R. Ackerley*, New York: Farrar, Straus and Giroux, 1990: 330

[18] John Knight (ed.), *Animals in Person: Cultural Perspectives on Human-Animal Intimacy*, New York: Oxford, 2005: 23

[19] www.tandfonline.com/doi/full/10.1080/00043249.2015.1067462?sr=recsys. Accessed March 21, 2018.

[20] Podberscek et al: 96

[21] Podberscek et al: 28ff

[22] Although touching as the circumstances of this appear, the Roman world buried its dead within only a very few days of death—so the dog either succumbed fairly swiftly to a broken heart or was helped upon its way to keep its young owner company in the afterlife.

[23] Tague: 172

[24] http://www1.nyc.gov/nyc-resources/service/1487/dead-animal. In New York

State, you can also have your pet's ashes interred with you in a human cemetery. See https://www.nytimes.com/2016/10/07/nyregion/new-york-burial-plots-will-now-allow-four-legged-companions.html.

[25] Podberscek et al: 28

[26] https://www.snopes.com/fact-check/all-dogs-go-to-heaven/. Accessed February 12, 2016.

[27] Walker-Meikle: 75-77

[28] Tague: 226

[29] Jennifer Walker, *Elizabeth of the German Garden, A Literary Journey*, Sussex: Book Guild Publishing, 2013

[30] For a fuller discussion of animal grief and scientific thought on the subject, see Barbara J. King, *How Animals Grieve*, Chicago: University of Chicago Press, 2013.

[31] parkhatch.com. Accessed March 29, 2018.

CHAPTER 9: IMAGINING

[1] Service: 5

[2] Marion Wolf, "Biblio Omni: Timeliness and Timelessness in the Work of Franz Marc," *Art Journal* 33, no. 3 (Spring 1974): 226–30

[3] Marc Rosenthal, *Franz Marc*, Berkeley, Calif.: University of California, University Art Museum, 1979: 39

[4] James Serpell, "Creatures of the unconscious: companion animals as mediators," in Podberscek et al: 115

[5] Radio 4, "Analysis," February 20, 2017

[6] Ansell: 11

[7] Franklin: 57

Captions and Picture Credits

Frontispiece

My mother, me at age 3, and my cat Freddy, also age 3, in our garden in Suffolk.
Author's collection

Chapter 1, opener

A boy and his dog from 26,000 years ago. The foot- and paw prints (on the right) from the Chauvet Cave, discovered June 7, 1999.
Photo by Alexis ORAND/Gamma-Rapho via Getty Images

Chapter 2, opener

"Jack Black, Her Majesty's ratcatcher," from Henry Mayhew's *London Labour and the London Poor* (1851). Note the "VR" on Jack Black's baldric, together with the silhouettes of two rats, and his indispensible companion, his terrier.
Private collection/Bridgeman Images

Chapter 3, opener

Two young men, possibly brothers, with that shared dimple in the chin, who chose to be photographed in 1910 with their baby raccoon. And very appealing they look, too, as a result.
Vintage Images/Alamy Stock Photo

Chapter 4, opener

Lieutenant Temple Godman of the 5th Light Dragoon Guards, his servant Kilburn, and "The Earl," photographed by Roger Fenton in 1855.

RCIN 25000424. Royal Collection Trust/© Her Majesty Queen Elizabeth II 2018

Chapter 5, opener

Louis Wain photographed at his drawing board in the 1890s. The date makes it possible that the cat photographed with him is indeed Peter.
Heritage Image Partnership Ltd/Alamy Stock Photo

Chapter 6, opener

A boy and his chicken, taking the air, from Morris Huberland's "Chicken in the City" series, taken in New York circa 1940.
Photo by Morris Huberland © The Miriam and Ira D. Wallach Division of Art, Prints and Photographs: Photography Collection, The New York Public Library

Chapter 7, opener

"Yes, I came back. I always come back."
New Yorker cartoon by Harry Bliss.
Harry Bliss/The New Yorker Collection/ The Cartoon Bank

Chapter 8, opener

The artist Dante Gabriel Rossetti lamenting the death of his wombat, 1869.
Private collection/Bridgeman Images

Chapter 9, opener

The Stanwick Horse Mask, c. 50 BC–AD 100
© The Trustees of the British Museum

Photo sections

Giovanni Savoldo, *Portrait of a Woman as Saint Margaret of Antioch*, 1525.
Musei Capitolini, Rome.
© Stefano Baldini/Bridgeman Images

One dog-man to another. Henry Scott, 3rd Duke of Buccleuch with a favorite dog, painted by Thomas Gainsborough c. 1760, and as engraved in mezzotint by John Dixon before 1771.
Art Collection 3/Alamy Stock Photo

A peasant family in relation to the natural world from 500 years ago, as depicted by a Flemish artist for "February," from *Grimani Breviary*, c. 1515.
Biblioteca Nazionale Marciana, Venice/Bridgeman Images

The Panel of Lions from Chauvet Cave, created 32,000–30,000 BC
Fine Art Images/Heritage Images/Getty Images

Sir Anthony van Dyck, *The Five Eldest Children of Charles I*, 1637
RCIN 404405. Royal Collection Trust/© Her Majesty Queen Elizabeth II 2018

Pieter Hugo, *Abdullahi Mohammed with Mainasara, Ogere-Remo, Nigeria*, 2007
© the photographer

Il Sodoma (Giovanni Antonio Bazzi), self-portrait with badgers and raven in the Life of St. Benedict frescoes, Monte Oliveto, 1502
Abbey of Monte Oliveto Maggiore, Asciano, Tuscany/Mondadori Portfolio/Archivio Lensini/Fabio e Andrea Lensini/Bridgeman Images

My brother cuddling a real-live lion cub in Harrods' Pet Kingdom.
Author's collection

More pawprints, from 500 years ago, photographed by Emir O. Filipović in 2011.
© Emir O. Filipović

Diego Velázquez's *Dwarf with a Dog*, c. 1645. Less than a decade separates this from Van Dyck's *Five Eldest Children of Charles I*; in essence, the elements of the paintings duplicate each other, yet their messages and implications could not be more different.
Prado, Madrid/Bridgeman Images

George V when he was the Duke of York, caught by an unknown photographer in c. 1895 being extremely irreverent with a pet pug.
RCIN 2107790. Royal Collection Trust/© Her Majesty Queen Elizabeth II 2018

Alexander Bassano, *Queen Victoria*, c. 1890
RCIN 2105786 Royal Collection Trust/© Her Majesty Queen Elizabeth II 2018

George Morland, *Selling Guinea Pigs*, c. 1789.
Yale Center for British Art/Paul Mellon Collection USA/Bridgeman Images

George Piner Cartland, *Princess Alice of Albany, later Countess of Athlone (1883–1981) with a dog*, photographed in April 1886.
RCIN 2904368. Royal Collection Trust/© Her Majesty Queen Elizabeth II 2018

Titian, *Federigo Gonzaga, Duke of Mantua*, c. 1525–30.
Prado, Madrid/Bridgeman Images

Jean-Jacques Bachelier, *A Dog of the Havana Breed*, 1768.
The Bowes Museum, Barnard Castle, County Durham/Bridgeman Images

William Hogarth, *The Painter and His Pug*, 1745. Tate Gallery, London.
World History Archive/Alamy Stock Photo

Jan van Eyck, *The Arnolfini Portrait*, 1434. National Gallery, London/Bridgeman Images

Daumier's cartoon: "Now he's one of the family, he needs his portrait too," which appeared in the illustrated magazine *Le Charivari* in January 1856.
Typ.815.32.2750, Janvier 1856, Houghton Library, Harvard University

Carl Kahler, *My Wife's Lovers*, 1891. Kate Birdsall Johnson, who commissioned the painting, reportedly owned 350 cats; just 42 are depicted here, including, in pride of place at the center of the composition, Sultan.
Historic Collection/Alamy Stock Photo

The Barrison sisters in the 1890s and their most risqué number. They advertised themselves in the United States as "The Wickedest Girls in the World."
The National Archives, ref. COPY1/420 (522)

Auguste Renoir, *Madame Georges Charpentier and Her children*, 1878. Georgette-Berthe is seated on the family dog, her brother Paul-Émile-Charles is seated next to their mother.
Catharine Lorillard Wolfe Collection, Wolfe Fund, 1907, Metropolitan Museum of Art, New York/Bridgeman Images

Johann de Critz, *Henry Wriothesley, 3rd Earl of Southampton*, 1603
Boughton House, Northamptonshire/Bridgeman Images

The perils of cats in the scriptorium—the 15th-century manuscript from Deventer bearing a monk's tale of woe.
© Cologne, Historisches Archiv der Stadt Köln Best. 7004, 249, fol. 68r

Auguste Renoir, *Mother Antony's Tavern*, 1866
Nationalmuseum, Stockholm, Sweden/Bridgeman Images

Jacques Callot, *A Blind Man with a Dog*, 1622.
National Gallery of Art, Washington DC/Bridgeman Images

Mark Gertler, *Gilbert Cannan at His Mill*, 1916. Luath is on the right; Sammy on the left.
Ashmolean Museum, University of Oxford/Bridgeman

The grave of Fanny the dog in Sir John Soane's Museum, Lincoln's Inn Fields, London, c. 1813. The inscription reads "Alas poor Fanny."
Bridgeman Images

The funeral procession of King Edward VII in 1910. The unknown photographer captured both Caesar and the King's horse as mourners in the cortege.
RCIN 2935437, Royal Collection Trust/© Her Majesty Queen Elizabeth II 2018

The Basse-Yutz Flagons, 450–400 BC, detail of the lid.
© The Trustees of the British Museum

Franz Marc, *The White Dog* (also known as *My Dog Before the World*), 1912.
Buhrle Collection, Zurich, Arthotek/Bridgeman Images

INDEX

Abuwtiyuw (dog), 121,
272n8
accessories for pets,
92–93, 95–96, 100,
196
Ackerley, J. R., 75, 105,
185, 207–208, 233
Adam, as first animal's
companion, 113–114
adoption, 74–78, 82–83,
137, 273n27
Agnelli, Carlo, 229
Aisholpan, 54, 116–117
Alex (parrot), 155–156,
157, 228
Alfonso X (king of
Castile), 47–48,
267n16
Alice (princess of
Albany), 82
animal graves, 23–24,
37–38, 39, 224–225,
229, 230, 237–241,
281n22, 281n24
animal rights, 259,
260
animals
acting like humans,
141–144
benefits of growing up
with, 5–6
in cave paintings,
29–30, 266n1
communication with,
41, 140–142, 145,
152–153, 156, 274n6
as food, 11, 12–14,
265n5
as having knowledge
humans do not, 42

human speech and, 11,
144–145, 147, 150, 154
humans instinctively
react against, 72–73
language, 157–158,
159–160, 276n42
as mirror of selves, 257
religion and, 41
speaking in fables and
fairy tales, 145
types of, purposely not
named, 115–117
Ansell, Mary, 205, 231,
258
anthropomorphism
animals in fables and
fairy tales, 145
ascribing opinions to
pets, 257–258
assigning human-values
to animals, 68
attributing emotions to
animals, 247–248
disposition of cats, 174
responses to images of
animals, 252–253
as revealing humans,
151–153, 275n31
when speaking to
animals, 148–149
appearances of animals,
62–64, 68, 69, 70–71,
109, 268n3
Archer, John, 1, 166–167,
234
Ashley-Cooper, Anthony,
146
Ashoka (Iron Age Indian
emperor), 24
Aubrey, John, 89

Augustus (Roman
emperor), 21
Aura (dog), 122, 229

Bachelier, Jean-Jacques,
93, 94
badgers, 48–49
Baldwin, William, 141
bantam hens, 70, 100
Barbary apes, 88
Barrett, Elizabeth, 71,
147, 184, 207
Barrie, J. M., 126–127
Barrison Sisters, 180
Basse-Yutz Flagons, 254
Baudelaire, Charles, 206
Bayly, Thomas Haynes,
165, 171
Bazzi, Giovanni Antonio,
26, 49
Beer, Frederick and
Rachel, 271n16
Beeton, Mrs., 81
Belaud (cat), 135
Bellay, Joachim du, 135, 225
Belyaev, Dmitry, 61, 62
Bentham, Jeremy, 127
Bingley, William, 154
Bird (cat), 44, 72, 82–83,
95, 124, 161, 187, 239,
257
"Birdman of Alcatraz," 98
birds, 43, 46, 49–50, 101,
154–155
Birkhead, Tim, 97
Black, Jack, 65
Black Shuck folktale, 35,
266n3
Blackstone, Sir William,
200